P9-EFG-875

Canadian Guide to UNIFORM LEGAL CITATION

3rd Edition

McGill Law Journal
Revue de droit de McGill

CARSWELL
Thomson Professional Publishing

© 1992 Trustees of the McGill Law Journal Trust Fund/ Fiduciaires du fonds en fiducie de la Revue de droit de McGill

All rights reserved. No part of this publication may be reproduced, stored in a retrieval system, or transmitted, in any form or by any means, electronic, mechanical, photocopying, recording, or otherwise, without the prior written permission of the publisher.

This publication is designed to provide accurate and authoritative information. It is sold with the understanding that the publisher is not engaged in rendering legal, accounting or other professional advice. If legal advice or other expert assistance is required, the services of a competent professional should be sought. The analysis contained herein should in no way be construed as being either official or unofficial policy of any governmental body.

Canadian Cataloguing in Publication Data

Main entry under title:

Canadian Guide to Uniform Legal Citation

3rd ed.
Text in English and French.
Title on added t.p., inverted: Manuel Canadien de la référence juridique.
"McGill Law Journal = Revue de droit de McGill"
Includes bibliographical references and index.

ISBN 0-459-55149-3 (bound) –
ISBN 0-459-55151-5 (pbk.)

1. Citation of legal authorities–Canada.
I. Title: Manuel canadien de la référence juridique.

KE259.C34 1992   808′ .06634   C92-094846-4F

CARSWELL
Thomson Professional Publishing

One Corporate Plaza
2075 Kennedy Road
Scarborough, Ontario
M1T 3V4

Customer service:
Toronto 1-416-609-8000
Elsewhere in Canada/U.S. 1-800-387-5164
Fax 1-416-298-5094

Officially adopted by:

Alberta Law Review
Canadian Journal of Law and Jurisprudence
Canadian Journal of Law and Society/Revue canadienne de droit et
société
McGill Law Journal/Revue de droit de McGill
Manitoba Law Journal
Osgoode Hall Law Journal
Ottawa Law Review/Revue de droit d'Ottawa
Queen's Law Journal
Saskatchewan Law Review
University of British Columbia Law Review
University of New Brunswick Law Journal/Revue de droit de
l'Université du Nouveau-Brunswick
University of Toronto Faculty of Law Review
British Columbia: Court of Appeal, Supreme Court and County
Court

TABLE OF CONTENTS

PREFACE

In the spring of 1984, the editors of the McGill Law Journal began a process of research and discussion on citation form which resulted, two years later, in the publication of the first edition of the *Canadian Guide to Uniform Legal Citation/Manuel canadien de la référence juridique*. The incentive for the citation project developed out of the recognition that although several citation systems had been proposed over the years, no one system had yet been accepted as standard. The editors believed that the formulation of a citation system which mirrored Canada's bilingual and bijuridical legal community would have the greatest likelihood of providing a nationally acceptable reference system.

The research for the citation project was initiated in the summer of 1984 when the Journal was awarded a Summer Canada Grant by the Department of Employment and Immigration. Researchers conducted a preliminary examination and comparison of existing citation styles. Rather than adopt the particular style of any one journal or publisher as a model, the incoming and outgoing editorial boards of the Journal chose the criteria of clarity, simplicity, consistency and brevity in order to guide their formulation of basic rules in four major areas: legislation, cases, secondary materials and government documents.

In order to achieve our aim that the citation project would result in a negotiated consensus on citation style across the country, in March 1985, the project coordinators distributed for comment a limited number of copies of a preliminary draft of the *Guide* in English and French. The new system was applied in the McGill Law Journal beginning in September 1984 in order to determine whether it was workable. Reasons supporting the rules were included in the initial draft in order to provide a basis for discussion.

The draft received a tremendous response. Editors of law reviews, journals and publishing houses, university law libraries, members of the Canadian Association of Law Libraries (CALL), judges of the courts of various provinces, legislative counsel, research directors at law firms and others expressed support for the project and submitted detailed comments.

During the summer of 1985, a research fellowship awarded to the McGill Law Journal by the Canadian Law Information Council (CLIC) enabled us to compile and consider the response to the draft and to research new areas: United Kingdom and international materials, and abbreviations. Chapter One, "Legislation", was rewritten in order to incorporate comment by legislative counsel and extensive fresh research. In view of the increasingly interdisciplinary nature of legal scholarship, the guidelines published by the International Organization for Standardization (ISO) were adopted and, accordingly, the inclusion of the place of publication and publisher is now recommended for the citation of books in Chapter Three, "Secondary Materials".

Preliminary drafts of the newly researched citation forms, with supporting reasons, were distributed in the fall of 1985 in both English and French. As well, copies of the *Guide* were printed for use by the McGill Legal Research and Writing program and the Mooting program. The regional Law Journal Conference, hosted by the Queen's Law Journal in February 1986, provided us with an opportunity to discuss citation form with several journals and to reach greater consensus. Response to the new sections of the *Guide* was considered and incorporated into the original manuscript which was finally submitted to Carswell for publication in April 1986.

A second Summer Canada Grant from the Department of Employment and Immigration allowed us to continue research on citation forms for legal materials of France as well as for international materials during the summer of 1986. Research in these areas, as well as additional research in the area of editorial guidelines, continued through to the summer of 1987.

With the support of the Office of the Dean of the Faculty of Law of McGill University, extensive revisions to the *Guide* were undertaken in the summer of 1987. Among the major changes introduced in the second edition was a modification of the "double-date" rule for the citation of cases; the year of decision no longer has to appear in all citations. The citation form for cases was also adapted to conform substantially with the Canadian Law Information Council's *Standards for Case Identification*. Numerous other revisions and additions were made to the chapters covering legislation, cases and Canadian government documents. The sections of the *Guide* dealing with legislation, cases and government documents of the United Kingdom were brought together to form a single chapter. A chapter establishing a system of reference for the legislation, jurisprudence and doctrine of France, and an introduction to legal footnotes, rounded out the additions to the second edition. A draft of the second edition was widely distributed for comment throughout the legal community – legal publications, courts, academics, practitioners.

Further support from the Office of the Dean, and another Summer Canada Grant from the Department of Employment and Immigration enabled us to begin general research and revision on the third edition of the *Guide* during the summer of 1990. A grant from the International Development Research Centre funded extensive research, expansion and revision work on the international materials chapter during the summers of 1990 and 1991. This chapter is now more comprehensive and features rules for citing documents and decisions of many organizations, courts and tribunals, including citation styles for the Organization of American States, the Canada-U.S. Free Trade Agreement and the General Agreement on Tariffs and Trade (GATT). Four new appendices dealing with international materials have also been added. An annotated draft of the new international materials chapter was widely distributed for comment throughout the legal community.

Many of the revisions made in this third edition are the result of comments received from users of the earlier editions. In response to requests from numerous readers, a chapter on citing American materials has been added (Chapter 7). The general editorial guidelines for citation which were found in the "Introduction" to the second edition, have been reworked and rendered more systematic in a section called "General Principles of Citation and Footnoting". With one minor exception, the various sections formerly scattered throughout the *Guide* dealing with the use of "hereinafter", "*supra*", "*ibid.*", etc., have been drawn together here in an attempt to avoid unnecessary duplication and potential contradictions.

While the other chapters of the *Guide* retain the basic rules and structure which led to the success of the earlier editions, an attempt has been made in the third edition to streamline the presentation. Many of the rules have been reworded in the interests of clarity. The bilingual format, whereby readers consulting the English half of the *Guide* were given rules for both English and French writing, has been abandoned: from now on, authors writing in French must use the French half of the *Guide*. It was felt that the former presentation was not only unnecessary but confusing, since an English-speaking reader could be led to believe that the "French" rules pertained to the citing of a French language source in an English text. This issue, i.e. that of citing foreign language sources, was not explicitly dealt with in the previous editions; a new section devoted to it can be found in the "General Principles of Citation and Footnoting".

The *Guide* Committee acknowledges the assistance it received in the initial stages of research through reference to the many learned authors and institutions who have, through their publications, recommended various systems of citation of legal materials. In particular, we would like to acknowledge the works of Mr. Chin-Shih Tang, Professors Margaret Banks, Douglass T. MacEllven and Ernest Caparros.

We are very pleased that the *Guide* continues to be used by more and more members of the legal community – practitioners, courts, professors and journals – as well as by Legal Research and Writing Programs at the majority of Canadian Law Faculties. We would like to emphasize that the citation project is an ongoing process of research and discussion, and that we would be most grateful to receive any suggestions or criticism which would allow us to improve the *Guide*. Any comments should be addressed to the Citations Editor, McGill Law Journal, 3644 Peel St., Montreal, Quebec, H3A 1W9.

ACKNOWLEDGEMENTS

We would like to thank the Canadian Law Information Council (CLIC) for the vital support and encouragement it provided during the preparation of the first and second editions of the *Guide*. We are also indebted to the International Development Research Centre for its grant which enabled the revision and expansion of the International Materials Chapter for the third edition. We also wish to acknowledge the importance of the grants received from the Department of Employment and Immigration. Through its support and encouragement, the Office of the Dean of the Faculty of Law of McGill University was also instrumental in the development of the project throughout its various stages.

An important role was played by Sonia Struthers and Robert Metcalfe, original project co-ordinators, who were central in initiating and sustaining the idea which became the first edition of this *Guide*. Summer researchers and members of the McGill Law Journal Boards of Volumes 30 through 33 performed initial research, verification of sources and revisions of the initial draft. Chantal Roy, Kathryn Sabo, Randall Hofley and Michael Waterston acted as project co-ordinators for the second edition. Louis Fortier and Nathalie Vézina provided translation services for the first and second editions respectively.

Co-ordination for work on the third edition of the *Guide* was initiated by James W.E. Doris and Timothy M. Egan, Citation Editors of Volume 35. Research and revisions in preparation for the third edition began during the summer of 1990 under the supervision of Julia E. Hanigsberg, Editor-in-Chief of Volume 36, with Lisa Yarmoshuk acting as project co-ordinator. Marie-Claude Goulet commenced research for the expansion of the chapter on international materials. In the summer of 1991, under the supervision of David Chemla, Editor-in-Chief of Volume 37, the work on the international chapter was completed by Nan Wang, and Mark Phillips revised the entire text of the *Guide* and added a chapter on American materials.

We would like to thank all those – judges, legislative counsel, research directors, professors, librarians, editors, lawyers and students – who so generously took time to respond to our questions and who submitted extensive and very helpful comments upon the various drafts of all three editions. Our gratitude further extends to Professors J.E.C. Brierley, P.-A. Crépeau, P.-G. Jobin, R.A. Macdonald, A.L.C. de Mestral, and the entire staff of the Faculty of Law, McGill University, for their encouragement and the critical comments supplied for various editions of the *Guide*. We are furthermore grateful to the librarians of the Law Library, McGill University, for their assistance and guidance during the research phases of the *Guide* project.

We would also like to thank Dean Y.-M. Morissette and Professors G.B. Baker, S.J. Toope and P. Healy, past and present Faculty Advisors, and the Trustees of the Journal for their assistance in the publication process. We thank them, along with the other members, past and present, of the Citation Guide Advisory Board – Jill Frank, Daniel Gogek, Jane Graham, Hélène Guay, Randall Hofley, Elizabeth Massey, Grant McCrea, Donald L. Munn, Peter Oliver, Raj Pande, Brian Pel, Chantal Roy, Kathryn Sabo and Henry K. Schultz.

David Chemla   Lisa Yarmoshuk
Editor-in-Chief   Citations Editor
Volume 37   Volume 37

GENERAL PRINCIPLES OF CITATION AND FOOTNOTING

INTRODUCTION

The objective of the *Canadian Guide to Uniform Legal Citation* is to provide a comprehensive system of reference for the citation of legal materials in general use in the Canadian legal community. The *Guide* seeks to assist authors in structuring their footnotes so as to enable the reader to locate the source with ease. While the citation styles given for legislation and cases are valid not only for footnotes but also for tables, bibliographies, lists of authorities, etc., the citation rules for books, articles and other secondary materials are applicable to footnotes only; for information on how to cite these sources in bibliographies, the reader is advised to consult a general style manual.

One major change is to be noted for those familiar with the earlier editions of the guide. The previous editions gave rules for both French and English writing in each half of the guide. In the present edition, the only rules and examples found in the English half of the guide are those which apply when one is writing in English. Someone writing in French must therefore consult the French half of the guide. For a discussion of how to cite French language sources when writing in English, see, below, the section entitled "Citing sources written in a language other than English".

Scholarly writing generally consists of both *text* and *footnotes*. Footnotes may be used any time the author wishes to give additional information or comments of any kind which would not be appropriately included in the text itself. A footnote *must* be used every time the author draws upon an outside source, whether or not that source is being quoted directly. In legal writing, the most common use of footnotes is to provide citations of statutes, cases, books, articles, government documents and other sources of legal authority. Citations never occur in the text itself but only in footnotes.

A citation consists of certain identifying elements which describe the source and ensure that the reader can easily find it in a library. The elements are shown in a set order and are set off by specific typefaces and marks of punctuation. For example, it may be required that a certain element be shown in italics, placed in parentheses, separated from the following element by a comma, etc. The citation styles presented in this guide aim at achieving clarity, simplicity, consistency and brevity in the references. **N.B. In accordance with well-established convention, underlining may always be used in lieu of italics.**

Footnotes are identified by number. As a general rule, these numbers run consecutively from the beginning of the piece to its end. In the text, footnote numbers appear as superscript numbers and may be placed after any word. There is no space between the word and the footnote number; if the word is followed by punctuation (including quotation marks), the footnote number follows the punctuation.

The footnotes themselves appear on each page beneath the text. Each note is preceded by its identifying number. If possible the note should begin on the page where its corresponding number appears in the text.

Citations to different sources are separated by a semi-colon, and the entire footnote ends with a period. A discursive or substantive footnote, i.e. one which contains prose commentary, must consist of one or more grammatical sentences.

INTRODUCTORY SIGNALS FOR CITATIONS

Examples   [25] **See** *Ford* v. *Quebec (A.G.)*, [1988] 2 S.C.R. 712, 54 D.L.R. (4th) 577. There the conclusion of the court seems to have been unequivocal. **Compare** *Irwin Toy* v. *Quebec (A.G.)*, [1989] 1 S.C.R. 927, 58 D.L.R. (4th) 577. **But see** *Mahe* v. *Alberta*, [1990] 1 S.C.R. 342, 68 D.L.R. (4th) 69.

Rules   In addition to citing a source, the author may wish to use an introductory signal before the citation to indicate the logical relationship between the authority cited and the proposition stated in the text. While in no way limited to a closed set of such signals, authors may wish to avail themselves of the following:

- **(No signal)**: The authority cited is being directly quoted in the text or states the proposition given in the text.
- **See**: The authority cited directly supports the proposition given in the text.
- **E.g.** or **See e.g.**: The authority cited is one of several which support the proposition given in the text.
- **See especially**: The authority cited is the strongest of several which lend support to the proposition in the text.
- **See also**: The authority cited provides added support for the proposition given in the text.
- **See generally**: The authority cited provides background information on the topic being discussed in the text.
- **Compare**: The authority cited provides useful contrast to illustrate the proposition given in the text.
- **But see**: The authority cited is in partial disagreement with the proposition stated in the text.
- **Contra**: The authority cited directly contradicts the proposition given in the text.

Do not italicize introductory signals (with the exception of *e.g.* and *contra*).

SUBSEQUENT REFERENCES

Example

² *Nova Scotia (A.G.)* v. *Phillips* (1987), 34 D.L.R. (4th) 633 (N.S.S.C. A.D.) [hereinafter *Phillips*].

⁴³ *Phillips, supra* note 2 at 655.

Rules

Very often a given source will be cited more than once in a piece of writing. The full citation appears only once, in the footnote accompanying the first reference to the source. Subsequent references refer back to this initial citation.

If the source has a long name, the author must choose a short but unambiguous way of identifying it in subsequent text and footnotes. See the section on the "hereinafter" rule below.

Subsequent footnotes will use various cross-referencing signals (*supra*, *ibid.*, etc.) to direct the reader to the footnote containing the complete reference. See the rules on footnoting subsequent references below.

The Hereinafter Rule

If the name of a source is short, the author may use it unchanged in all text and footnotes. If it is long, however, the author should choose a shortened version of the name which will be placed in square brackets at the end of the first citation introduced by "hereinafter". This short name will be used for all subsequent references to the source, both in text and footnotes.

The names of different types of sources are shortened in different ways:

Legislation

Examples

3 *Museums Act*, S.C. 1990, c. 3.

8 *Nordion and Theratronics Divestiture Authorization Act*, S.C. 1990, c. 4 **[hereinafter *Nordion Act*]**.

10 *Canadian Charter of Rights and Freedoms*, Part I of the *Constitution Act, 1982*, being Schedule B to the *Canada Act 1982* (U.K.), 1982, c. 11 **[hereinafter *Charter*]**.

12 *Charter of the French Language*, R.S.Q. c. C-11 **[hereinafter *Bill 101*]**.

Rules

If a statute has an official short title, this should always be used in the initial citation. If it is sufficiently short, it may be used in subsequent references as well; no "hereinafter" indication is necessary in such a case. Where the statute does not have a short name or where the author wishes to use a designation other than the official short form, a short but distinctive name should be used, introduced by "hereinafter".

Cases

Examples

15 *R.* v. *Lavallée*, [1990] 1 S.C.R. 852, 76 C.R. (3d) 329 **[hereinafter *Lavallée* cited to S.C.R.]**.

23 See *Société des Acadiens du Nouveau-Brunswick Inc.* v. *Association of Parents for Fairness in Education*, [1986] 1 S.C.R. 549, 27 D.L.R. (4th) 406 **[hereinafter *Société des Acadiens* cited to S.C.R.]** for a discussion of this issue.

Rules Subsequent references should refer to one of the party names or a distinctive part thereof.

If the full citation contains parallel references to various law reporters, the author must indicate to which of these subsequent pinpoint references are directed ("cited to ..."). For this purpose, the author should choose the most official reporter in which the case is found.

Secondary Materials

Examples [3] J.P. Humphrey, *No Distant Millennium: The International Law of Human Rights* (Paris: UNESCO, 1989).

[6] Humphrey, *supra* note 3 at 25.

OR

[3] J.P. Humphrey, *No Distant Millennium: The International Law of Human Rights* (Paris: UNESCO, 1989) **[hereinafter *No Distant Millennium*]**.

[6] *No Distant Millennium, supra* note 3 at 25.

[10] G.J. Postema, "On the Moral Presence of our Past" (1991) 36 McGill L.J. 1153 **[hereinafter "Moral Presence"]**

[15] "Moral Presence", *supra* note 10 at 1156.

[25] R. Veinott, "Child Custody and Divorce: A Nova Scotia Study, 1866-1910" in P. Girard & J. Phillips, eds., *Essays in the History of Canadian Law*, vol. 3, *Nova Scotia* (Toronto: University of Toronto Press, 1990) 273.

[31] K.S. Maynard, "Divorce in Nova Scotia, 1750-1890", **in Girard & Phillips, eds., *supra* note 25**, 232 at 239.

Rules Secondary materials can always be subsequently referred to by the author's name; no "hereinafter" indication is required for this.

If several works by the same author are being cited, it becomes necessary to use a shortened form of the title for subsequent references. A "hereinafter" marker is therefore required. The shortened form is set off in the same typographical form as the full title, i.e. italics for books and quotation marks for articles.

If a piece forming part of a collection of essays has already been cited, other essays within the same collection may be cited merely by referring to the editor(s) of the collection and cross-referencing back to the initial citation.

Government Documents

Example   25 Alberta, *Interim Report of the Special Legislative Committee on Professions and Occupations* (Edmonton: Queen's Printer, May 1973) (Chair: C. Chichak) **[hereinafter Chichak Committee]** or **[hereinafter *Professions and Occupations*]**.

Rule   The short name may be based on the chairperson's name or a short form of the title.

United Kingdom

Example   45 *Woolmington* v. *D.P.P.*, [1935] A.C. 462 (H.L.) **[hereinafter *Woolmington*]**.

Rule   The rules for Canadian sources also apply to materials from the United Kingdom.

France

Examples   *Loi nº 78-23 du 10 janvier 1978 sur la protection et l'information des consommateurs de produits et de services*, J.O., 11 January 1978, 301, D.1978.Lég.86 **[hereinafter *Loi du 10 janvier 1978*]**.
Décret nº 84-854 du 21 septembre 1984, J.O., 23 September 1984, 2977, D.1984.Lég.538 **[hereinafter *Décret du 21 septembre 1984*]**.
Cass. Ch. réun., 13 February 1930, *Jeand'heur*, S.1930.I.121 (Annot. Esmein), D.P.1930.I.57 (Annot. Ripert) **[hereinafter *Jeand'heur*]**.

Rules   The short form for French legislative materials should consist of an identification of the type of legislation ("Loi", "Arrêté", "Ordonnance", "Décret") and the date on which it was enacted.

If reference is made to two pieces of legislation enacted the same day, subsequent references must contain the number of the legislation or a shortened form of the title.

For French jurisprudence, use one of the party names if possible. Otherwise, simply use the name of the court and the date. In the latter case, no "hereinafter" indication is required.

For information on subsequent references for French encyclopedias, see chapter 6.

United States

Examples	[12] 42 U.S.C. 1983 (1988). [13] 42 U.S.C. 1985(3) (1988). [15] *Griggs* v. *Duke Power Company*, 401 U.S. 424 (1971) **[hereinafter *Griggs*]**.
Rule	The rules for Canadian sources apply. For codified U.S. legislation, however, it is often simplest to provide a full reference in each citation.

International materials

Examples	*Agreement between the Government of Canada and the Government of the Republic of Poland for the Promotion and Reciprocal Protection of Investments*, 6 April 1990, Can. T.S. 1990 No. 43 **[hereinafter *Investment Protection Agreement*]**. UN GAOR, 13th Spec. Sess., 7th Plen. Mtg. UN Doc. A/S-13/PV.7 (1986) **[hereinafter UN Doc. A/S-13/PV.7]**.
Rules	Treaties may be referred to by a shortened form of the title. Other documents may be cited by a shortened title or by number.

Footnoting subsequent references

Example	[10] *Sansregret, supra* note 3 at 502.
Rules	It is not necessary to provide a footnote for each subsequent reference to a source in the text. One need only be provided if a specific part of the source is being quoted or alluded to and therefore a new pinpoint page reference is required. With legislative materials, pinpoint references to different sections are often incorporated right into the text; in such a case no footnote is needed. When a footnote for a subsequent reference is needed, it may contain up to four elements: 1) Identification of the source; 2) Cross-referencing signal (*supra, ibid.*, etc.);

3) Number of the footnote to which the reader is referred;

4) Pinpoint reference.

Place a comma after the identification of the source.

As indicated below, one or more of these elements can be omitted in certain situations.

Supra (Latin – above)

Examples

1 *Reference re Education Act of Ontario and Minority Language Education Rights* (1984), 47 O.R. (2d) 1, 10 D.L.R. (4th) 491 (Ont. C.A.) [hereinafter *Ontario Reference* cited to O.R.].

32 *Ontario Reference*, **supra** note 1 at 13.

37 See also **supra** note 28 and accompanying text.

Rules

If the source is already identified unequivocally in the text, no identification is needed in the footnote.

"*Supra* note #" directs the reader to the original footnote in which the relevant material was cited. "**Supra**" **must always direct the reader back to the full citation.**

Use "*supra* note # and accompanying text" to refer the reader first to the material contained in the cited note and then to the accompanying material in the text.

Ibid. (Latin "ibidem" – in the same place)

Examples

12 See *Commission des Écoles Fransaskoises Inc.* v. *Saskatchewan,* [1988] 3 W.W.R. 354, 48 D.L.R. (4th) 315, 64 Sask. R. 123 (Sask. Q.B.) [hereinafter *Écoles Fransaskoises* cited to W.W.R.].

13 *Ibid.* at 358. See also *R.* v. *Big M Drug Mart,* [1985] 1 S.C.R. 295 at 326, 18 D.L.R. (4th) 321 [hereinafter *Big M* cited to S.C.R.].

14 *Big M,* **ibid.** at 330.

15 *Ibid.*

16 *Ibid.* at 331.

41 Compare *R.* v. *Oakes,* [1986] 1 S.C.R. 103, 26 D.L.R. (4th) 200 [hereinafter *Oakes* cited to S.C.R.]. The test for section 1 of the *Charter* was also discussed in that case (*ibid.* at 135-142).

Rules "*Ibid.*" directs the reader back to the immediately preceding footnote; there is therefore no need to provide the number of that note.

The source need only be identified if there is more than one source mentioned in the preceding footnote.

"*Ibid.*" can be used after the original full citation, or after a note referring back to the original reference by means of "*supra*", or after another note using "*ibid.*"

When "*ibid.*" is used without a pinpoint reference, it is understood that the pinpoint reference is the same as in the preceding note.

"*Ibid.*" is also used when the same source is referred to twice within the same note.

Infra (Latin – below)

Examples 10 For other examples of restrictions on advertising, see *infra* note 53.

53 In 1988, the federal government imposed a ban on cigarette advertising by passing the *Tobacco Products Control Act*, S.C. 1988, c. 20.

Rules As the full citation generally occurs in the first note in which a source is mentioned, one does not normally refer the reader to notes occurring later in a piece of writing. There may, however, be instances where the author will wish to refer the reader to a subsequent note, for example if there are relevant discursive comments to be found there. The cross-reference to a subsequent note is effected with "*infra* note #", or to a subsequent note and the text accompanying it with "*infra* note # and accompanying text".

Above, Below

Examples 23 See Part II, **above**, for a discussion of this issue.

43 On pp. 405-410, **below**, the reader will find a compilation of the relevant statistics.

51 For an analysis of the holding in *Bernard*, see text accompanying note 72.

Rules The English words "above" and "below" direct the reader to portions of the *text* (not footnotes). If the text lacks easily identifiable section or paragraph markers and if

the final pagination of the text is unclear at the time of
writing, the author may use the footnotes as guideposts
by saying "see text accompanying note #".

CITING SOURCES WRITTEN IN A LANGUAGE OTHER THAN ENGLISH

The following principles should be borne in mind when citing
sources written in a language other than English:

Firstly, it should be stressed that regardless of the language of the
source, one must always cite according to the rules given in the English
half of the *Guide* when writing in English. If, for example, one wanted to
cite a French book in an English article, one should not flip the *Guide* over
and cite it according to the rules shown in the French half of the guide.
Those rules only apply when one is writing in French.

Secondly, it is important to know what may be translated and what
must stay in the original language. Let us briefly examine each of the
major types of legal authority.

With respect to legislation, it must first be noted that in Canada all
jurisdictions pass their laws in English. For countries which do not have
an English version of their laws, the rule is that the title of the legislation
must be given in the original language while other elements should be
given in English.

Example   ***Loi n° 91-593 du 25 juin 1991***, J.O., 27 June 1991, 8271,
D.1991.Lég.276.

This example is from the legislation of France. Notice that the title
of the statute is given in French; this includes the first date, since it
forms an integral part of the title of the statute. The second date, however, is merely part of the reference necessary to find the law in the *Journal Officiel* and is therefore given in English.

As to caselaw, it should be noted that in English one should always
use "v." (never "c.") to separate the names of the parties. Titles of reporters and names of courts must be given in the original language unless
they have an official English name.

Example   ***Jean-Louis Boucher*** v. ***Rivière-du-Loup (Ville de)***,
[1990] R.L. 533 at 535 (Que. C.A.), Vallerand J.A.

With respect to secondary materials, the title must of course be
given in the original language. Other elements which are not in the nature of a title or a proper noun should appear in English.

Example   J.-L. Baudouin, *Les obligations*, 3d ed. (Cowansville, Que.: Yvon Blais, 1989) at 240.

GENERAL PRINCIPLES

QUOTATIONS

The following rules apply in both text and footnotes:

Short quotations (four lines or less) are incorporated directly into the flow of the text and are set off by quotation marks. The footnote number appears after the final quotation marks. Long quotations (more than four lines) are indented from both margins and single-spaced without quotation marks. Quotations of legislative provisions, although fewer than four lines, may also be set off in this way.

All quotations must correspond exactly to the original source in terms of spelling, capitalization, and internal punctuation. Any departures from the original must be explicitly indicated. Except where the beginning of a quoted passage is omitted, use ellipsis points, (i.e., three periods: "...") to indicate the omission of any part of a quoted passage. Use square brackets to indicate any editorial modifications such as changes in spelling, punctuation or capitalization of quoted material, including corrections of errors. Where the material cited contains an error, enclose the correction or *sic* in square brackets. Expressions such as "emphasis added", "emphasis in original", "footnotes omitted", etc. appear in square brackets following the citation.

When placing a quotation within a sentence, if the quoted material begins with a capital letter, change it to lower case. Enclose the change in square brackets. When opening a sentence with quoted material which does not already begin with a capital letter, change the lower case letter to a capital, enclosing the change in square brackets.

Examples   He said that "[t]he judgment at first instance was overturned".[5]

"[A] question of mixed fact and law"[10] was the expression used by the judge.

1

LEGISLATION

A. STATUTES

General form

Judges Act,	R. S.	C.	1985,	c. J-1,	s. 4.
title	statute volume	jurisdiction	year	chapter	pinpoint

Elements

1. Title
2. Statute volume
3. Jurisdiction
4. Year
5. Chapter
6. Pinpoint (section, paragraph, etc.)
7. Amendments and repeals
8. Appendix
9. Statutes within statutes

1. TITLE

Examples ***Indian Act****, R.S.C. 1985, c. I-5, s. 19(a).*
City of Moncton Pension Act, 1990*, S.N.B. 1990, c. 69.*

> *The Emergency Planning Act*, S.S. 1989-90, c. E-8.1.
> *Archives Act*, S.N.W.T. 1981 (3d Sess.), c. 2.

Rules   The title of the statute is italicized and followed by a comma.

Use the short title if the statute has one. If none is provided, use the title found at the head of the statute.

A year which forms part of the title should be included. Include the definite article only if it forms part of the title.

Capitalize the first letter of all words except prepositions, articles and connectives.

If the title of the statute is provided in the text, omit this element from the footnote citation.

Note   Change the word "Ordinance" to "Act" when citing Northwest Territories or Yukon legislation originally enacted as an ordinance.

2.   STATUTE VOLUME

(a)   Revised Statutes

Examples   *Courts of Justice Act*, **R.S.O.** 1990, c. C.43.
Interpretation Act, **R.S.C.** 1985, c. I-21.
The Manitoba Evidence Act, **R.S.M.** 1987, c. E150.

Rules   Cite the Revised Statutes (in Manitoba the Re-enacted Statutes) when possible in preference to the sessional or annual volumes.

Both "Revised Statutes" and "Re-enacted Statutes" are abbreviated "R.S."

Note   In Quebec, the preferred citation is to the looseleaf (see Rule 2(c) (viii) below).

(b)   Sessional or annual volumes of statutes

Examples   *Police Act*, **S.B.C.** 1988, c. 53.
The Public Utilities Act, **S.N.** 1989, c. 37, s. 4.
Transportation of Dangerous Goods Act, 1990, **S.N.W.T.** 1990, c. 36.

Rules   Statutes which have not been revised or re-enacted must be cited to the sessional or annual volume.

Abbreviate "Statutes" to "S."

Note "S." for "Statutes" (not "O." for "Ordinances") is now used when referring to any volume past or present of Northwest Territories or Yukon Legislation.

(c) Looseleafs

(i) Canada

1

Rule Do not cite the looseleaf.

(ii) Alberta

Rule Do not cite the looseleaf.

(iii) British Columbia

Rule Use the same form of citation when referring to the looseleaf and bound publications.

(iv) Manitoba

Examples *The Highway Traffic Act*, S.M. 1985-86, c. 3, **C.C.S.M. c. H60**.
   The Municipal Assessment Act, S.M. 1989-90, c. 24, **C.C.S.M. c. M226**.

Rule The looseleaf reference is optional. Acts included in the Continuing Consolidation of the Statutes of Manitoba may be cited "C.C.S.M." followed immediately by the chapter number, with no indication of the year.

Note Statutes included in the Re-enacted Statutes of Manitoba are designated by the same chapter number in the C.C.S.M.

(v) New Brunswick

Rule Use the same form of citation when referring to the looseleaf and bound publications.

(vi) Nova Scotia

Rule Use the same form of citation when referring to the looseleaf and bound publications.

(vii) Prince Edward Island

Examples   *Emergency Measures Act*, S.P.E.I. 1990, c. 60, **R.S.P.E.I. 1988, c. E-6.1**.
Agricultural Development Corporation Act, S.P.E.I. 1990, c. 11, **R.S.P.E.I. 1988, c. A-8.1**.

Rules   The looseleaf reference is optional and should always be preceded by the reference to the bound volume.
Cite the looseleaf as "R.S.P.E.I. 1988" followed by the chapter number.

(viii) Quebec

Examples   *Penal Actions Act*, **R.S.Q. c. A-5**.
Cultural Property Act, **R.S.Q. c. B-4, s. 26**.

Rules   Statutes in their current form should always be cited to the looseleaf.
"R.S.Q." followed immediately by the chapter number, with no indication of the year, indicates the looseleaf. The citation "R.S.Q. 1977", followed by the chapter number, directs the reader to the unamended form of the statute as it is found in the bound volumes of the Revised Statutes.

(ix) Saskatchewan

Rule   Do not cite the looseleaf.

(x) Other Jurisdictions

Newfoundland, the Northwest Territories, Ontario and the Yukon Territory do not at present publish looseleaf editions of their statutes.

3.   JURISDICTION

Examples   *Canada Labour Code*, R.S.C. 1985, c. L-2, s. 14.
The Co-operatives Act, 1989, **S.S.** 1989-90, c. C-37.2, s. 3.
Livestock Brands Act, R.S.N.S. 1989, c. 261.

Rules   Place the jurisdiction immediately after the statute volume.
No comma follows the jurisdiction.

Abbreviate the jurisdictions as follows:

Canada	C.
Province of Canada	**Prov. C.**
Lower Canada	L.C.
Upper Canada	U.C.
Alberta	A.
British Columbia	B.C.
Manitoba	M.
New Brunswick	N.B.
Newfoundland	N.
Northwest Territories	N.W.T.
Nova Scotia	N.S.
Ontario	O.
Prince Edward Island	P.E.I.
Quebec	Q.
Saskatchewan	S.
Yukon Territory	Y.

4. YEAR

Examples   *Construction Lien Act*, R.S.O. **1990**, c. C.30.
Motor Transport Act, S.Y. **1988**, c. 18.
BUT
Registry Office Act, R.S.Q. c. B-9, s. 19.
The International Sale of Goods Act, S.M. 1989-90, c. 18,
C.C.S.M. c. S11.

Rules   Place the year after the jurisdiction.

The year is omitted when citing the looseleaf editions of the statutes of Manitoba ("C.C.S.M.") or Quebec ("R.S.Q.") (see Rule 2(c) above).

A comma follows the indication of the year, unless a session or supplement is indicated parenthetically after the year, in which case the comma follows this indication (see Rules 4(c) and (d) below).

(a) Calendar year

Example   *Freedom of Information Act*, S.N.S. **1990**, c. 11.
NOT
Freedom of Information Act, S.N.S. **39 Eliz. II**, c. 11.

Rule   For all Canadian statutes, provide the calendar year rather than the regnal year.

(b)   When a session spans more than one year

Examples   *The Agrologists Act*, S.S. **1984-85-86**, c. 57, s. 7.
             Statutory Instruments Act, S.C. **1970-71-72**, c. 38.
Rule   Cite the full date span of the volume.

(c)   When there is more than one session in a single year

Example   *An Act to amend the Business Licence Act*, S.N.W.T. 1985 **(3d Sess.)**, c. 1.
Rules   If a statute volume is broken down into several sessions with independent chapter numbering, it is necessary to indicate the session by placing the number of the session ("1st", "2d", "3d", etc.) and the abbreviation "Sess." in parentheses following the year.
            A comma follows the closing parenthesis.

(d)   Supplement

Examples   *Customs Act*, R.S.C. 1985 **(2d Supp.)**, c. 1.
             Gas Burning Devices Act, R.S.Y. 1986 **(Supp.)**, c. 9.
Rules   Cite to the supplement for acts and amendments which were passed during the year in which the Revised Statutes were issued but which were not included in the revision.
             Place the supplement number and the abbreviation "Supp." in parentheses after the date.
             A comma follows the closing parenthesis.

5.   CHAPTER

Examples   *Loan Companies Act*, R.S.N.S. 1989, **c. 264**.
             County of Oxford Act, R.S.O. 1990, **c. C.42**.
             The Ground Water and Water Well Act, R.S.M. 1987, **c. G110**, s. 11.
             Financial Administration Act, R.S.Q. **c. A-6**, s. 12.
Rule   Abbreviate "chapter" to "c." and include the numeric or alpha-numeric chapter designation as shown in the statute volume.

Exception Statutes in Newfoundland sessional volumes are designated by number (abbreviated to "No.") rather than by chapter between 1934 and 1975-76.

Example *The Development Areas (Lands) (Amendment) Act, 1976*, S.N. 1975-76, **No. 18**.

6. PINPOINT (SECTION, PARAGRAPH, ETC.)

Examples *Election Act*, R.S.P.E.I. 1988, c. E-1, **s. 3(2)(h)**.
An Act to amend the Official Languages Act, S.N.W.T. 1990, c. 7, **ss. 2-3, 8, 10-14**.
Copyright Act, R.S.C. 1985, c. C-42, **s. 2, para. 4**.
Canadian and British Insurance Companies Act, R.S.C. 1985, c. I-12, **preamble**.
Appropriation (Interim Supply) Act, 1988, S.A. 1988, c. 13, **sch. A**.

Rules A pinpoint reference follows the chapter indication, the two being separated by a comma.

Abbreviate "section" to "s." and "sections" to "ss." If several consecutive sections are being referred to, give the first and last of these separated by a hyphen; if the sections are not consecutive, separate the numbers with commas.

Numbered or lettered subsections are placed in parentheses immediately after the section number.

Unnumbered or unlettered subdivisions are labelled "paragraph", abbreviated to "para."

Give the word "preamble" in full.

Abbreviate "schedule" to "sch."

Note The provisions of Quebec codes are termed "articles" not "sections". Use "art." and "arts." for "article" and "articles" (see part C, "Codes of Quebec", below).

7. AMENDMENTS AND REPEALS

(a) Amended acts

(i) When amendments are assumed

Example **Railway Act, R.S.C. 1985, c. R-3.**
NOT
Railway Act, R.S.C. 1985, c. R-3, as am.

Rule	As a rule, citations are presumed to be to the statute as amended.
Note	For Quebec statutes, the citation "R.S.Q. 1977" refers to the unamended statute found in the bound volumes. To indicate the amended statute, one must always refer to the looseleaf, cited "R.S.Q." and chapter number, with no mention of the year (see Rule 2(c) above).

(*ii*) When to indicate amendments

Examples	*Social Services Tax Act*, R.S.B.C. 1979, c. 388, **as am. by S.B.C. 1988, c. 25**. *Municipal Taxation Act*, R.S.A. 1980, c. M-31, s. 24, **as am. by *School Act*, S.A. 1988, c. S-3.1, s. 249(a)**.
Rules	If an amendment is relevant to a point being discussed, it should be cited. Place the citation to the original act first, followed by "as am. by" and the citation of the new act. Include the name of the amending statute only if it has a different title from the original act (i.e. other than "An Act to Amend ...").

(b)   An act that amends an earlier act

Example	*An Act to amend the Automobile Insurance Act and other legislation*, S.Q. 1989, c. 15, **amending R.S.Q. 1977, c. A-25**.
Rules	Use "amending" when referring specifically to an act which amends an earlier act. The title of the amended act may be omitted if it appears in the title of the amending statute.

(c)   Repealed acts

Example	*War Measures Act*, R.S.C. 1985, c. W-2, **as rep. by *Emergencies Act*, S.C. 1988, c. 29, s. 80**.
Rules	When referring to an act which has been repealed, include notice of the repeal in the citation. Abbreviate "as repealed by" to "as rep. by". The title of the repealing statute may be omitted if it contains the title of the repealed statute or is substantially similar to it.

(d) **An act repealing an earlier act**

Example   *Schools Act*, S.N.B. 1990, c. S-5.1, s. 83, **repealing R.S.N.B. 1973, c. S-5.**

Rules   Use "repealing" followed by the reference to the earlier act.

The title of the repealed statute may be omitted if it is contained in the title of the repealing statute or is substantially similar to it.

8. APPENDIX

Example   *Canadian Bill of Rights*, S.C. 1960, c. 44, **reprinted in R.S.C. 1985, App. III.**

Rules   Do not cite to an appendix alone; always provide the official citation first.

The phrase "reprinted in" introduces the appendix reference.

Indicate the statute revision or volume to which the appendix is attached, followed by a comma.

Abbreviate "Appendix" to "App."

9. STATUTES WITHIN STATUTES

Example   **Enterprise Cape Breton Corporation Act (being part II of the *Government Organization Act, Atlantic Canada, 1987*, S.C. 1988, c. 50), s. 27.**

Rules   Provide the title of the act within the act.

In parentheses indicate the relevant part of the containing act and its full citation.

Any pinpoint references to section numbers follow the parentheses and are preceded by a comma.

B. CONSTITUTIONAL STATUTES

1. *CANADA ACT 1982*

Example   **Canada Act 1982 (U.K.), 1982, c. 11.**

Rule   This act is cited according to the rules for United Kingdom statutes (see chapter 5). Note that there is no comma in the title of the act.

2.   *CONSTITUTION ACT, 1982*

   Example   **Constitution Act, 1982, being Schedule B to the Canada Act 1982 (U.K.), 1982, c. 11.**

   Rule   Cite as shown.

3.   *CANADIAN CHARTER OF RIGHTS AND FREEDOMS*

   Example   **Canadian Charter of Rights and Freedoms, Part I of the Constitution Act, 1982, being Schedule B to the Canada Act 1982 (U.K.), 1982, c. 11.**

   Rule   As the *Charter* is not an independent enactment, cite as Part I of the *Constitution Act, 1982*.

4.   OTHER CONSTITUTIONAL STATUTES

   Examples   **Constitution Act, 1867 (U.K.), 30 & 31 Vict., c. 3.**
                Constitution Act (No. 2), 1975, S.C. 1974-75-76, c. 53.
                Newfoundland Act (U.K.), 12 & 13 Geo. 6, c. 22 (formerly British North America Act, 1949).
                Statute of Westminster 1931, (U.K.), 22 & 23 Geo. 5, c. 4, reprinted in R.S.C. 1985, App. II, No. 27.

   Rule   Follow the rules for Canadian and United Kingdom statutes (for the latter, see chapter 5).
                Use the new title provided in the Schedule to the *Constitution Act, 1982*, retaining the balance of the reference. The old title may be provided parenthetically if desired ("formerly ...").
                The author may include a reference to Appendix II of R.S.C. 1985 after the official citation.

5.   PINPOINT CITATION

   Examples   *Canadian Charter of Rights and Freedoms*, **s. 33**, Part I of the *Constitution Act, 1982*, being Schedule B to the *Canada Act 1982* (U.K.), 1982, c. 11.
                Constitution Act, 1982, **s. 52**, being Schedule B to the *Canada Act 1982* (U.K.), 1982, c. 11.
                Canada Act 1982 (U.K.), 1982, c. 11, **s. 4**.

Rules   Place pinpoint section references to the *Charter* and the *Constitution Act, 1982* immediately after the title.

Place pinpoint section references to the *Canada Act 1982* and other constitutional statutes after the chapter number.

C. CODES OF QUEBEC

1. CIVIL CODE OF LOWER CANADA (1866)

Examples   **Art. 1024 C.C.L.C.**
Arts. 1053-1057 C.C.L.C.

Rules   The indication of the article precedes the title of the code.

Abbreviate "article" to "art." and "articles" to "arts."

Abbreviate the *Civil Code of Lower Canada*, as amended, to C.C.L.C.

2. CIVIL CODE OF QUEBEC

Example   **Art. 435 C.C.Q.**

Rule   Cite an *Act to Establish a New Civil Code and to Reform Family Law*, S.Q. 1980, c. 39, as the *Civil Code of Quebec*, abbreviated to C.C.Q.

3. CODE OF CIVIL PROCEDURE

Example   **Art. 710 C.C.P.**

Rule   Cite the *Code of Civil Procedure of Quebec*, R.S.Q. c. C-25 as the *Code of Civil Procedure*, abbreviated to C.C.P.

4. CODE OF PENAL PROCEDURE

Example   **Art. 210 C.P.P.**

Rule   Use C.P.P. for the *Code of Penal Procedure*.

D. BILLS

(a) General form

Bill 82,	*An Act ...,*	1st Sess.,	35th Leg.,	Ontario,	1991.
number	title	session	legislature	jurisdiction	year

Examples   **Bill 5, *An Act to Amend the Motor Vehicle Act*, 4th sess., 51st Leg., New Brunswick, 1991, cl. 2.**
Bill C-231, *An Act to amend the Family Allowance Act*, 3d Sess., 34th Parl., 1991.
Bill 15, *Alberta Foundation for the Arts Act*, 3d Sess., 22d Leg., Alberta, 1991.
Bill S-5, *An Act to amend certain statutes of Canada to recognize the war-time service of the veterans of the Canadian merchant navy*, 3d Sess., 34th Parl., 1991.

Rules   The elements are separated by commas.
In the case of federal bills, the number of the bill is preceded by a "C" for bills originating in the House of Commons and an "S" for those originating in the Senate.
Italicize the title.
Unlike statutes, bills should always be referred to by the long title.
Reference to the jurisdiction is omitted in federal bills.
Do not include the regnal year.

Note   The subdivisions which will be called "sections" once the bill is enacted into law, are referred to as "clauses" (abbreviated "cl." in the singular and "cls." in the plural) in bills.

(b)   Additional information

Examples   Bill C-208, *An Act to amend the Department of Agriculture Act*, 3d Sess., 34th Parl., 1991 **(1st reading 27 May 1991)**.
Bill 151, *An Act to amend the Workmen's Compensation Act and the Act respecting industrial accidents and occupational diseases*, 1st Sess., 34th Leg., Quebec, 1991 **(assented to 20 June 1991, S.Q. 1991, c. 35)**.

Rules   Include additional information in parentheses at the end of the citation. This could include such things as the stage reached in the passage of the bill, the fact that a bill already assented to will come into force only upon proclamation, etc.
When citing an act passed and promulgated but not yet bound in a statute volume, cite to the bill and include reference to the assent date at the end of the cite in parentheses. If the chapter number of the bill is known, the future statute citation can be given parenthetically after the assent date.

E. REGULATIONS

1. FEDERAL REGULATIONS

(a) Not revised

1

Examples   **SOR/90-822.**
St. Andrew's Lock Regulations, **SOR/91-144, s. 6.**
Taxes, Duties and Fees (GST) Regulations, **SOR/91-34.**

Rules   [*Title* optional], SOR/last two digits of the year-number.

Abbreviate "Statutory Orders and Regulations" to "SOR".

Federal regulations promulgated subsequent to the Consolidation are found in the Canada Gazette Part II. It is not necessary to include a direct reference to the Gazette in the citation.

(b) Revised

Examples   *Canada Corporations Regulations*, **C.R.C., c. 424, s. 23.**
Seaway Regulations, **C.R.C., c. 1379.**

Rules   *Title*, C.R.C., chapter number.

Abbreviate "Consolidated Regulations of Canada" to "C.R.C."

Indication of the year is optional. Unless otherwise specified, references are assumed to be to the latest revision.

2. PROVINCIAL AND TERRITORIAL REGULATIONS

(a) Alberta

(i) Not revised

Examples   **Alta. Reg. 312/90.**
Alta. Reg. 207/91.

Rule   Alta Reg. number/last two digits of the year.

(*ii*)   **Revised**

Examples   **Alta. Reg. 77/91.**
Alta. Reg. 254/90.
Rule   Cite revised regulations in the same manner as unrevised regulations.

(b)   **British Columbia**

(*i*)   **Not revised**

Examples   **B.C. Reg. 154/91.**
B.C. Reg. 210/88.
Rule   B.C. Reg. number/last two digits of the year.

(*ii*)   **Revised**

Rule   There is no revised edition at present. Cite the looseleaf consolidation in the same manner as the unrevised regulations.

(c)   **Manitoba**

(*i*)   **Not re-enacted**

Examples   **Man. Reg. 84/90.**
Man. Reg. 285/89.
Rule   Man. Reg. number/last two digits of the year.

(*ii*)   **Re-enacted**

Examples   **Man. Reg. 203/87 R.**
Man. Reg. 75/88 R.
Rule   Man. Reg. number/last two digits of the year R.
Note   Most of Manitoba's regulations were re-enacted in English and French in 1987 and 1988. There has been no revision since.

(d) New Brunswick

(i) **Not revised**

Examples	**N.B. Reg. 90-119.**
	N.B. Reg. 89-104, s. 10.
Rule	N.B. Reg. last two digits of the year-number.

(ii) **Revised**

Rule	New Brunswick regulations were last revised in 1963. Cite as above.
Note	The looseleaf of New Brunswick regulations is not an official revision.

(e) Newfoundland

(i) **Not revised**

Examples	**Nfld. Reg. 112/90.**
	Nfld. Reg. 256/90, s. 5.
Rule	Nfld. Reg. number/last two digits of the year.

(f) Northwest Territories

(i) **Not revised**

Examples	**N.W.T. Reg. 063-91.**
	N.W.T. Reg. 031-91.
Rule	N.W.T. Reg. three digit number-last two digits of the year.

(ii) **Revised**

Example	**R.R.N.W.T. 1990, c. A-10.**
Rule	R.R.N.W.T. 1990, chapter number.

(g) Nova Scotia

(*i*) Not revised

> *Examples*   **N.S. Reg. 211/90.**
>   **N.S. Reg. 131/91, s. 10.**
> *Rule*   N.S. Reg. number/last two digits of the year.

(h) Ontario

(*i*) Not revised

> *Examples*   **O. Reg. 45/91.**
>   **O. Reg. 10/91.**
> *Rule*   O. Reg. number/last two digits of the year.

(*ii*) Revised

> *Examples*   **R.R.O. 1990, Reg. 71.**
>   **R.R.O. 1990, Reg. 105.**
> *Rule*   R.R.O. 1990, Reg. number.

(i) Prince Edward Island

(*i*) Not revised

> *Examples*   EC346/89.
>   *Environmental Protection Act Water Well Regulations* (EC188/90).
>   *Natural Areas Protection Act Regulations* (EC54/89).
> *Rules*   [*Title* optional, but usually included] (EC number/last two digits of the year).
>   If the title is not included, omit parentheses.

(*ii*) Revised
> *Rule*   The looseleaf is not an official revision. Cite as above.

(j) Quebec

(i) **Not revised**

Examples O.C. 646-91, 8 May 1991, G.O.Q. 1991.II.1695.
O.C. 826-90, 13 June 1990, G.O.Q. 1990.II.2445.

Rules O.C. number-last two digits of the year, date in full, Gazette citation.
Abbreviate "Order in Council" to "O.C."
The citation to the "Gazette officielle du Québec" follows the general form for Gazette citation (see Part F below).

(ii) **Revised**

Examples *Regulation respecting the quality of the atmosphere,* R.R.Q. 1981, c. Q-2, r. 20.
Regulation respecting fiscal administration, R.R.Q. 1981, c. M-31, r. 1.

Rules [*Title* optional], R.R.Q. 1981, c. number, r. number.
The inclusion of the title is optional but recommended. Abbreviate "Revised Regulations of Quebec" to "R.R.Q."

(k) Saskatchewan

(i) **Not revised**

Examples Sask. Reg. 49/91.
Sask. Reg. 66/90.

Rules Sask. Reg. number/last two digits of the year.

(ii) **Revised**

Examples R.R.S. c. W-13.1, Reg. 49, Sask. Gaz. 1991.II.423.
R.R.S. c. E-0.1, Reg. 10, Sask. Gaz. 1990.II.563.

Rule R.R.S. c. number, Reg. number, Gazette reference.
See Part F, below, for the rules regarding Gazette citation.

Note Amendments to revised regulations are cited in the same manner as unrevised regulations (above).

(l)   Yukon Territory

(i)   **Not revised**

    Examples   **Yukon O.I.C. 1991/141.**
                Yukon O.I.C. 1984/171.
    Rules   Yukon O.I.C. year in full/number.
                Abbreviate "Order in Council" to "O.I.C."

F.   INFORMATION PUBLISHED IN GAZETTES (OTHER THAN REGULATIONS)

1.   GENERAL FORM

Notice	,	C. Gaz.	1991	.	I	.	2337.
Title		Gazette abbreviation	year		part of Gazette		page

    Examples   **Ministerial Order 36/91, A. Gaz. 1991.I.1609.**
                Notice, N.B. Gaz. 1990.I.946.
                Ministerial Order, SI-004-90, N.W.T. Gaz. 1990.I.77.
    Rules   The title should be given if appropriate.
                If the item in question is numbered in some way, this number should be included with the title.
                If the Gazette is not published in parts, cite the page number immediately after the year.
                Use the following abbreviations:

Canada: The Canada Gazette . . . . **C. Gaz.**
Alberta: The Alberta Gazette . . . . **A. Gaz.**
British Columbia:
    The British Columbia Gazette . . . . . . **.B.C. Gaz.**
Manitoba: The Manitoba Gazette . . . . **.M. Gaz.**
New Brunswick: The Royal Gazette . . . . . **N.B. Gaz.**
Northwest Territories:
    Northwest Territories Gazette . . . . **N.W.T. Gaz.**
Newfoundland: The Newfoundland
    Gazette . . . . **N. Gaz.**
Nova Scotia: Royal Gazette . . . . **N.S. Gaz.**
Ontario: The Ontario Gazette . . . . **O. Gaz.**
Prince Edward Island: Royal Gazette . . . . **.P.E.I. Gaz.**
Quebec: Gazette officiel du Québec . . . . **G.O.Q.**
Saskatchewan: The Saskatchewan Gazette . . **S. Gaz.**

Yukon Territory: The Yukon Gazette . . . . . . **Y. Gaz.**

2.   PROCLAMATIONS

Examples   *Canadian Space Agency Act,* S.C. 1990, c. 13, **proclaimed in force 14 December 1990, SI 91-5, C. Gaz. 1991.I.74. Proclamation, 9 August 1969, C. Gaz. 1969.I.1998. Proclamation, 1 April 1991, S. Gaz. 1991.I.1174.**

Rules   Include the date and the Gazette citation.
For federal proclamations from 1972 to date, also include the statutory instrument ("SI") number.
The word "Proclamation" may be included as a title if it is appropriate in the context.

3.   ORDERS IN COUNCIL

(a)   Federal

Examples   **P.C. 1979-1823, C. Gaz. 1979.I.4610.**
***After Hour CFR Fee Remission Order,* SI/90-104, C. Gaz. 1990.II.3526.**

Rules   P.C. year-number, citation of Gazette as set out above.
Include the title if there is one.
Include the statutory instrument ("SI") number if there is one.

(b)   Provincial

Examples   ***The Municipal Government Act, Annexation of Lands,* O.C. 164/80, A. Gaz. 1980.I.759.**
O.I.C. 1989/19, Y. Gaz. 1989.II.57.

Rules   O.C. (or O.I.C.) number, citation of Gazette as set out above.
Cite the abbreviation for "Order in Council" as it appears in the Gazette.
Cite the number as it appears in the Gazette; this may include the year or the last two digits of the year.
Additional information such as name of the act under which the order in council is made may be included.

G. MUNICIPAL BY-LAWS

Examples   **City of Ottawa, By-law No. 103-78,** *A by-law of The Corporation of the City of Ottawa respecting the establishment of The City of Ottawa Spay/Neuter Clinic for the spaying or neutering of cats and dogs* **(5 April 1978).**

City of St.John's, *Heritage By-Law* **(22 June 1977), s. 8.**

Rules   Name of municipality, By-law No., *title* (full date), pinpoint.

Include the by-law number if there is one.

Give the full title if no short title is provided.

H. RULES OF COURT

General form

Manitoba,	Court of Queen's Bench Rules,	r. 275(2)
jurisdiction	title	rule

Examples   **Federal Court Rules, r. 41(1).**

Alberta Rules of Court, r. 154.

Ontario, Rules of Civil Procedure, r. 70.26(3)(b).

Rules   Indicate the jurisdiction unless it is part of the title of the rules. It is also not necessary to indicate "Canada" in the case of the Supreme Court of Canada or Federal Court rules.

The jurisdiction is followed by a comma.

Cite the official title of the Rules (see below), followed by a comma.

Abbreviate "rule" to "r."

Note   To cite the Quebec *Code of Civil Procedure* and *Code of Penal Procedure*, see Part C above.

Titles of Rules

Canada
- Rules of the Supreme Court of Canada
- Federal Court Rules

Alberta
- Alberta Rules of Court

British Columbia
- Rules of Court
- Court of Appeal Rules
- Family Relations Act Rules and Regulations
- British Columbia Court of Appeal Criminal Appeal Rules, 1986
- Small Claims Rules

Manitoba
- Court of Appeal Rules
- Provincial Court (Family Division) Rules
- Court of Queen's Bench Rules

New Brunswick
- Rules of Court

Newfoundland
- Rules of the Supreme Court, 1986

Northwest Territories
- The Supreme Court Rules
- Probate Rules
- Rules of the Court of Appeal Respecting Civil Appeals
- Summary Conviction Appeal Rules of the Supreme Court of the Northwest Territories
- Rules for the Court of Appeals of the Northwest Territories as to A. Criminal Appeals B. Bail on Appeals
- Northwest Territories Supreme Court Rules Respecting Pre-Trial Conferences

Nova Scotia
- Civil Procedure Rules

Ontario
- Rules of Civil Procedure

Prince Edward Island
- Civil Procedure Rules

Quebec
- Rules of Practice of the Court of Appeal in Civil Matters
- Rules of Practice of the Superior Court of Quebec in Civil Matters
- Rules of Practice of the Superior Court of the District of Montreal in Civil and Family Matters
- Rules of Practice of the Superior Court of the District of Quebec in Civil and Family Matters
- Rules of Practice of the Superior Court of Quebec in Family Matters
- Rules of Practice of the Court of Quebec (Civil Division)

Saskatchewan
- Rules of Court

Yukon Territory
- Rules of Court
- Court of Appeal Rules, Yukon Territory, 1974
- Criminal Appeal Rules, 1973
- Small Claims Court Regulations

2

CASES

A. BASIC FORM FOR CANADIAN CASES

Masson v. *Kelly*	(1991),	85	D.L.R.	(4th)	214	(Ont. C.A.).
style of cause	year	volume	reporter	series	page	jurisdiction and court

R. v. *Landry*, [1991] 1 S.C.R. 99	at 110,	62 C.C.C. (3d) 117,	Lamer C.J.
first citation	pinpoint	parallel citation	judge

Elements

1. Style of cause
2. Year of decision
3. Volume
4. Reporter
5. Series
6. Page
7. Pinpoint
8. Parallel citation
9. Jurisdiction and court
10. Judge
11. History of case

1. STYLE OF CAUSE

(a) Omission of the style of cause

Exemple **[1953] 2 S.C.R. 107 at 109-10, 107 C.C.C. 93.**

Rule If the style of cause is already provided in the text, do not repeat it in the footnote citation.

(b) "v."

Example *Barcan* **v.** *Zorkin* (1991), 79 Alta. L.R. (2d) 119 (Alta. Q.B.)
NOT
Barcan v. Zorkin (1991), 79 Alta. L.R. (2d) 119 (Alta. Q.B.)

Rules A "v." separates the names of the parties.
Italicize the names of the parties.
Do not italicize "v."
Never use "c." when writing in English.

(c) Capitalization

Examples ***Canadian Imperial Bank of Commerce* v. *Otto Timm Enterprises Ltd.*** (1991), 79 D.L.R. (4th) 67 (Ont. Ct. (Gen. Div.)).
Re Murphy and Minister of Consumer and Commercial Relations (1985), 22 D.L.R. (4th) 240 (Ont. H.C. Div. Ct.)

Rule Capitalize the first letter of a party name and the first letter of all words other than prepositions, connectives and words in procedural phrases.

(d) Punctuation

Examples *R.* v. *Kumar* (1990), 80 C.R. (3d) 204 (B.C.S.C.).
BUT
Poiré v. *Laflamme,* [1990] R.J.Q. 2703 (C.S.).

Rule No comma follows the style of cause if the year of decision is included. However, if the year of decision is omitted (see rule 2 below), it becomes necessary to place a comma immediately after the style of cause.

(e)   Selection of style of cause and the *sub nom.* rule

Examples   *Laliberté* v. *Larue* (1930), [1931] S.C.R. 7, (*sub nom. Lafontaine Apts.* v. *Larue*) [1931] 2 D.L.R. 12.
Martineau v. *Matsqui Institution Disciplinary Board* (1979), [1980] 1 S.C.R. 602, (*sub nom. Martineau* v. *Matsqui Institution Disciplinary Board No. 2*) 106 D.L.R. (3d) 385.

Rules   Include the party names as provided in the first-cited reporter.
If parallel citations appear under different styles, enclose the second-cited style in parentheses introduced by the phrase "*sub nom.*"

2

(f)   Consolidations, etc.

Examples   R. v. **Fotheringham**
Murray v. **Smith**
NOT
R. v. *Fotheringham and Sun Publishing Co.*
Murray v. *Smith et al.*
BUT
Smith v. **Steal, Grab, Pilfer & Cheat Barristers**

Rules   If the case is a consolidation of two or more actions, cite only the first action listed.
Omit all expressions, such as "et al.", which indicate that there are multiple parties.
Include, however, each element in a partnership name.

(g)   Indications of quality

Examples   **McGill** v. *Shea*
A.G. Canada ex rel. McWhirter v. *Independent Broadcasting Authority*
NOT
Doe dem. McGill v. *Shea*
McWhirter v. *Independent Broadcasting Authority*

Rule   Omit any indications of the quality in which the parties act, but always include the first-named relator, introduced by the phrase "ex rel."

(h) Procedural phrases

Examples   **Re** *Crisan Estate*
Ex parte *Delhasse:* **Re** *Megevand*
Perkins v. *Perkins*
NOT
In re Crisan Estate
Ex. p. Delhasse: In Re Megevand
Re Perkins v. Perkins

Rules   Shorten procedural phrases such as "In re", "In the matter of", and "Dans l'affaire de" to "Re".
"Ex parte" is written out in full.
Omit any procedural phrase which appears before the first-named party in an adversarial style of cause.

(i) Constitutional references

Example   **Reference Re Section 94(2) of the Motor Vehicle Act, R.S.B.C. 1979**, [1985] 2 S.C.R. 486, [1986] 1 W.W.R. 481.

Rule   Use the phrase "Reference Re" to introduce a constitutional reference.

(j) Given names and company names

Examples   **Smith** v. **Jones**
Roncarelli v. **Duplessis**
NOT
Bob Smith v. *Martha Jones*
Frank Roncarelli v. *The Honourable Maurice Duplessis*
BUT
Wickman Machine Tool Sales Ltd. v. *L. Schuler A.G.*

Rule   Omit given names and initials of individuals, except when they form part of the name of a corporation or business firm.

(k) Compound surnames

Examples   *Richard* v. **Beaudoin-Daigneault**
Cannon-Callaghan v. *Mercier*

Rule   Give compound surnames in full.

(l)   Undisclosed party names

Examples   ***Droit de la famille – 871***, [1990] R.J.Q. 2107 (C.A.).
D.L.* v. *M.L., [1990] R.L. 566 (Que. C.A.)

Rules   If the parties' names are not disclosed, use the title and numerical designation provided in the reporter.
Use initials if available.

(m)   Omission of the definite article

Examples   ***Société de développement de la Baie James*** v. *Kanatewat*
NOT
La société de développement de la Baie James v. *Kanatewat*
BUT
The Mihalis Angelos

Rules   Omit "The", "Le", "La", "L'","Les" as the first word of any party name, whether it is part of a company name or not.
The definite article, however, is retained when it is a part of the name of an object proceeded against *in rem* (i.e. ships).

(n)   The Crown

Examples   ***R.*** v. *Romeo*, [1991] 1 S.C.R. 86, 62 C.C.C. (3d) 1.
Doyle v. ***M.N.R.*** (1989), [1990] 1 F.C. 94.
Quebec (A.G.) v. *Lippé*, [1990] R.J.Q. 2200 (C.A.).
Caron v. ***Canada (Employment and Immigration Commission)***, [1991] 1 S.C.R. 48, 77 D.L.R. (4th) 172.
Ontario (Employment Standards Officer) v. *Equitable Management Ltd.* (1990), 75 O.R. (2d) 506 (Ont. Ct. (Gen. Div.) Div. Ct.).

Rules   Refer to the Crown as "R." in criminal cases.
Use "M.N.R." for cases involving the Minister of National Revenue.
In other cases, simply use the name of the jurisdiction followed by a parenthetical indication of the governmental authority involved. Use the abbreviation "A.G." for the Attorney General.
Never use expressions such as "The Queen", "The Crown", "The Queen in Right of", etc.

Also omit phrases such as "Province of".

(o) Place names

(i) Countries, provinces, etc.

Example *Italy* v. *Piperno*
NOT
Government of the Republic of Italy v. *Piperno*

Rules Omit "State of", "People of", "Government of", etc., retaining only the name of the jurisdiction which is a party to the action.
For Canadian jurisdictions, see the rules shown under "Crown" (rule 1(n) above).

(ii) Municipalities

Examples *Smith* v. *Toronto (City of)*
Eadie v. *Brantford (Township of)*

Rule For municipalities, place designations such as "City of", "County of", "District of", "Township of", etc., in parentheses after the place name.

(iii) Other prepositional phrases of location

Examples *Roman Catholic Separate Schools **of Ottawa*** v. *Mackell*
Phillips v. *Blue Cross **of Atlantic Canada***
*Société de développement **de la Baie James*** v. *Kanatewat*
NOT
Roman Catholic Separate Schools v. *Mackell*
Phillips v. *Blue Cross*
Société de développement v. *Kanatewat*

Rule Include all prepositional phrases of location.

(p) Corporate status

Examples ***International Nickel Co. of Canada*** v. *Smith*
Cie Immobilière Viger v. *Lauréat Giguère Inc.*
NOT
International Nickel Co. of Canada Ltd. v. *Smith*
Cie Immobilière Viger Ltée v. *Lauréat Giguère Inc.*
BUT

Phillips & Wang Bros. Inc. v. R.
NOT
Phillips & Wang Bros. v. R.

Rules   Omit "Inc.", "Ltd." or "Ltée" when the name of the party also contains the word "Co." (or "Cie"), which already indicates the corporate status of the party.
But retain "Inc.", "Ltd." or "Ltée" after "Bros.", "Ass'n", "Industries", and other phrases which do not sufficiently indicate the corporate status of the party.

2

(q) Institutions

Examples   *Damus* v. *St. Boniface School Division No. 4*
McBeth v. *Dalhousie College & University*
NOT
Damus v. *Board of Trustees of St. Boniface School Division No. 4*
McBeth v. *Governors of Dalhousie College & University*

Rule   Omit terms such as "Board of Trustees of" and "Governors of", citing only the name of the institution.

(r) Union names

Examples   *Premier Cable Systems Ltd.* v. *I.B.E.W., Local 213*
Boisvert v. *A.E.C.R.*
NOT
Premier Cable Systems Ltd. v. *International Brotherhood of Electrical Workers, Local 213*
Boisvert v. *Association des employés du Conseil de recherches*

Rule   If possible, abbreviate the name of the union according to Labour Canada's annual *Directory of Labour Organizations in Canada.*

2.   YEAR OF DECISION

Examples   *Kruger* v. R. **(1977)**, [1978] 1 S.C.R. 104, [1977] 4 W.W.R. 300, 34 C.C.C. (2d) 377.
R. v. *Cooper* **(1981)**, 49 N.S.R. (2d) 221, 96 A.P.R. 221, 65 C.C.C. (2d) 254 (S.C.A.D.).
BUT
R. v. *Keegstra*, [1990] 3 S.C.R. 697.
NOT
R. v. *Keegstra* (1990), [1990] 3 S.C.R. 697.

Rules   Place the year of decision in round brackets after the style of cause, followed by a comma.

The year of decision is omitted if the first reporter cited is one whose volumes are organized by year (see rule 3(a) below) and the year of the volume (shown in square brackets) is the same as the year of decision.

3. VOLUME

(a) Reporters organized by year

Examples   *Côté* v. *Proulx*, **[1990]** R.L. 191 (Que. C.A.).

R. v. *Landry*, **[1991]** 1 S.C.R. 99.

Canada (A.G.) v. *Lavell* (1973), **[1974]** S.C.R. 1349.

Rules   Many reporters are organized by year. This year (placed in square brackets) identifies the volume of the reporter. With some reporters (e.g. S.C.R. and F.C.), this indication may also be followed by a volume number.

As stated in rule 2, above, the year of decision (shown in round brackets) is omitted if the first reporter cited is organized by year and this year is the same as the year of decision.

(b) Reporters organized by volume number

Examples   *Lightburn* v. *Belmont Sales Ltd.* (1969), **6** D.L.R. (3d) 692, **69** W.W.R. 734 (B.C.S.C.).

Cardinal Construction Ltd. v. *R.* (1981), **38** O.R. (2d) 161, **128** D.L.R. (3d) 662 (C.A.).

Rules   Other reporters are simply identified by volume number.

Place the volume number after the year of decision and before the reporter abbreviation.

4. REPORTER

Example   *Beauregard* v. *R.,* **[1981]** 2 **F.C.** 543, 130 **D.L.R.** (3d) 433 (T.D.).

Rule   Provide the reporter abbreviation (see appendix 2).

5. SERIES

Examples *Re Children's Aid Society of Western Manitoba and Corrigan* (1983), 148 D.L.R. (**3d**) 114 (Man. C.A.).
R. v. *Andrushko* (1977), 40 C.R.(**N.S.**) 216 (Man. C.A.).

Rule If the reporter has been published in more than one series, indicate the series in parentheses (1st, 2d, 3d, 4th, etc.; abbreviate "New Series" to "N.S.").

6. PAGE

2

Example *Ford* v. *Quebec (A.G.),* [1988] 2 S.C.R. **712**.

Rule Indicate the number of the first page of the decision.

7. PINPOINT

Examples *Canada (A.G.)* v. *Lavell* (1973), [1974] S.C.R. 1349 **at 1388**, 38 D.L.R. (3d) 481.
Doyle v. *Sparling*, [1986] R.D.J. 585 **at 587ff** (Que. C.A.).
R. v. *Big M Drug Mart Ltd.*, [1985] 1 S.C.R. 295 **at 351-53**, 18 D.L.R. (4th) 321.

Rules "at" appears before a pinpoint page reference.
"at" is not preceded by a comma.
Abbreviate "and following" to "ff".
Cite specific page references to the first-cited reporter. Parallel pinpoint references may be added at the author's discretion.

8. PARALLEL CITATIONS

(a) Order of reporters

Examples *General Motors Products of Canada Ltd.* v. *Kravitz*, [1979] 1 **S.C.R.** 790, 93 **D.L.R.** (3d) 481.
R. v. *Kulbacki* (1965), 52 **D.L.R.** (2d) 283, [1966] 1 **C.C.C.** 167 (Man. C.A.).
Sealand of the Pacific Ltd. v. *Robert C. McHaffie Ltd.* (1974), 51 **D.L.R.** (3d) 702, [1974] 6 **W.W.R.** 724 (B.C.C.A.).

Rules Include at least one parallel citation if possible.
Cite to an official or semi-official reporter before an unofficial reporter. (See Appendix 1 for a list of official and semi-official reporters.)

Cite to a general reporter before a specific reporter.
Cite to reporters covering larger geographical areas before those covering smaller geographical areas.
The last three rules are subject to the author's discretion.

(b)   The *sub nom.* rule

Examples   **Laliberté v. Larue** (1930), [1931] S.C.R. 7, (*sub nom. Lafontaine Apts. v. Larue*) [1931] 2 D.L.R. 12.
Martineau v. Matsqui Institution Disciplinary Board (1979), [1980] 1 R.C.S. 602, (*sub nom. Martineau v. Matsqui Institution Disciplinary Board No. 2*) 106 D.L.R. (3d) 385.

Rule   If a parallel citation appears under a different style of cause, this style should be given in parentheses at the beginning of the parallel citation, introduced by the phrase "*sub nom.*" (see Rule 1(e) above).

9.   JURISDICTION AND COURT

Examples   *Canadian Imperial Back of Commerce v. Otto Timm Enterprises Ltd.* (1991), 79 D.L.R. (4th) **(Ont. Ct. (Gen. Div.))**.
Murphy v. Penney Motors Ltd. (1979), 23 Nfld. & P.E.I.R. 152 **(Nfld. S.C.T.D.)**.
BUT
Lasby v. Walsh (1920), 13 **Sask.** L.R. 201 **(C.A.)**.
Faubert v. Brown (1938), 76 **C.S.** 328.
Field v. Zien, [1963] **S.C.R.** 632.
NOT
Lasby v. Walsh (1920), 13 Sask. L.R. 201 (Sask. C.A.).
Faubert v. Brown (1938), 76 C.S. 328 (Que. Sup. Ct.).
Field v. Zien, [1963] S.C.R. 632 (S.C.C.).

Rules   Indicate the jurisdiction and the court in parentheses following the page reference. Use the abbreviations found at Appendices 3 and 4.
If the jurisdiction is obvious from the title of any of the reporters cited, reference need only be made to the court. If the court itself is obvious, this too is omitted.

10. JUDGE

Examples R. v. *Landry*, [1991] 1 S.C.R. 99 at 110, **Lamer C.J.**
R. v. *Sorensen* (1984), 56 A.R. 180 at 181 (Q.B.), **Purvis J.**

Rules If the name of the judge appears in the footnote, place it at the end of the citation, preceded by a comma, followed by his or her office in abbreviated form.

No punctuation separates the judge's name and his or her office.

Abbreviate offices as follows:

Chief Justice/Judge . . . . C.J.
Justice/Judge . . . . J.
Justices/Judges . . . . JJ.
Justice/Judge of Appeal . . . . J.A.
Justices/Judges of Appeal . . . . JJ.A.

Optionally, the abreviation for Chief Justice may be followed by an indication of the jurisdiction (for example, "Lamer C.J.C.")

11. HISTORY OF CASE

(a) Subsequent history

Examples *Gay Alliance Toward Equality* v. *Vancouver Sun* (1975), Report of a Board of Inquiry under the *Human Rights Code of British Columbia*, **aff'd [1976] W.W.D. 160 (B.C.S.C.), rev'd (1977), 77 D.L.R. (3d) 487 (B.C.C.A.), rev'd [1979] 2 S.C.R. 435.**
Asselin v. *Davidson* (1912), 13 Que. P.R. 423 (Sup. Ct.), **aff'd (1914), 23 B.R. 274.**

Rules If relevant, indicate the subsequent history of a case as the last element of the citation.

The subsequent dispositions are introduced by "aff'd" (affirmed) or "rev'd" (reversed).

"Aff'd" or "rev'd" always refer back to the primary citation. In the first example above, for instance, the Supreme Court of Canada agreed with the British Columbia Court of Appeal that the initial decision should be reversed; it did not reverse the decision of the Court of Appeal.

Parallel citations may or may not be included when appending the history of a case to the primary citation.

(b) Prior history

Examples   *Multiple Access Ltd.* v. *McCutcheon*, [1982] 2 S.C.R. 161, 138 D.L.R. (3d) 1, 44 N.R. 181, **rev'g (1978), 19 O.R. (2d) 516, 86 D.L.R. (3d) 160 (C.A.).**
Lapierre v. *Quebec (P.G.)*, [1985] 1 S.C.R. 241, 58 N.R. 161, **aff'g [1983] C.A. 631.**

Rules   Append the prior history of a case, if relevant, to the primary citation.
Abbreviate the signals as follows:
"affirming" to "aff'g"
"reversing" to "rev'g"

(c) Prior and subsequent history

Examples   *Ludditt* v. *Ginger Coote Airways Ltd.*, [1942] S.C.R. 406, [1942] 4 D.L.R. 353, **rev'g (1942) B.C.R. 176 (C.A.) (rev'g (1941), 56 B.C.R. 401 (S.C.)), aff'd [1947] A.C. 233 (P.C.).**
National Drying Machinery Co. v. *Wabasso Ltd.* (1978), [1979] C.A. 279, **rev'g [1977] C.S. 782, rev'd [1981] 1 R.C.S. 578, 38 N.R. 224.**

Rules   If prior and subsequent history are appended to the primary citation, indicate the prior history before the subsequent history.
Enclose history which does not refer back to the primary disposition in parentheses.

(d) Different style of cause

Examples   *Glover* v. *Glover* (No. 1) (1980), 29 O.R. (2d) 392, 113 D.L.R. (3d) 161 (C.A.), aff'd (***sub nom. Glover v. M.N.R.***) [1981] 2 S.C.R. 561.
Oakwood Development Ltd. v. *St François Xavier (Municipalité rurale de)*, [1985] 2 S.C.R. 164, 20 D.L.R. (4th) 641, aff'g (***sub nom. Oakwood Development Ltd. v. St François Xavier (Rural Municipality of)***) (1982), 17 Man. R. (2d) 241 (C.A.).

Rule   If the case appears under a different style of cause at any point in its history, this style should be included in parentheses introduced by the phrase "*sub nom.*"

B. UNPUBLISHED DECISIONS

1. GENERAL FORM

(a) Common law provinces and territories

Examples   ***Stephenson*** v. ***Stephenson*** **(6 December 1984), Nanaimo 5920/004143 (B.C.S.C.).**
R. v. ***Rao*** **(24 November 1983), (Ont. C.A.) [unreported].**

Rules   Include the full date of the decision in parentheses, followed by a comma.
This is followed by the name of the judicial district and the docket number. The abbreviated jurisdiction and court are placed in parentheses.
If the docket number of a case does not appear on the title page of an offprint of an unreported common law decision, place the word "unreported" in square brackets following the court.

(b) Quebec

Examples   ***St-Pierre*** v. ***Services des affaires sociales de la Ville de Montréal*** **(12 March 1982), Montreal 500-05-006810-806, J.E. 82-371 (Sup. Ct.).**
Fredette v. ***Montreal Dress and Sportswear Manufacturers' Guild*** **(15 December 1977), Montreal 500-09-001461-771, J.E. 78-14 (C.A.).**

Rules   Follow the rules shown above for common law jurisdictions.
Give the Jurisprudence Express number, if available, after the docket number.

2. CASES IN ELECTRONIC FORM

Rule   Cite to a database only if the case does not exist in printed form, observing the following rules.

(a)   QL Systems

Examples   **R. v. *Butler*, [1992] S.C.J. No. 15 (QL).**
R. v. *Howard*, [1991] A.J. No. 1025 (QL).
***Atlas Copco Aktiebolag* v. *CIL Inc.*, [1986] F.C.J. No. 987 (QL).**

Rules   Give the QL citation after the style of cause. This consists of the year in square brackets as it appears on the screen, the database abbreviation and the number of the judgment.
Place "QL" in parentheses at the end of the citation.

Note   Pinpoint page references are problematic and should be avoided if possible. The page number shown on the screen may vary depending on the choice of segments.

(b)   CAN/LAW

Rule   Most decisions in CAN/LAW databases can also be found in printed form. Cases found only in electronic form should be cited according to the rules given above for unreported judgments.

(c)   SOQUIJ

Rule   Most decisions in SOQUIJ databases can also be found in printed form. For those which cannot, cite according to the rules given above for Quebec unreported judgments, indicating the Jurisprudence Express number if possible.

C.   ADMINISTRATIVE TRIBUNALS

1.   REPORTED DECISIONS

Examples   ***Wilpark Farms Ltd.* v. *Manitoba (Department of Highways)* (1990), 44 L.C.R. 130 (Manitoba Land Value Appraisal Commission).**
***Citric Acid and Sodium Citrate (review)* (1987), 10 C.E.R. 88 (C.I.T.).**

Rules   Follow the basic rules for case citation.
Indicate the style of cause, whether adversarial or non-adversarial, as shown by the particular reporter cited. If

there is no style of cause, substitute the decision number.

Include the name of the tribunal in parentheses at the end of the citation if it is not evident from the title of the cited law reporter.

Include one or more parallel citations if available.

At the author's discretion, additional information such as the decision number or the name of the committee responsible for the decision, may be placed at the end of the citation as parenthetical information.

2

2. UNREPORTED DECISIONS

Examples   ***In the Matter of an Application under the National Energy Board Act of Ontario Hydro*** (April 1991), No. EW-3-90 (N.E.B.).

Hyacinth v. ***Treasury Board*** (15 May 1987), No. 166-2-15746 (P.S.S.R.B.).

Rules   The date of the decision should be given as precisely as possible. It is included in parentheses after the style of cause and followed by a comma.

This should be followed by the decision number and, in parentheses, the abbreviated name of the tribunal.

Any other information which will facilitate locating the source may by included at the author's discretion.

3

SECONDARY MATERIALS

A. BOOKS

General form

P.W. Hogg,	*Constitutional Law of Canada,*	2d ed.	(Toronto: Carswell, 1985)	at 73.
Author	Title	Edition	Publication information	Pinpoint

Elements

1. Author
2. Title
3. Volume number (if it describes a separate book)
4. Edition
5. Publication information
6. Pinpoint reference

1.   AUTHOR

(a)   Single author

Examples   **M.H. Ogilvie**, *Canadian Banking Law* (Toronto: Carswell, 1991).
Lord A.T. Denning, *What Next in the Law* (London: Butterworths, 1982).
J.-L. Baudouin, *Les obligations*, 3d ed. (Cowansville, Que.: Yvon Blais, 1989).

Rules   Full initials precede the author's last name.
Honourary titles, if any, are also included.

(b)   Joint authors

Examples   **R.H. Floyd, C.S. Gray & R.P. Short**, *Public Enterprises in Mixed Economies* (Washington, D.C.: International Monetary Fund, 1984).
BUT
J.B. Laskin *et al.*, *Debtor and Creditor: Cases, Notes and Materials*, 2d ed. (Toronto: University of Toronto Press, 1982).
NOT
J.B. Laskin, E. Gertner, B.J. Reiter, M.A. Springman, M.J. Trebilcock, *Debtor and Creditor: Cases, Notes and Materials*, 2d ed. (Toronto: University of Toronto Press, 1982).

Rules   List up to three authors, including all initials.
To separate the last two authors' names, use an ampersand (&).
If there are more than three authors, cite only the first and use "*et al.*"
There is no comma between the author's last name and "*et al.*"
Place a comma after "*et al.*"

(c)   Editor of a collection as author

Examples   **E. McWhinney, ed.**, *Canadian Jurisprudence: The Civil and Common Law in Canada* (Toronto: Carswell, 1958).
R. Adams & S. Cullin, eds., *The Final Epidemic: Physicians and Scientists on Nuclear War* (Chicago: Educational Foundation for Nuclear Scientists, 1981).

Rules   List up to three editors; if there are more than three, indicate the first followed by "*et al.*".
Abbreviate "editor" to "ed.", "editors" to "eds."
Set off "ed." or "eds." with commas.

(d)   Editor or reviser of a standard text

(*i*)   Author's name as part of title

Example   **L.C. Warmington, ed.,** *Stephen's Commentaries on the Laws of England*, 21st ed. (London: Butterworths, 1950).

Rules   If the author's name has become part of the title, the editor is cited as author.
Include the initials of the editor as well as the indication "ed."

3

(*ii*)   Author's name separate from title

Example   S.A. De Smith, *Judicial Review of Administrative Action*, **4th ed. by J.M. Evans** (London: Stevens, 1980).

Rules   If the author's name has not become part of the title, place the editor's name after the edition statement: author, *title*, # ed. by editor, etc.
Include full initials for the editor(s) and the author(s).

(e)   Translator

Example   E. Durkheim, *The Division of Labour in Society*, **trans. G. Simpson** (Glencoe, Ill.: Free Press, 1933).

Rules   Author, *title*, edition trans. name of translator (publication information).
The inclusion of the translator is at the discretion of the author.

2.   TITLE

Example   M. Jackson, ***Prisoners of Isolation: Solitary Confinement in Canada*** (Toronto: University of Toronto Press, 1983).

Rules   Author, *title*, etc.
Cite the main title in full, in italics.

Do not use abbreviations.
Include the subtitle, preceded by a colon, if it helps to identify the book.
Capitalize the first letter of all words except connectives, articles and prepositions.

3.   VOLUME NUMBER

(a)   **English books**

(*i*)   **The volume is a separate book**

Example   S.A. Schiff, *Evidence in the Litigation Process*, **vol. 1** (Toronto: Carswell, 1978) at 69-70.

Rules   Author, *title*, vol. # (publication information), etc.
The volume number appears before the publication information if it designates a separate book.
Cite the volume number in arabic numerals.
Abbreviate "volume" to "vol." and "volumes" to "vols."
Separate the title and the volume with a comma.

(*ii*)   **The volumes are contained in one book**

Example   K. Marx, *Capital* (New York: International, 1967) **vol. 1** at 15.

Rules   Author, *title* (publication information) vol. #, etc.
The volume designation appears after the publication information if the volume is a subdivision of a single book.
No comma separates the publication information and the volume number.

(b)   **French books**

Examples   F. Laurent, *Principes de droit civil*, **vol. 10**, 5th ed. (Brussells: Bruylant-Christophe, 1893).
H., L. and J. Mazeaud, *Leçons de droit civil*, **t. 3, vol. 2**, 6th ed. by M. de Juglart (Paris: Montchrestien, 1984).

Rules "Vol." may be used to translate the word "tome" in French language works, whether the "tomes" are separate volumes of a work or divisions within a work.

If, however, the "tomes" are further subdivided into "volumes", retain the French designation, abbreviating "tome" to "t."

Indication of tome and volume are placed immediately after the title, set off by commas.

4. EDITION

(a) Two or more editions

Examples J.G. Fleming, *The Law of Torts*, **7th ed.** (Sydney: Law Book, 1987) at 104.

M.A. Tancelin, *Jurisprudence sur les obligations*, **2d ed.** (Quebec City: Presses de l'Université Laval, 1981) at 7.

Rule If the work has appeared in several editions, the number of the edition (1st, 2d, 3d, 4th, 5th, etc.) follows the title.

(b) Unnumbered Revised edition

Example W. Goodsell, *A History of Marriage and the Family*, **rev. ed.** (New York: Macmillan, 1934) at 174-75.

Rule An unnumbered revised edition is indicated by "rev. ed."

5. PUBLICATION INFORMATION

(a) Place of publication

Examples M. Jackson, *Prisoners of Isolation: Solitary Confinement in Canada* **(Toronto**: University of Toronto Press, 1983).

P. Lemieux, *Les contrats de l'administration fédérale, provinciale et municipale* **(Sherbrooke, Que.**: R.D.U.S., 1981).

Rules Open a parenthesis before the place of publication.

Include the place of publication as it appears on the title page or on the verso of the title page. If more than one place of publication is listed, include the first place name only.

When the name of the city alone is insufficient identification, include additional geographical information such as the province, state or country.

Place a colon after the place of publication.

(b) Publisher

Examples   S.A. Schiff, *Evidence in the Litigation Process*, vol. 1 (Toronto: **Carswell**, 1978).

P. Garant, *Droit administratif*, 2d ed. (Montreal: **Yvon Blais**, 1985).

NOT

S.A. Schiff, *Evidence in the Litigation Process*, vol. 1 (Toronto: The Carswell Co. Ltd, 1978).

P. Garant, *Droit administratif*, 2d ed. (Montreal: Les Éditions Yvon Blais Inc., 1985).

BUT

R. St. J. MacDonald, G.L. Morris & D.M. Johnston, eds., *Canadian Perspectives on International Law and Organization* (Toronto: **University of Toronto Press**, 1974).

J.-L. Baudouin, *Les obligations*, 1st ed. (Montreal: **Presses de l'Université de Montréal**, 1970).

Rules   Cite the publisher's name as it appears on the title page or on the verso of the title page.

Omit the definite article ("The", "Le", "La", "L'", "Les") even if it is the first word of the name.

Omit terms such as "Inc.", "Ltd." or "Ltée." which indicate corporate status.

Omit "Publishing" or "Publishers". For French language publishers, omit the word "Éditions" unless it forms part of an indivisible phrase ("Yvon Blais" NOT "Éditions Yvon Blais" BUT, of course, "Éditions de l'homme").

Include "Press" in English and "Presses" in French.

Place a comma after the name of the publisher.

(c) Year

Example   D.T. MacEllven, *Legal Research Handbook*, 2d ed. (Toronto: Butterworths, **1986**).

Rules   Indicate the year of the edition, not the year of the impression.

Close the parentheses after the year.

6.   PINPOINT REFERENCE

Examples   R.J. Delisle, *Evidence: Principles and Problems* (Toronto: Carswell, 1984) **at 129**.
G. Calabresi & P. Bobbitt, *Tragic Choices* (New York: W.W. Norton, 1978) **at 32-35**.
C. Lasch, *The Culture of Narcissism* (New York: W.W. Norton, 1978) **at 3ff**.
E.P. Thompson, *Whigs and Hunters: The Origin of the Black Act* (London: Penguin Books, 1975) **c. 5**.
M.A. Tancelin, *Des obligations: Contrat et responsabilité*, rev. ed. (Montreal: Wilson & Lafleur, 1986) **para. 708**.
D. Bradet *et al.*, *Droit de la santé et de la sécurité du travail* (Cowansville, Que.: Yvon Blais, 1986) **c. 3, para. 3**.

Rules   The pinpoint reference follows the publication information.

A page reference is introduced by "at".

Consecutive page references are separated by a hyphen, retaining at least two digits at all times (*e.g.*, 30-33, NOT 30-3).

The symbol "ff" ("and following") is placed immediately after the page number.

Chapter is abbreviated "c." in both the singular and plural.

Cite the chapter number in arabic numerals regardless of how it appears in the text.

For works with numbered paragraphs, use the abbreviation "para." in the singular and "paras." in the plural.

B.   ARTICLES IN JOURNALS

General form

L.E. . Weinrib,	"Learning to Live with the Override"	(1990)	35	McGill L.J.	541	at 562.
Author	Title of article	Year	Volume	Name of Journal	Page	Pinpoint

Elements

1.   Author

2.   Title of article
3.   Year of publication
4.   Volume number
5.   Name of journal
6.   First page of the article
7.   Pinpoint page reference

1.   AUTHOR

(a)   Single author

Examples   **M. Meltsner**, "Feeling Like a Lawyer" (1983) 33 J. Legal
Educ. 624.
A.L.C. de Mestral, "Le rôle de la pratique dans la formation du droit international public" (1984) 14 R.D.U.S.
441.

Rules   Initial(s) surname, "title" *etc.*
Include full initials and honorary titles.

(b)   Joint authors

Example   **G.A. Ferguson & D.W. Roberts**, "Plea Bargaining: Di-
rections for Canadian Reform" (1974) 52 Can. Bar Rev.
497.

Rules   List up to three authors, including all initials. Use an
ampersand (&) to separate the last two names shown.
If there are more than three authors, cite the first author
and use "*et al.*" to indicate the others.
No comma separates the author's surname and "*et al.*"
Place a comma after "*et al.*"

2.   TITLE

Examples   I. Hunter, **"Liberty and Equality: A Tale of Two
Codes"** (1983) 29 McGill L.J. 1.
A. Popovici, **"De la mutabilité du régime matrimonial
étranger"** (1975) 35 R. du B. 77.

Rules   Author, "title" etc.
Place the title of the article in quotation marks.
No comma follows the title.

3. YEAR OF PUBLICATION

Examples   S.N. Hosenball, "The Space Shuttle in Perspective" **(1981)** 9 J. Space L. 69.

G.E. White, "The Evolution of Reasoned Elaboration: Jurisprudential Criticism and Social Change" **[1973]** Va. L. Rev. 279.

Rules   If a journal is identified by volume numbers, include the year of publication of the article in parentheses.

If a journal is not identified by volume number but rather merely by the year, enclose the year (that shown on the spine of the volume) in square brackets.

4. VOLUME NUMBER

Examples   S.R. Derham, "Set-off and Agency" (1985) **44** Cambridge L.J. 384.

L. Threlfall, "How Have Comparative Living Costs Changed Since 1981?" (1983) **10:3** Can. Bus. Rev. 29.

Rules   Place the volume number between the year of publication and the name of the journal.

Where issues within a volume of a journal are not consecutively paginated, place the issue number immediately after the volume number, separated by a colon.

5. NAME OF JOURNAL

Examples   The Honourable Madame Justice B.M. McLachlin, "Crime and Women – Feminine Equality and the Criminal Law" (1991) 25 **U.B.C. L. Rev.** 1.

Madeleine Caron, "L'égalité sous le Code civil : l'incidence des Chartes" (1990) 24 **R.J.T.** 433.

Rules   Author, "title" (year) volume, journal etc.

Abbreviate the name of the periodical (see appendix 6). Do not italicize the abbreviation.

6. FIRST PAGE OF ARTICLE

(a) General form

Example   H. Kotz, "Taking Civil Codes Less Seriously" (1987) 50 Mod. L. Rev. **1**.

Rule   Indicate the first page number of the article after the name of the journal.

(b)   When the article is published in parts

Examples   R.A. Macdonald, "Enforcing Rights in Corporeal Moveables: Revendication and Its Surrogates" (1986) 31 McGill L.J. **573**, (1986) 32 McGill L.J. **1**.
S. Massé, "Les régimes matrimoniaux au Canada – Analyse comparative des législations provinciales" (1985-86) 88 R. du N. **103, 223**.

Rules   When parts of the article are published in different volumes, indicate the author and title as above, followed by the full journal citation for each part.
When the article is published in parts in one volume, indicate the author, title, etc., as above, including the first page number of each part, separated by commas.

7.   PINPOINT REFERENCE

Example   M.G. Bridge, "Discharge for Breach of the Contract of Sale of Goods" (1983) 28 McGill L.J. **867 at 913**.
Rule   A pinpoint page reference is introduced by "at".

C.   ENCYCLOPEDIC DIGESTS

Examples   *Halsbury's Laws of England*, vol. 34, 4th ed. (London: Butterworths, 1980) at 60, para. 71.
American Jurisprudence, vol. 17A, 2d ed. (Rochester: Lawyers Cooperative, 1991) "Contracts", § 97.
Corpus Juris Secundum, vol. 96 (Brooklyn: American Law Book, 1957) at 397, § 934.

Rules   Follow the rules set out for books, omitting the first element (author).
Pinpoint references can refer to the page and/or paragraph number (abbreviated "para." or "§"). Mention may also be made of the title of the part in question.
For French encyclopedias, see chapter 6 – France.

D. COLLECTIONS OF ESSAYS

Examples   R. Veinott, "Child Custody and Divorce: A Nova Scotia Study, 1866-1910" in P. Girard & J. Phillips, eds., *Essays in the History of Canadian Law*, vol. 3, *Nova Scotia* (Toronto: University of Toronto Press, 1990) 273.

L. Panitch, "The Role and Nature of the Canadian State" in L. Panitch, ed., *The Canadian State: Political Economy and Political Power* (Toronto: University of Toronto Press, 1977) 3 at 14.

Rules   The initials and name of the author of the essay and the title of the essay precede the full reference to the collection, which includes the initials and name of the editor. The first page of the essay and any pinpoint reference follow the reference to the collection.

3

The title of the essay is enclosed in quotation marks; the title of the collection is italicized.

If the author of the essay is also the author of the collection, he or she is cited twice.

Note   If another essay in the collection has already been cited, it is not necessary to repeat the citation to the collection (see General Principles of Citation and Footnoting – Subsequent references at page xxv).

E. BOOK REVIEWS

Examples   S.M. Waddams, **Book Review** (1982) 32 U.T.L.J. 115.

D.M. Paciocco, **Book Review of *Law of Trusts in Canada*, 2d ed. by D.W.M. Waters** (1985) 30 McGill L.J. 335.

D. Schachter, **"Rule and Purpose in International Society"** (1985) 85 Colum. L. Rev. 894.

Rules   Author, Book Review (year) volume journal first page of review.

Include all initial(s) of the author of the book review. The indication "Book Review", which is never followed by a comma, may be followed by the title and author of the book in question. It may also be replaced entirely by the title of the review, if there is one, placed in quotation marks.

F.   FOREWORDS, PREFACES, ETC.

Examples   J. de Larosière, "**Foreword**" in R.H. Floyd, C.S. Gray & R.P. Short, *Public Enterprise in Mixed Economies* (Washington, D.C.: International Monetary Fund, 1984) v at v. Mr. Justice M. Proulx, "**Préface**" in P. Béliveau, *Les garanties juridiques dans les chartes des droits* (Montreal: Thémis, 1991) ix.

Rules   Author, "Foreword", etc. in author, *title* (publication information) first page of foreword at #.
Include full initials of both authors.
Enclose the words "Foreword", "Preface", "Introduction", etc., in quotation marks.

G.   COMMENTS ON LEGISLATION AND CASE COMMENTS

Examples   R. Smith, **Case Comment** (1974) 52 Can. Bar Rev. 315.
M. Gochnauer, **Case Comment on *R.* v. *Roche*** (1984) 62 Can. Bar Rev. 211.
C.E.S. Franks, "**Parliamentary Control of Security Activities**" (1984) 29 McGill L.J. 326.

Rules   Include the full initial(s) of the author.
If the comment has a title, place it in quotation marks: Author, "title" (year) volume journal first page of comment/case comment.
If it has no title, name it "Comment" or "Case Comment" without quotation marks.
The name of the case, preceded by "on", may be included at the discretion of the author:
Author, Comment/Case Comment (year) volume journal first page of comment.
OR
Author, Case Comment on *X* v. *Y* (year) volume journal first page of comment.

H. REMARKS, NOTES, ETC.

Examples   E.L. Meyrowitz, **Remarks** (1981) 75 Proc. Am. Soc. Int'l L. 214.

Note, "Round and 'Round the Bramble Bush: From Legal Realism to Critical Legal Scholarship" (1982) 95 Harv. L. Rev. 1669.

Rules   Author, Remarks (year) volume journal first page.

Include full initial(s) of the author.

If there is no author: Note, "title" (year) volume number journal first page.

Do not enclose "Remarks", "Commentaires" or "Note" in quotation marks.

I. ADDRESSES AND PAPERS DELIVERED AT CONFERENCES

3

(a) Titled

Examples   **B. Laskin C.J.C., "Public Perceptions of the Supreme Court of Canada" (Address to the Canadian Press Annual Association, 20 April 1977) [unpublished].**

J.W. Higham, "Environmental Assessment and Management on Indian Reserve Lands in Canada" (Paper presented to the International Association for Impact Assessment, 1989) [unpublished].

Rules   Speaker, "title" (Address to whom, where, date).

Include the full initial(s) of the speaker.

The office of the speaker may be omitted; if it is relevant, it will usually be included in the text of the article.

Enclose the title in quotation marks.

No comma separates the title and the opening parenthesis.

If the address is unpublished, indicate that fact in square brackets at the end of the citation.

(b) Untitled

Example   **B. Laskin C.J.C., Address (Canadian Bar Association Annual Meeting, 2 September 1982) [unpublished].**

Rules   Speaker, Address (to whom, where, date).

Include full initial(s).

The office of the speaker may be omitted.
There is no comma between "Address" and the opening parenthesis.
Separate the place and the date of the address by a comma, and enclose them in parentheses.
If the address is unpublished, indicate that fact in square brackets at the end of the citation.

J. UNPUBLISHED DISSERTATIONS, LETTERS, THESES, INTERVIEWS

Examples   J.E.C. Brierley, *Bibliographical Guide to Canadian Legal Materials* (Faculty of Law, McGill University, 1968) [unpublished].
R. Cullen, *Federalism in Action: The Canadian and Australian Offshore Disputes Compared* (LL.M. Thesis, York University, 1986).
Letter of B. Diamond to Premier R. Lévesque (30 November 1982.)

Rules   Unpublished manuscripts:
Author, *title* (degree for which the manuscript was written (if any), institution, year) [unpublished].
Letters or Interviews:
Letter from X to Y [or interview with X] (date) location.
Provide the full initials of all persons referred to in the citation.
In citing the location, provide either the place of the interview or "reprinted in" author, *title*, publication information page number.

K. NEWSPAPER ARTICLES

(a) Signed

Example   J. Grey, "Yes to Quebec, No to Its Extreme Demands" *The [Montreal] Gazette* (17 April 1991) B3.

Rules   Author(s), "title" *newspaper* (day month year) page.
Include full initial(s) of the author(s). The author's name is followed by a comma.
Enclose the title of the article in quotation marks.
Italicize the name of the newspaper. Include in square brackets any geographical information, not properly a

part of the newspaper's name, which helps to identify the source.

The page reference must also indicate the section if sections are paginated independently.

If the article is contained on a single page, it is not necessary to repeat that page for a pinpoint citation.

Include the column number if it is useful.

(b) Unsigned

Example "Charter a Poor Safeguard to Citizens, Ex-Justice Says" *The [Toronto] Globe and Mail* (13 February 1982) 11.

Rules "Title" *newspaper* (day month year) page reference.
Same as for signed articles, except that the author is not named.

(c) Untitled

Example B. Savoie, Letter to the Editor, *Le Devoir [Montreal]* (13 August 1985) 6.

Rules Author(s), description of the piece cited, *newspaper* (day month year) page reference.
Include full initial(s).
The description is not enclosed in quotation marks.

L. PRESS RELEASES

Example National Energy Board, News Release 91/30, "NEB Issues Electricity Export Permits to Ontario Hydro" (14 May 1991).

Rules Issuing body, generic designation of document #, "title" (full date).
Title is optional.
Indicate generic designation as it appears on the document ("Press Release", "Release", "Communiqué", etc.).
Provide document number if available.

3

4

CANADIAN GOVERNMENT DOCUMENTS

A. DEBATES AND JOURNALS

Elements

1. Jurisdiction
2. Name of legislative assembly
3. Title
4. Issue (where applicable)
5. Full date of debate
6. Page reference

Examples   **Nova Scotia, House of Assembly, *Debates and Proceedings*, No. 85-29 (18 April 1985) at 1343.**
Journals of the House of Assembly of the Province of New Brunswick (20 February 1875) at 19.
House of Commons Debates (14 June 1991) at 1741.
Debates of the Senate (20 July 1988) at 4057.

Rules   Indicate the jurisdiction, followed by a comma. This element is omitted for federal (House of Commons and Senate) debates as well as any time the jurisdiction is mentioned in the name of the legislative assembly or in the title of the debates.

Indicate the name of the legislative assembly, followed by a comma. This element is omitted if it is mentioned in the title of the debates.

Cite the title, in italics, as it appears on the title page of the document. It is followed by a comma only if the issue number is included in the citation.

If the document is published in numbered issues, cite the issue number.

The full date is enclosed in parentheses.

Cite the pinpoint page reference at the end of the citation introduced by "at".

B.   PARLIAMENTARY PAPERS

1.   IF THE REPORT IS COLLECTED IN THE PUBLICATION OF THE MAIN BODY

(a)   Debates

Example   **Ontario, Legislative Assembly, Standing Committee on Supply, "Estimates, Ministry of Consumer and Commercial Relations" in *Debates*, No. S-56 (28 June 1972) at S-1791.**

Rules   Follow the rules for debates (see part A above) noting the following points:

Two additional elements are inserted into the citation between the name of the legislative assembly and the title of the debates journal, namely the name of the issuing body and the title of the report.

The name of the issuing body, which may be shortened if too long, is followed by a comma.

The title of the report is set off in quotation marks.

The word "in" connects the title of the report with the title of the debates journal.

(b)   Sessional Papers

Example   **Ontario, Legislative Assembly, "Report on Workmen's Compensation for Injuries" by J. Mavor in *Sessional Papers* (1900) at 6-7.**

Rules   Jurisdiction, name of legislative assembly, "title of report" in *Sessional Papers* (date) pinpoint.
The jurisdiction and the name of the legislative assembly are followed by commas.
Place the title in quotation marks followed by "in".
The year is placed in parentheses.
At the author's discretion, additional information such as the sessional number of the paper or the author may also be included.

Note   Most jurisdictions ceased the publication of *Sessional Papers* by 1940.

2. IF THE REPORT IS PUBLISHED UNDER SEPARATE COVER

Follow the rules set out below for papers which do not emanate directly from a legislature.

C. NON-PARLIAMENTARY DOCUMENTS

4

1. GENERAL FORM

Examples   **Alberta, *Interim Report of the Special Legislative Committee on Professions and Occupations* (Edmonton: Queen's Printer, May 1973) at 25.**
***Report of the Canadian Committee on Correction: Toward Unity: Criminal Justice and Corrections* (Ottawa: Queen's Printer, 31 March 1969) at 16-21.**

Rules   Jurisdiction, issuing body, *title* (place of publication: publisher, full date) pinpoint citation.
Cite the jurisdiction unless disclosed in another element of the citation.
Cite the issuing body unless it is named in the title of the report.
Include the breakdown of the issuing body only to the extent that it is informative.
Cite the title of the report as it appears on the title page, including all informative subtitles.
In parentheses, cite full publication information, including place of publication, publisher, and as complete a date as is available.
Pinpoint citations are introduced by "at".

Other elements may also be added to the citation, including those outlined in the following rules.

2. WORKING PAPERS, STUDY PAPERS, ETC.

Example Royal Commission on Matters of Health and Safety Arising From the Use of Asbestos in Ontario, *Living with Contradictions: Health and Safety Regulation and Implementation in Ontario* **(Study No. 5)** by G.B. Doern, M.J. Prince & G. McNaughton (Ottawa: Centre for Policy and Program Assessment, Carleton University, February 1982) at 5.6–5.7.

Rule If an indication of the nature of the publication ("Working Paper", "Study", etc.) appears on the title page, include that indication immediately after the title within parentheses.

3. INDIVIDUAL AUTHOR(S)

Example Law Reform Commission of Canada, *Consent to Medical Care* **by M.A. Somerville** (Hull, Que.: Supply & Services Canada, 1980).

Rule If an individual has had subordinate responsibility for the authorship of the paper, the name of the individual follows the title preceded by the word "by".

4. PARENTHETICAL INFORMATION

Example Special Joint Committee of the Senate and the House of Commons on the Constitution of Canada, *Final Report* (Ottawa: Queen's Printer, 1972) **(Co-chairs: G.L. Molgat & M. MacGuigan)**.

Rule Include the name of the minister, chair, commissioner, etc. at the end of the citation as parenthetical information.

5. SUBDIVISIONS OF A LARGER WORK

(a) With one title

Example   Ontario, ***Report of the Royal Commission on Certain Sectors of the Building Industry***, vols. 1, 2 (Toronto: Queen's Printer, 1974) (Commissioner: H. Waisberg).

Rules   When a publication includes sub-divisions under separate covers, cite as above, including the elements which distinguish the sub-divisions, i.e. volume and date.

Is the word "Book", "Livre" or "Cahier" appears on the title page of the paper, include that word immediately after the title.

(b) With different titles

Example   Ontario, Royal Commission on Electric Power Planning, ***Report: Concepts, Conclusions, and Recommendations***, vol. 1 (Toronto: Queen's Printer, 1980); Ontario, Royal Commission on Electric Power Planning, ***Report: Decision-Making, Regulation, and Public Participation: A Framework for Electric Power Planning in Ontario for the 1980's***, vol. 8 (Toronto: Queen's Printer, 1980).

Rule   When citing subdivisions with different titles, include a full citation for each subdivision separated by a semicolon.

6. PUBLIC PAPERS OF INTER-GOVERNMENTAL CONFERENCES

Example   **Meeting of the Continuing Committee of Ministers on the Constitution, *The Canadian Charter of Rights and Freedoms – Discussion Draft, July 4, 1980,* Document No. 830-81/027 (Ottawa, 8-12 September 1980).**

Rules   Issuing body, *title*, Document No. (location, full date).

Cite the name of the conference or continuing committee in full.

Place a comma between the issuing body and the title, and between the title and the document number.

Include the location and date of the conference or meeting in parentheses, set off by a comma.

5

UNITED KINGDOM

A. LEGISLATION

1. STATUTES

Examples   ***Companies Act*** **(U.K.), 1980, c. 22, s. 4.**
Finance Act 1981 **(U.K.), 1981, c. 35, s. 2(1)(2).**

Rule   Cite United Kingdom statutes in the same manner as Canadian statutes, noting the following points:

(a) Punctuation when the title includes the year

Examples   ***Covent Garden Market Act, 1961*** (U.K.), 1961, c. 49.
Criminal Justice (Amendment) Act 1981 (U.K.), 1981, c. 27, s. 2(1).

Rules   If a date is included in the title of an act enacted before 1 January 1963, the date is preceded by a comma. No comma precedes the date included in the title of an act enacted after 1 January 1963.

(b) Placement of "U.K."

Example   *Sale of Goods Act 1979* **(U.K.),** 1979, c. 54, s. 4.
NOT
Sale of Goods Act 1979, 1979, c. 54, s. 4, (U.K.).

Rule   "U.K." is placed in parentheses and immediately follows the title. A comma follows the closing parenthesis.

(c)   Regnal year or calendar year

Examples   *Law of Property Act, 1925* (U.K.), **15 & 16 Geo. 5**, c. 20.
Policyholders Protection Act 1975 (U.K.), **1975**, c. 75.

Rules   Cite the regnal year for all legislation enacted before 1 January 1963.
Cite the calendar year for all legislation enacted after 1 January 1963.

2.   REGULATIONS

Examples   **S.I. 1980/726.**
Fabrics (Misdescription) Regulations 1980, S.I. 1980/958.
Iso-propyl Alcohol Regulations 1927, S.R. & O. 1927/783.

Rules   *Title*, S.I. [or S.R. & O.] year/#.
The title is optional.
1948 to date – Abbreviate "Statutory Instruments" to "S.I."
Pre-1948 – Abbreviate "Statutory Rules & Orders" to "S.R. & O."

B.   CASES

INTRODUCTION

Examples   **Constantine v. Imperial Hotels Ltd, [1944] 1 K.B. 693, [1944] 2 All E.R. 171.**
John Summers & Sons v. Frost, [1955] A.C. 740, [1955] 1 All E.R. 870 (H.L.).

Rule   Cite United Kingdom cases in the same manner as Canadian cases, noting the following points:

1. MODERN ENGLISH REPORTERS

(a) General form

Examples   *R. v. Brittain* (1971), [1972] 1 **Q.B.** 357, [1972] 2 **W.L.R.** 450, [1972] 1 **All E.R.** 353 (C.A.).
R. v. Bullock (1954), [1955] 1 **W.L.R.** 1, [1955] 1 **All E.R.** 15, 119 **J.P.** 65 (C.C.A.).

Rules   Cite a semi-official reporter before an unofficial reporter.
Cite the Law Reports before the Weekly Law Reports.
Cite to a general before a specialized reporter.
Include two parallel citations, if available.
These rules may be varied at the discretion of the author.

(b) Law Reports

(i) The present five series

Examples   *Co-op. Committee on Japanese Canadians* v. *Canada (A.G.)* (1946), [1947] **A.C.** 87 (P.C.).
Re Robson (1915), [1916] 1 **Ch.** 116.
Hongkong Fir Shipping Co. v. *Kawasaki Kisen Kaisha Ltd.* (1961), [1962] 2 **Q.B.** 26 (C.A.).
E. & S. Ruben Ltd. v. *Faire Bros.* (1948), [1949] 1 **K.B.** 254.
Countess De Gasquet James v. *Duke of Mecklenburg-Schewerin*, [1914] **P.** 53.
Ansah v. *Ansah* (1976), [1977] **Fam.** 138 (C.A.).
Re Associated Transformer Manufacturers' Agreement (1961), **L.R. 2 R.P.** 295.
H.T.V. Ltd. v. *Price Commission*, [1976] **I.C.R.** 170 (C.A.).

Rules   Include "Court of Appeal", abbreviated to "C.A.", at the end of each reference to a case heard in that court; there is no separate reporter for the Court of Appeal.
Abbreviate the Law Reports series from 1891 to date as follows:
Appeal Cases (House of Lords and Judicial Committee of the Privy Council) to "A.C."
Chancery (Chancery Division and appeals therefrom in the Court of Appeal) to "Ch."

5

Queen's (King's) Bench (Queen's Bench Division and appeals therefrom in the Court of Appeal) to "Q.B." or "K.B."

Family to "Fam." (1972 to date) and *Probate* to "P." (1891 to 1971): Family Division, Probate, Divorce and Admiralty Division, appeals therefrom, and Ecclesiastical Courts.

Industrial Cases Reports to "I.C.R." (1975 to date), *Industrial Court Reports* to "I.C.R." (1972 to 1974), and *Law Reports Restrictive Practices* to "L.R. R.P." (1957 to 1972): National Industrial Relations Court and Restrictive Practices Court, appeals therefrom and decisions of the High Court relevant to industrial relations.

Insert the volume number before "R.P." for cases reported in the *Law Reports Restrictive Practices*.

(*ii*)   Law Reports from 1875 to 1890

Examples *Derry* v. *Peek* (1889), 14 **App. Cas.** 337 (H.L.).
Boston Deep Sea Fishing and Ice Co. v. *Ansell* (1888), 39 **Ch.D.** 339, [1886-90] All E.R. Rep. 65 (C.A.).
R. v. *Keyn* (1876), 2 **Ex.D.** 63 (C.C.R.).
Heaven v. *Pender* (1883), 11 **Q.B.D.** 503 (C.A.).
Foulkes v. *Metropolitan District Railway Co.* (1879), 4 **C.P.D.** 267 (Div. Ct.), aff'd (1880), 5 **C.P.D.** 157 (C.A.).
The Moorcock (1889), 14 **P.D.** 64, [1886-90] All E.R. Rep. 530 (C.A.).

Rules Include "Division" abbreviated to "D." in order to distinguish the 1875-1890 series of reports from the later series of reports of the same name.

Include the volume number of the report.

Abbreviate the Law Reports' series from 1875 to 1890 as follows:

Appeal Cases (House of Lords and the Judicial Committee of the Privy Council) to "App. Cas."

Chancery (Chancery Division and appeals therefrom) to "Ch.D."

Exchequer (Exchequer Division and appeals of Inferior Courts before the Divisional courts of Appeal) to "Ex.D."

Queen's Bench (Queen's Bench Division and Crown Cases Reserved) to "Q.B.D."

Common Pleas (Common Pleas and appeals therefrom) to "C.P.D."

Probate (Probate, Divorce, Admiralty and Ecclesiastical and appeals therefrom in the Court of Appeal and Privy Council) to "P.D."

(iii) Law Reports from 1865 to 1875

Examples

Evans v. *Smallcombe* (1868), **L.R. 3 H.L.** 249.

Rowley v. *Rowley* (1866), **L.R. 1 Sc. & Div.** 63 (H.L.).

Dow v. *Black* (1875), **L.R. 6 P.C.** 272.

Alexander v. *Mills* (1870), **L.R. 6 Ch.** 124.

Wilkinson v. *Joughin* (1866), **L.R. 2 Eq.** 319.

Powell Duffryn Steam Coal Co. v. *Taff Vale Railway Co.* (1874), **L.R. 9 Ch. App.** 331.

Baylis v. *Lintott* (1873), **L.R. 8 C.P.** 345.

George v. *Skivington* (1869), **L.R. 5 Ex.** 1.

R. v. *Allen* (1872), **L.R. 1 C.C.R.** 367.

Cattle v. *Stockton Waterworks Co.* (1875), **L.R. 10 Q.B.** 453.

The American and The Syria (1874), **L.R. 4 A. & E.** 226, on app. **L.R. 6 P.C.** 127.

Hyde v. *Hyde* (1866), **L.R. 1 P. & D.** 130 (Ct. Div. & Matr.).

Rules

Include "Law Reports" abbreviated to "L.R." before the volume number and abbreviation of the reporter in order to distinguish this series of reports from the later series of the same name.

Abbreviate the Law Reports' series from 1865 to 1875 as follows:

House of Lords (cases before the House of Lords) to "L.R. H.L." (entitled English and Irish Appeal Cases).

Scotch and Divorce (Scotch and Divorce Appeal cases before the House of Lords) to "L.R. Sc. & Div.".

Privy Council (cases heard by the Judicial Committee of the Privy Council) to "L.R. P.C."

Chancery (cases heard in Chancery) to "L.R. Ch."

Equity (Equity Cases before the Master of the Rolls and the Vice-Chancellor) to "L.R. Eq."

Chancery Appeal Cases (Chancery Appeal Cases and the Court of Appeal in Chancery) to "L.R. Ch. App."

Common Pleas (cases in the Court of Common Pleas) to "L.R. C.P."

Exchequer (cases in the Court of Exchequer) to "L.R. Ex."

Crown Cases Reserved (cases determined by the Court for Crown Cases Reserved) to "L.R. C.C.R."

Queen's Bench (cases in the Court of Queen's Bench) to "L.R. Q.B."

Admiralty and Ecclesiastical (cases in the High Court of Admiralty and Ecclesiastical Courts) to "L.R. A. & E."

Probate & Divorce (cases in the courts of Probate and Divorce) to "L.R. P. & D."

2.   THE NOMINATE REPORTERS (1537-1865)

(a)   General form

Examples   *Baglehole* v. *Walters* (1811), 3 **Camp.** 154, 170 E.R. 1338, [1803-13] All E.R. Rep. 500, 13 R.R. 778 (K.B.).

Ayre v. *Craven* (1834), 2 **Ad. & E.** 2, 4 **N. & M.** 220, 111 E.R. 1, 41 R.R. 359 (K.B.).

Rules   Cite first to the nominate reporter even if it was not consulted. The order of parallel citations is as follows: cite to the *English Reports* abbreviated to "E.R.", then to the *All England Reports Reprints* abbreviated to "All E.R. Rep." or the *All England Reports Reprints Extension* abbreviated to "All E.R. Rep. Ext." and then to the *Revised Reports* abbreviated to "R.R."

(b)   A case included in two or more nominate reporters

Examples   *Barnett* v. *Allen* (1858), 3 **H. & N.** 376, 1 **F. & F.** 125, 157 E.R. 516, 175 E.R. 655, 117 R.R. 736 (Ex. Div.)

Christ's Hospital v. *Grainger* (1849), 1 **Mac. & G.** 460, 1 **H. & Tw.** 533, 41 E.R. 1343, 47 E.R. 1521, [1843-60] All E.R. Rep. 204, 84 R.R. 128 (Ch.).

Rule   Cite the reprints in parallel order to the nominate reporters.

3.   YEARBOOKS

(a)   General form

Examples   **Waldon v. Marshall** (1370), **Y.B. Mich. 43 Edw. 3, pl. 38, fol. 33.**

Doige's Case (1422), **Y.B. Trin. 20 Hen. 6, pl. 4, fol. 34.**

Rules   Case name if it is available (Gregorian year of decision), yearbook term regnal year, plea number, folio number. Abbreviate "Yearbook" to "Y.B."
Indicate the term and abbreviate as follows: Michaelmas to "Mich.", Hilary to "Hil.", Easter to "Pach.", and Trinity to "Trin."
Abbreviate "plea" to "pl."
Abbreviate "folio" to "fol."

(b) Reprints of Yearbooks

Examples   *Beauver* v. *Abbot of St Albans* (1312), Y.B. Mich. 6 Edw. 2, **reprinted in (1921) 38 *Selden Society* 32.**
Jordan's Case (1528), Y.B. Mich. 19 Hen. 8, pl. 3, fol. 24, **translated in C.H.S. Fifoot, *History and Sources of the Common Law: Tort and Contract* (London: Stevens, 1949) at 353.**

Rule   Cite the original yearbook including as many elements as are available before citing to the reprint.

4. SCOTTISH CASES

(a) General form

Examples   **M'Lean v. Bell, [1932] Sess. Cas. 21, [1932] S.L.T. 286 (H.L.).**
Urquhart v. Baxter & Sons (Contractors), [1961] Sess. Cas. 149, [1961] S.L.T. 331 (Ct. Sess.).
Gray v. Caledonian Railway Co. (1911), [1912] Sess. Cas. 339, [1912] S.L.T. 1 Reports 76 (Ct. Sess.).

Rules   Cite to the semi-official reporter (*Session Cases*) before the general reporter (*Scottish Law Times*) and then to any specialized reporter.
Include the court and/or the jurisdiction, "Scotland" abbreviated to "Scot.", after the page citation if either is not obvious from the title of the cited reporter.

(b) Cases Reported in Session Cases

Examples   *A.E. Abrahams Ltd.* v. *Campbell* (1910), [1911] **Sess. Cas. 353 (Ct. Sess., Scot.).**
Thompson v. *Great North of Scotland Railway* (1899), 2 **F. 22 (Ct. Just., Scot.).**
Brownlie v. *Miller* (1880), 7 **R. 66 (H.L., Scot.).**
Fernie v. *Robertson* (1871), 9 **M. 531 (Ct. Sess., Scot.).**
Thompson v. *Fowler* (1859), 21 **D. 265 (Ct. Sess., Scot.).**
Ferrier v. *Graham's Trustees* (1828), 6 **S. 818 (Ct. Sess., Scot.).**

Rules   Abbreviate the six series of Session Cases reporters as follows:
"Session Cases" to "Sess. Cas." (1906 to present).
"Fraser" to "F." (1898 to 1906).
"Rettie" to "R." (1873 to 1898).
"MacPherson" to "M." (1862 to 1873).
"Dunlop" to "D." (1838 to 1862).
"Shaw" to "S." (1821 to 1838).
Include the name of the court because each volume is divided into parts according to the court reported and because the parts are separately paginated.

5.   IRELAND TO 1924 AND NORTHERN IRELAND

Examples   ***Walker*** v. ***Glass*, [1979] N.I. 129 (Ch.D.).**
Johnson v. ***Egan*, [1894] 2 I.R. 480 (Q.B.D.).**
Hardman v. ***Maffett*** (1884), 13 L.R.Ir. 499 (Ch.D.).
Leclerc v. ***Greene*** (1870), I.R. 4 C.L. 388 (Ex.).

Rules   Abbreviate the reporters as follows:
Northern Ireland Law Reports to "N.I." (1924 to date).
Irish Law Reports to "I.R." (1894 to 1924).
Law Reports (Ireland) to "L.R.Ir." (1878 to 1893).
Irish Reports Common Law Series to "I.R. C.L." (1867 to 1878).
Irish Reports Equity Series to "I.R. Eq."(1867 to 1878).
Irish Law Times Reports to "Ir. L.T.R."
Cite in the same manner as Canadian cases.
Cite to a semi-official reporter before a general reporter and to a general reporter before a specialized reporter. Include the jurisdiction, "Ireland" abbreviated to "Ir.", and court in parentheses after the page citation if either is not obvious from the title of the cited reporter.

C. GOVERNMENT DOCUMENTS

INTRODUCTION

Examples U.K., Standing Committee D, "Minutes of Proceedings on the Contracts of Employment Bill" No. 189 in *Sessional Papers* (1962-63) vol. 4, 787.

U.K., Law Revision Committee, "Fifth Interim Report (Statutes of Limitation)" Cmd 5334 in *Sessional Papers* (1936-37) vol. 13, 37.

Rule Follow the basic form set out in Chapter 4 for Canadian Government Documents.

1. DEBATES

(a) 1803 to present

Examples U.K., H.C., *Parliamentary Debates*, 5th ser., vol. 362, col. 1177 (10 July 1940).

U.K., H.L., *Parliamentary Debates*, 3d ser., vol. 185, col. 1011 at col. 1018 (26 February 1867, Earl of Carnarvon).

Rules Jurisdiction, issuing body, *Parliamentary Debates*, # ser., vol. #, col. # (date of debate, other parenthetical information).

Abbreviate "United Kingdom" to "U.K."

Abbreviate "House of Commons" to "H.C."

Abbreviate "House of Lords" to "H.L."

Cite the title as *Parliamentary Debates* for all six series.

Place the series number immediately after the title and separate the two with a comma.

Abbreviate "series" to "ser."

Place the volume number after the series number and separate the two with a comma.

Include the column number.

Abbreviate "column" to "col."

Include the full date of the debate in parentheses.

For a pinpoint reference, cite "at col. #" following the initial column number and place the name of the speaker in parentheses after the date.

5

(b)   Pre-1803

Examples	U.K., H.C., *Parliamentary History of England*, vol. 12, col. 1357 (27 May 1774).
Rules	Cite to the *Parliamentary History of England*.
	Include the jurisdiction, the issuing body, *Parliamentary History of England*, vol. #, col. # (date of debate).

2.   JOURNALS

Examples	U.K., *Journals of the House of Commons*, vol. 185 at 424 (3 July 1930).
	U.K., *Journals of the House of Lords*, vol. 118 at 313 (24 June 1886).
Rules	Jurisdiction, *title*, vol. # at [page] # (full date).
	Do not include the issuing body as a separate element; it appears in the title.
	Cite to either *Journals of the House of Commons* or *Journals of the House of Lords* followed by a comma.

3.   PARLIAMENTARY PAPERS

(a)   Sessional Papers

Examples	U.K., H.C., "Copy of the Reply of Mr Doyle to Miss Rye's Report on the Emigration of Pauper Children to Canada" No. 263 in *Sessional Papers* (1877) vol. 71, 1.
	U.K., H.C., "Reports of the Commissioners Appointed to Inquire into the Grievances Complained of in Lower Canada" No. 50 in *Sessional Papers* (1837) vol. 24, 1.
Rules	Jurisdiction, issuing body (if it does not appear in the title) "title" No. # in *Sessional Papers* (date) vol. #, first page of report, (specific page reference within paper).
	Cite the title as it appears on the title page of the report.
	Place the sessional number of the paper after the title.
	Separate the volume number and the first page of the paper by a comma.
	Cite to the internal pagination of the paper for a pinpoint citation.

Cite to the House of Commons' bound *Sessional Papers* unless the paper appears only in the House of Lords' *Sessional Papers*.

(b)   Command Papers

Examples   U.K., H.L., "Reports from Her Majesty's Representatives Abroad Showing the Earliest Age at Which Marriages Can Be Legally Solemnized in Each of the States of the Continent of Europe" C. 1096 in *Sessional Papers* (1874) vol. 28, 201.

U.K., Law Revision Committee, "Fifth Interim Report (Statutes of Limitation)" Cmd 5334 in *Sessional Papers* (1936-37) vol. 13, 37.

U.K., H.C., "Report of the Committee on the Law Relating to Rights of Light" Cmnd 473 in *Sessional Papers* (1957-58) vol. 17, 955 (President: C.E. Harman).

Rules   Follow the form set out for Sessional Papers.

Abbreviate "Command" as follows:

1833 to 1869 1st series (1 – 4222) – "c."
1870 to 1899 2d series (1 – 9550) – "C."
1900 to 1918 3d series (1 – 9239) – "Cd"
1919 to 1956 4th series (1 – 9889) – "Cmd"
1957 to present 5th series (1 –) – "Cmnd"

The name of the chair may be included in parentheses at the end of the citation.

The appropriate abbreviation for each series is set out at the first page of each Command Paper.

4.   NON-PARLIAMENTARY PAPERS

Examples   U.K., *Royal Commission on the Press, Studies on the Press* (Working Paper No. 3) by O. Boyd-Barrett, C. Seymour-Ure & J. Turnstall (London: H.M.S.O., 1978).

U.K., Commission on the Constitution, *Research Papers 2: Federalism in the United States, Canada and Australia* by M.J.C. Vile (London: H.M.S.O., 1973).

Rules   Jurisdiction, issuing body, *title* by individuals responsible (publication information).

Include the full title as it appears on the title page of the document.

If an individual has had subordinate responsibility for the authorship of the paper, the name(s) of the individual(s) follows the title of the paper introduced by the word "by".

Include the place of publication and the publisher followed by as full a date as possible.

6

FRANCE

A. LEGISLATION

General form

Loi nº 91-593 du 25 juin 1991,	J.O., 27 June 1991, 8271,	D.1991.Lég.276.
Title	Journal officiel	Parallel citation

Elements

1. Title
2. Reference to the "Journal officiel de la République Française"
3. Parallel citation

1. TITLE

Examples   *Loi nº 81-4 du 7 janvier 1981*, J.O., 8 January 1981, 192, Gaz. Pal. 1981. 1er sem. Lég.83.
Arrêté du 6 avril 1984 fixant le taux de la taxe intérieure de consommation sur les produits pétroliers dt assimilés, J.O., 10 April 1984, 1107, D.1984.Lég.293.
Ordonnance nº 45-174 du 2 février 1945 relative à l'enfance délinquante, J.O., 9 February 1945, 652, D.1945.Lég.41.

Rules   Cite the elements of the title (type of enactment, number, date and descriptive title) in French.
The title is italicized.
When the legislation has a number, its descriptive title is optional.
When the legislation does not have a number, cite its descriptive title in full after the date.
The title is not shortened.
There is no comma between the title of the legislation and the number.
There is no comma between the date and the number of the legislation.
Capitalize only the first letter of the title and the first letter of proper nouns.

2.   JOURNAL OFFICIEL DE LA RÉPUBLIQUE FRANÇAISE

(a)   Regular publication

Example   *Décret n⁰ 84-854 du 21 septembre 1984*, **J.O.**, **23 September 1984, 2977**, D.1984.Lég.538.

Rules   Always cite first to the "Journal officiel de la République Française", abbreviated to "J.O."
Cite the publication date in full and the page number.
Place commas after each of the above elements.

(b)   Supplements

Example   *Décret du 5 décembre 1978 portant classement d'un site pittoresque*, **J.O., 6 December 1978 (N.C.), 9250**.

Rules   The indication "N.C." (for "numéro complémentaire") is placed in parentheses following the publication date.
A comma follows the parentheses.

3.   PARALLEL CITATION

Examples   *Décret n⁰ 78-160 du 10 février 1978*, J.O., 14 February 1978, 719, **Gaz. Pal. 1978. 1er sem. Lég.185**.
Loi n⁰ 68-978 du 12 novembre 1968, J.O., 13 November 1968, 10679, **D.1968.317**.

Rules   Cite the volumes "Dalloz", "Sirey", "Gazette du Palais" and "Semaine Juridique" according to the rules in part C, Jurisprudence, below.

Refer to the "Recueil de législation Sirey" as "S."

B. CODES

Examples   **Art. 1713 C. civ.**

Arts. 1382-1384 C.N.

Art. 49 C. proc. pén.

Rules   The number of the article precedes the code abbreviation.

Use the following abbreviations:

Code civil . . . . **C. civ.**

Code civil des Français (1804) . . . . **C.N.**

Code pénal . . . . **C. pén.**

Nouveau Code de procédure civile . . . **N.C. proc. civ.**

Code de procédure pénale . . . . **C. proc. pén.**

C. JURISPRUDENCE

General form

Cass. com.,	30 June 1953,	J.C.P.	1953	.	II	.	7811	(Annot. R. Savatier).
Court	Date	Reporter	Year		Section		Page	Annotation

Elements

1. Court
2. Date of decision
3. Style of cause (where applicable)
4. Abbreviation of the reporter
5. Year of publication of the reporter
6. Section of the reporter
7. Page and/or decision number
8. Parallel citation (where applicable)
9. Annotation, report or conclusions

1.   COURT

(a)   General form

Examples **Cass. com.**, 27 February 1973, Bull. civ. 1973.IV.89, No.
105, J.C.P. 1973.II.17445 (Annot. R. Savatier).
Lyon, 18 December 1952, D.1953.Jur.241.
Cass. civ. 2e, 5 June 1971, Bull. civ. 1971.II.145, No. 203.
Trib. com. Seine, 16 April 1953, Gaz. Pal. 1953. 2e sem.
Jur.121.

Rule Indicate the name of the court followed by a comma and
the date of the decision.

(b)   Court of first instance

Examples **Trib. civ. Cholet**, 17 February 1954, D.1954.Jur.308.
Trib. gr. inst. Aix-en-Provence, 21 October 1982, Gaz.
Pal. 1983. 2e sem. Jur.623 (Annot. H. Vray).
Trib. com. Paris, 27 April 1983, Gaz. Pal. 1983. 2e sem.
Jur.375.
Trib. admin. Nantes, 27 November 1981, Mme Robin,
Rec. 1981.544.

Rules Abbreviate the names of the courts as follows:
Tribunal civil or *Tribunal de première instance* (Civil court of
original general jurisdiction prior to 1958) as "Trib. civ."
Tribunal de grande instance (Civil court of original general
jurisdiction after 1958) as "Trib. gr. inst."
Justice de Paix (Small claims court prior to 1958) as "J.P."
Tribunal d'instance (Small claims court after 1958) as "Trib.
inst."
Tribunal commercial as "Trib. com."
Tribunal administratif as "Trib. admin."
Indicate the city in which the court sits.

(c)   Court of appeal

Examples **Paris**, 3 March 1976, D.1978.Jur.233 (Annot. J. Massip).
Toulouse, 11 February 1977, D.1978.Jur.206 (Annot. J.
Mestre), J.C.P. 1978.II.18898 (Annot. J.-P. Verschaeve).

Rules Indicate only the name of the city in which the court
sits.
Omit the name of the court.

(d) Cour de cassation

Examples **Cass. civ.**, 3 January 1951, S.1952.I.58.

Cass. civ. 1re, 26 January 1983, Bull. civ. 1983.I.33, No. 38, D.1983.Jur.436 (Annot. J. Massip).

Cass. civ. 2e, 4 June 1984, Bull. civ. 1984.II.73, No. 103.

Cass. civ. 3e, 11 May 1976, Bull. civ. 1976.III.155, No. 199, D.1978.Jur.269 (Annot. J.-J. Taisne).

Cass. com., 27 February 1973, Bull. civ. 1973.IV.89, No. 105, J.C.P. 1973.II.17445 (Annot. R. Savatier).

Cass. soc., 29 October 1980, Bull. civ. 1980.V.586, No. 796.

Cass. Req., 21 October 1925, D.P. 1926.I.9.

Cass. Ch. réun., 17 March 1954, Bull. civ. 1954. Ch. réun., No. 2, D.1954.Jur.328.

Cass. Ass. plén., 15 April 1983, Bull. civ. 1983. Ass. plén., No. 4, D.1983.Jur.461 (Annot. F. Derreda).

Cass. Ch. mixte, 23 March 1973, Bull. civ. 1973. Ch. mixte, No. 1.

Rules Abbreviate the chambers as follows:

"Chambre civile" as "civ. 1re", "civ. 2e" or "civ. 3e", depending on whether the decision is from the first, second or third chamber (post-1952).

"Chambre commerciale" as "com."

"Chambre sociale" as "soc."

"Chambre criminelle" as "crim."

"Chambre des requêtes" as "Req."

"Chambres réunies" (pre-1967) as "Ch. réun."

"Assemblée plénière" (post-1967) as "Ass. plén."

"Chambre mixte" as "Ch. mixte".

6

(e) Conseil d'État

Example **Cons. d'État,** 15 October 1982, *Ministère de l'éducation nationale,* Rec. 1982.341.

Rule "Conseil d'État" is abbreviated to "Cons. d'État".

2.   DATE OF DECISION

Examples   Bordeaux, **27 June 1983**, Gaz. Pal. 1983. 2e sem. Jur.467 (Annot. J.-P. Marchi).
Cass. civ., **2 December 1891**, D.1892.I.161 (Annot. L. Sarrut), S.1892.I.92.

Rules   Indicate, in English, the full date on which the decision was rendered.
Place a comma after the date.

3.   STYLE OF CAUSE

Examples   Cass. civ. 3e, 28 November 1978, Bull. civ. 1978.III.275, No. 358.
Cons. d'État, 27 May 1977, **Pagoaga Gallastegui**, Rec. 1977.244.
Cass. Ass. plén., 3 June 1983, **C.P.A.M. de la Corrèze** v. **Garoux**, Bull. civ. 1983. Ass. plén., No. 6, Gaz. Pal. 1983. 2e sem. Jur.462.

Rules   Generally, omit the style of cause.
Indicate the name of the plaintiff when citing a decision from an administrative tribunal or the Conseil d'État.
When citing an unpublished decision or one which is merely summarized in the section "Sommaire" of a reporter, indicate the style of cause.
The author may, at his discretion, indicate the style of cause where the decision is better known by the names of the parties or where confusion might otherwise result (e.g., when two decisions are rendered on the same date by the same court).
Indicate the style of cause in italics, set off by commas, after the date of the decision.

4.   REPORTER

(a)   General form

Examples   Trib. gr. inst. Caen, 30 October 1962, **S.1963.Jur.152**.
Trib. admin. Dijon, *Commune de Saint-Denis-les-Sens*, 12 May 1981, **Rec. 1981.527**.
Cass. com., 16 October 1973, **Bull. civ. 1973.IV.256, No. 285, J.C.P. 1974.II.17846**.

Rules   Indicate the abbreviated title of the reporter, the year of publication, the number of the section or the abbreviation of the section title, and the page and/or decision number.

Separate the elements with periods.

Refer to an official reporter before an unofficial reporter. Parallel citations may be included at the author's discretion.

(b) Title

Examples   Cass. civ., 12 November 1884, **D.P.** 1885.I.357.

Anger, 9 July 1935, **D.H.** 1935.513.

Paris, 4 February 1941, **D.A.** 1941.Jur.216.

Cass. civ., 10 November 1942, **D.C.** 1943.Jur.21.

Trib. gr. inst. Basse-Terre, 26 October 1982, **D.**1983.Jur.92 (Annot. J.-C. Groslière).

Trib. civ. Riom, 9 November 1950, **S.**1952.II.28.

Cons. d'État, 28 February 1964, *Ministère des Armées*, **A.J.D.A.** 1964.580.

Aix-en-Provence, 10 May 1983, **Gaz. Pal.** 1983. 2e sem. Jur.620 (Annot. C. Dureuil).

Cass. civ. 1re, 9 March 1964, **Bull. civ.** 1964.I.105, No. 139.

Cass. com., 30 June 1953, **J.C.P.** 1953.II.7811 (Annot. R. Savatier).

Trib. admin. Dijon, 12 May 1981, *Commune de Saint-Denis-les-Sens*, **Rec.** 1981.527.

Cass. Req., 11 March 1931, **Sem. Jur.** 1931.605.

Rules   Abbreviate the different reporters as follows:

"Recueil périodique et critique Dalloz" (1845 to 1940) as "D.P."

"Recueil hebdomadaire Dalloz" (1924 to 1940) as "D.H."

"Recueil analytique Dalloz" (1941 to 1944) as "D.A."

"Recueil critique Dalloz" (1941 to 1944) as "D.C.

"Recueil Dalloz" and "Recueil Dalloz et Sirey" (1945 to date) as "D."

"Recueil Sirey" (to 1964) as "S."

"Gazette du Palais" as "Gaz. Pal."

"Bulletin de la Cour de cassation, section civile" as "Bull. civ."

"Semaine Juridique" (1927 to 1936) as "Sem. Jur."

"Semaine Juridique" (1937 to date) as "J.C.P."

"Recueil des décisions du Conseil d'État" or "Recueil Lebon" as "Rec."
"Actualité juridique de droit administratif" as "A.J.D.A."

5.   YEAR

Examples   Cass. civ. 1re, 19 January 1965, D.**1965**.Jur.389.
Cass. com., 31 May 1949, Bull. civ. **1949**.II.502, No. 221.
Trib. admin. Dijon, *Commune de Saint-Denis-les-Sens*, 12 May 1981, Rec. **1981**.527.
Rouen, 20 March 1959, Gaz. Pal. **1959. 2e sem.** Jur. 117.

Rules   Cite the volume by indicating the year of publication after the abbreviation of the title of the reporter.
Omit the volume number where more than one volume appears in the same year (i.e., for the "Recueil Dalloz" from 1972, the "Bulletin civil" and the "Semaine Juridique" from 1968).
Indicate the session number after the year of publication when citing the "Gazette du Palais".

6.   SECTION

Examples   Rouen, 28 November 1925, D.P. **1927**.II.172 (Annot. G. Lepargneur).
Cass. Req., 7 October 1940, D.H. **1940**.Jur.180.
Poitiers, 9 February 1942, D.A. **1942**.Jur.114.
Trib. civ. Seine, 13 July 1944, D.C. **1944**.Jur.173 (Annot. H. Lalou).
Cass. Ass. plén., 15 April 1983, D.**1983**.Jur.461 (Annot. F. Derrida).
Cass. civ., 12 November 1884, S.**1886**.I.149.
Trib. gr. inst. Caen, 30 October 1962, S.**1963**.Jur.152.
Cass. Req., 5 June 1929, Gaz. Pal. **1929. 2e sem. Jur**.433.
Cass. com., 2 May 1984, Bull. civ. **1984**.IV.123, No. 145.
Trib. Seine, 22 January 1930, Sem. Jur. **1930**.Jur.578.
Trib. gr. inst. Nancy, 15 October 1976, J.C.P. **1977**.II.18526 (Annot. R. Lindon).
Cass. Ass. plén., 15 avril 1983, Bull. civ. **1973. Ass. plén.**, No. 4.

Rules   When the sections in the volume are numbered, indicate the section number in roman numerals after the year of publication.

When the sections in the volume are not numbered, give the abbreviation of the section title.

Abbreviate the section titles as follows:

"Jurisprudence" as "Jur."

"Législation", "Lois et décrets", "Textes de lois" etc. as "Lég."

"Chroniques" as "Chron."

"Doctrine" as "Doctr."

"Sommaire" as "Somm."

"Informations rapides" as "Inf."

"Panorama de jurisprudence" as "Pan."

"Chambre des requêtes" as "Req."

"Chambres réunies" as "Ch. réun."

"Assemblée plénière" as "Ass. plén."

"Chambre mixte" as "Ch. mixte"

Set off the section title with periods.

Exception   Do not indicate the section when citing the "Recueil Lebon" or the "Actualité juridique de droit administratif".

7.   PAGE AND/OR DECISION NUMBER

Examples   Cass. civ. 1re, 26 January 1983, Bull. civ. 1983.I.33, No. 38, D.1983.Jur.**436** (Annot. J. Massip).

Cass. soc., 27 January 1939, J.C.P. 1940.**1393**.

Cass. Ch. mixte, 23 March 1973, Bull. civ. 1973. Ch. mixte, **No. 1**.

Cass. crim., 31 March 1981, D.1983.Jur.**39 at 40**.

Rules   Indicate the page number after the section reference or the year of publication.

When referring to the "Semaine Juridique", provide the decision number instead.

Cite both the page and decision number separated by a comma for the "Bulletin de la Cour de cassation".

Note   Pinpoint citations are rarely used given the brevity of most decisions. Should one be required, it is always placed immediately after the page number introduced by "at".

8.   PARALLEL CITATION

Example   Cass. com., 16 October 1973, Bull. civ. 1973.IV.256, No. 285, **J.C.P. 1974.II.17846.**

Rules   Refer to an official reporter before an unofficial reporter. Parallel citations may be provided at the author's discretion.

9.   ANNOTATIONS, REPORTS AND CONCLUSIONS

Examples   Cass. civ. 1re, 13 February 1985, J.C.P. 1985.II.20388 **(Concl. Gulphe),** D.1985.Inf.403 **(Annot. J. Penneau).** Cass. com., 27 October 1970, Bull. civ. 1970.IV.249, No. 285, J.C.P. 1971.II.16655 **(Annot. P.L.).**

Rules   As the last element in the citation, indicate in parentheses any annotations, reports or conclusions which follow the decision.

Refer to "Annot.", "Rep." or "Concl." followed by the name of the author.

Note   If one wishes to refer directly to such commentary, see rule D 2 below.

D.   DOCTRINE

INTRODUCTION

Examples   **J. Mestres, "La pluralité d'obligés accessoires" (1981) 79 R.T.D.C. 1.**
P. Dubois, "La responsabilité civile des dirigeants de sociétés anonymes du secteur public" (1986) 8 Rev. soc. 47.

Rule   Cite the doctrine of France according to the rules set out in Chapter 3, "Secondary Materials", noting the following exceptions.

1.   ARTICLES PUBLISHED IN GENERAL REPORTERS

Examples   **R. Savatier, "Les contrats de conseil professionnel en droit privé" D.1972.Chron.137, No. 10.**
R. Meurisse, "Les interférences du rapport à fin d'égalité et du rapport à fin de réduction" S.1962.Chron.61.

M.P. Malinvaud, "La responsabilité civile du fabriquant en droit français" Gaz. Pal. 2e sem. 1973.Chron.463, No. 15ff.

J. Robert, "L'avant-projet du Code pénal" J.C.P. 1976.I.281 at 283.

Rules   Provide the author and title of the comment according to the rules set out in Chapter 3, "Secondary Materials". Cite the "Dalloz", "Sirey", "Gazette du Palais" and "Semaine Juridique" according to the rules set out in Part C, "Jurisprudence", above.

When a volume contains two sections entitled "Chroniques", cite the case comments section as "Chron. jur." and the legislative comments section as "Chron. lég."

Pinpoint references refer either to the paragraph number or to the page.

2.   ANNOTATIONS ACCOMPANYING THE TEXT OF A DECISION

Examples   P. Jestaz, Annotation of Cass. civ. 3e, 23 March 1968, D.1970.Jur.663 at 665.

M. Boitard & J.-C. Dubarry, Annotation of Paris, 15 May 1975, J.C.P. 1976.II.18265.

Rules   Author, "Annotation of" name of the court, date of the decision, abbreviated title of the reporter.year.section.page.

Cite the decision which is annotated following the rules for citing French cases in Part C, "Jurisprudence", above. Pinpoint references follow the indication of the first page of the annotation, introduced by "at".

E.   ENCYCLOPEDIAS

INTRODUCTION

Examples   *Encyclopédie juridique Dalloz: Répertoire de droit civil*, 2d ed., "Astreintes", by J. Bauré.

Juris-classeur civil, art. 3, fasc. N, by P. Malaurie, No. 38.

Rules   *Title of the collection,* edition [if applicable], subject heading, by Author of the section of the encyclopedia, pinpoint.

Do not provide a parallel citation, even when a section is published in more than one collection of the "Juris-classeur".

Refer to the "Juris-classeur civil" before any other collection of the "Juris-classeur".

1.   TITLE OF THE COLLECTION

Examples   ***Juris-classeur commercial: Banque et crédit,*** vol. 2, fasc. 32, by J. Stoufflet, No. 1-5.
Juris-classeur civil, art. 1315 à 1316, by G. Wiederkehr.
Encyclopédie juridique Dalloz: Répertoire de droit civil, 2d ed., "Publicité foncière" by M. Donnier, No. 528.

Rules   *Title of the collection,* edition [if applicable], subject heading, by author of the section, pinpoint.

Provide the full title of the collection.

Place the title in italics.

2.   "HEREINAFTER" RULE

Example   *Encyclopédie juridique Dalloz: Répertoire de droit civil,* 2d ed., "Publicité foncière", by M. Donnier **[hereinafter *Rép. Civ. Dalloz*]**.

Rules   To make subsequent references to the encyclopedia in the text, use the expression "hereinafter" to indicate the abbreviated title of the encyclopedia that will be employed.

Abbreviate the principal collections as follows:
"Juris-classeur civil" to "J.-cl. civ."
"Juris-classeur commercial" to "J.-cl. com."
"Juris-classeur commercial : Banque et crédit" to "J.-cl. com. : Banque et crédit"
"Juris-classeur responsabilité civile" to "J.-cl. resp. civ."
"Juris-classeur civil annexe" to "J.-cl. civ. annexe"
"Juris-classeur répertoire notarial" to "J.-cl. rép. not."
"Juris-classeur administratif" to "J.-cl. admin."
"Encyclopédie juridique Dalloz : Répertoire de droit civil" to "Rép. civ. Dalloz"

"Répertoire de droit commercial" of the Encyclopédie Dalloz to "Rép. com. Dalloz"
"Repertoire de droit administratif" to "Rép. admin. Dalloz"
Place the abbreviated title of the collection in italics.

3. EDITION

Examples   *Encyclopédie juridique Dalloz: Répertoire de droit civil*, **2d ed.**, "Publicité foncière", by M. Donnier.
Encyclopédie juridique Dalloz: Répertoire de droit commercial, **2d ed.**, "Ventes commerciales", by L. Bihl, No. 256ff.

Rules   When there is more than one edition, refer to the number of the edition in the abbreviated form indicated in Chapter 3 of the *Guide*.
Provide the reference to the edition after the title of the collection.

4. SUBJECT HEADING

(a) The sections are organized in alphabetical order

Examples   *Encyclopédie juridique Dalloz: Répertoire de droit international*, **"Propriété littéraire et artistique"**, by H. Desbois.
Juris-classeur civil annexes, **"Associations" fasc. 1-A**, by R. Brichet.

Rules   Provide the name of the section (key-word under which the cited section is found) in quotations.
Capitalize only the first letter of the first word.
Indicate "fasc. #" after the name of the section if there is a fascicule number corresponding to the section.
Do not refer to the date of the revision of the fascicule.

(b) The sections are organized by articles of a Code

Examples   *Juris-classeur civil*, **app. art. 3, fasc. 4**, by Y. Luchaine.
Juris-classeur civil, **art. 1354 à 1356, fasc. A**, by R. Perrot.

Rules   Indicate the article (or articles) under which the section is classified following the form used in the collection, e.g. "art. #", "app. art. #", "art. # à #", etc.
If applicable, indicate "fasc. #" after the reference to the article.

(c)   The sections are classified according to a numerical system

Examples   *Juris-classeur commercial: Concurrence consommation,* **vol. 1, fasc. 360**, by V. Sélinsky.

Juris-classeur administratif, **vol. 6, fasc. 530**, by J. Dufau, No. 29-30.

Rules   Provide the number of the volume in which the section is found.

Indicate the number of the fascicule after the number of the volume.

Place a comma between the title of the collection and the volume reference.

Place a comma between the volume reference and the fascicule number.

7

UNITED STATES

A. CONSTITUTIONS

Examples **U.S. Const. preamble.**
U.S. Const. art. IV, § 2, cl. 3.
U.S. Const. amend. XX, § 2.
La. Const. art. V, § 14.

Rules Abbreviate "United States Constitution" to "U.S. Const."

Use "art." for "article", "amend." for "amendment", "§" or "s." for "section" and "cl." for "clause".

Give article and amendment numbers in capital Roman numerals, section and clause numbers in Arabic numerals.

Cite state constitutions in similar fashion, abbreviating the name of the state.

B. STATUTES

INTRODUCTION

Rule In descending order of preference, cite statutes to:
1. An official code. The official federal code is *United States Code* (U.S.C.).

2. An unofficial code. For federal statutes, there are two:
United States Code Annotated (U.S.C.A.) and *United States Code Service* (U.S.C.S.).
3. Session laws. The official federal session laws are called the *Statutes at Large.*
4. A secondary source. At the federal level, the most important such source is the *United States Code Congressional and Administrative News.*
5. A looseleaf service.

1.   CITING TO CODES

General form

17 U.S.C. § 201(b) (1988).
Conn. Gen. Stat. Ann. § 38-376 (West 1987).

Elements

(a)   Name of statute (exceptionally)
(b)   Title, chapter or volume number (if applicable)
(c)   Abbreviated code name
(d)   Section number
(e)   Publisher (unofficial codes only)
(f)   Year of publication

(a)   Name of statute (exceptionally)

Example   ***Deepwater Ports Act***, 33 U.S.C. § 1517(m)(4) (1988).
Rules   The original name of a statute is not normally provided once it has been codified. Include it only for some special reason (for example, because it is commonly known by that name).
              Italicize the title.

(b)   Title, chapter or volume number

Examples   **15** U.S.C. § 4 (1988).
             Pa. Stat. Ann. **tit. 63,** § 425.3 (Supp. 1986).

Rules   If the code is divided into separate titles, chapters or volumes, the number of that division must be indicated. This element is placed either before or after the title, depending on the citation style indicated for the particular code.

(c)   Abbreviated code name

Examples 17 **U.S.C.** § 104 (1988).
           W. Va. Code § 30-3C-2 (1986).
Rules   Abbreviate the name of the code.
           Do not italicize it.

(d)   Section number

Examples Utah Code Ann. § **58-12.43(8)** (1986).
           29 U.S.C. §§ **701-796** (1988).
Rule   Indicate the relevant section or sections with "§" or "§§", or alternatively by "s." or "ss."

(e)   Publisher

Examples Cal. Penal Code § 4500 (**West** 1982).
           S.C. Code Ann. § 40-71-10 (**Law. Co-op.** 1986).
Rules   Enclose the name of the publisher in parentheses after the section number when citing to an unofficial code. When citing to an official code such as U.S.C., no mention of the publisher need be made.

(f)   Year of publication

Examples 21 U.S.C. § 34 (**1988**).
           Fla. Stat. Ann. § 448.075 (West **1981**).
           Wash. Rev. Code Ann. § 4.24.240 (**Supp. 1987**).
           28 U.S.C.A. § 991 (West **Supp. 1987**).
Rules   Include the year in parentheses after the name of the publisher.
           When citing a bound volume, use the year on the spine of the volume.
           When citing a supplement or pocket insert, give the year shown on the title page of the supplement in question preceded by the qualifier "Supp."

2.   CITING TO SESSION LAWS

General form

Economic Recovery Tax Act of 1981, Pub. L. No. 97-34, 95 Stat. 172.
The Indian Child Welfare Act of 1978, Pub. L. No. 95-608, 92 Stat. 3069 (codified as amended at 25 U.S.C. §§ 1901-1963 (1988)).

Elements

(a)   Name of statute
(b)   Public law or chapter number
(c)   Volume number
(d)   Abbreviated name of session laws
(e)   Page number
(f)   Year
(g)   Section
(h)   Codification information (optional)

(a)   Name of statute

Examples	*Water Quality Act of 1987*, Pub. L. No. 100-4, 100 Stat. 7.
	Act of Aug. 21, 1974, ch. 85, 1974 N.J. Laws 385.
Rules	Give the name of the statute in italics.
	If it has no official name, identify it by its date of enactment.
	The name of the statute is followed by a comma.

(b)   Public law or chapter number

Examples	*Employee Retirement Income Security Act*, **Pub. L. No. 93-406**, 88 Stat. 829 (1974) (codified as amended at 29 U.S.C. §§ 1001-1461 (1988)).
	Federal Trademark Act, **ch. 79-540**, 60 Stat. 427 (1946).
Rule	Provide the public law number or chapter number of the statute.

(c)   Volume number

Example	*Omnibus Budget Reconciliation Act of 1986*, Pub. L. No. 99-509, **100** Stat. 1874.

Rule   Indicate the volume number in the session laws.

(d) Abbreviated name of session laws.

Example   *The Deficit Reduction Act of 1984*, Pub. L. No. 98-369, 98 **Stat.** 494 (1984) (codified as amended at 26 U.S.C. §§ 1-9504 (1988)).

Rule   Give the abbreviated name of the session laws. The federal *Statutes at Large* are abbreviated "Stat."

(e) Page number

Example   *The Balanced Budget and Emergency Deficit Control Act of 1985*, Pub. L. No. 99-177, 99 Stat. **1037**.

Rule   Indicate the page number of the statute in the session laws.

(f) Year of publication

Examples   *National Labor Relations Act*, ch. 372, 49 Stat. 449 **(1935)** (codified as amended at 29 U.S.C. §§ 151-169 (1988)). *National Environmental Policy Act of 1969*, Pub. L. No. 91-190, 83 Stat. 852 **(1970)**.

Rule   Note the year in parentheses, unless it is already part of the name of the statute.

Note   A year in the title of the statute may not exactly coincide with the year of publication, in which case the year of publication must be included.

(g) Section

7

Example   *National Environmental Policy Act of 1969*, Pub. L. No. 91-190, § **102**, 83 Stat. 852 **at 853** (1970).

Rule   To refer to a particular section, indicate the section number between the public law number and the statute volume, as well as a pinpoint page reference following the number of the first page.

(h)   Codification information (optional)

> *Example*   *Health Insurance for the Aged and Disabled,* Pub. L. No. 89-97, 79 Stat. 290 (1965) **(codified as amended at 42 U.S.C. §§ 1395-1396(d) (1988), and in scattered sections of 26 U.S.C. and 45 U.S.C.).**
>
> *Rule*   If known, codification information can be provided parenthetically. Quite often a single statute is split up and codified in various portions of the code.

3.   CITING *UNITED STATES CODE CONGRESSIONAL AND ADMINISTRATIVE NEWS*

> *Examples*   **Persian Gulf Conflict Supplemental Authorization and Personnel Benefits Act of 1991, Pub. L. No. 102-25, 1991 U.S.C.C.A.N. (105 Stat.) 75.**
> **Act of March 22, 1991, Pub. L. No. 102-16, 1991 U.S.C.C.A.N. (105 Stat.) 48.**
>
> *Rules*   Include the name of the statute or, if there is no name, the date of enactment.
> Provide the public law number.
> Give the year and the abbreviated form of *United States Code Congressional and Administrative News*: U.S.C.C.A.N.
> Lastly, indicate as shown in the above examples, the volume and page number of *Statutes at Large* at which the law will subsequently appear.

C.   QUASI-LEGISLATIVE SOURCES

> *Examples*   **U.C.C. § 6-109 (1991).**
> ***Uniform Partnership Act* § 23 (1969).**
> ***Restatement (Second) of Agency* § 78 (1957).**
> ***Restatement (Second) of Torts* § 599 (1976).**
> ***Restatement of Contracts* § 104 (1932).**
>
> *Rules*   For uniform codes and acts as well as the Restatements, provide the title of the source followed by the section number and, in parentheses, the year of adoption or promulgation, which is often indicated on the title page. Italicize the title unless it is a code.
> Where more than one Restatement has been produced on a given area of the law, indicate the number in parentheses after the word "Restatement".

D. CASES

General form

Lojuk v. Quandt,	706	F.2d	1456	(7th Cir.	1983).
Style of cause	Volume	Reporter and series	Page	Court	Year

Elements

1. Style of cause
2. Volume
3. Reporter and series
4. Page
5. Pinpoint
6. Court
7. Year

1. STYLE OF CAUSE

Example **United States v. Nixon**, 418 U.S. 683 (1974).

Rules Italicize the names of the parties but not the "v."
Place a comma after the style of cause.

2. VOLUME

Examples *Jackson* v. *People's Republic of China*, **794** F.2d 1490 (11th Cir. 1986).
Marbury v. *Madison*, **5** U.S. **(1 Cranch)** 137 (1803).

Rules Refer to the volume number of the reporter.
For *U.S. Reports* prior to 1875, the volumes are also numbered consecutively for each editor. Place this number and the editor's name in parentheses after "U.S."

3. REPORTER AND SERIES

Examples *Henningsen* v. *Bloomfield Motors, Inc.*, 32 **N.J.** 358, 161 **A.2d** 69 (1960).
Shaffer v. *Heitner*, 433 **U.S.** 186 (1977).

Rule Abbreviate the reporter name, including the series number if any.

The principal reporters and their abbreviations are:

United States Reports .... **U.S.**
Supreme Court Reporter .... **S. Ct.**
Lawyers' Edition .... **L. Ed.**
Federal Reporter .... **F.**
Federal Supplement .... **F. Supp.**
Atlantic Reporter .... **A.**
Pacific Reporter .... **P.**
North Eastern Reporter .... **N.E.**
North Western Reporter .... **N.W.**
South Eastern Reporter .... **S.E.**
South Western Reporter .... **S.W.**
Southern Reporter .... **So.**
New York Supplement .... **N.Y.S.**
California Reporter .... **Cal. Rptr.**

4.   PAGE

Example   *Miranda* v. *Arizona*, 384 U.S. **436** (1966).
Rule   Refer to the first page of the decision.

5.   PINPOINT

Examples   *Morrissey* v. *Curran*, 567 F.2d 546 **at 549** (2d Cir. 1977).
South Carolina v. *Gathers*, 490 U.S. 805 **at 824** (1989).
Rule   A pinpoint citation follows the indication of the first page of the judgment, introduced by "at".

6.   COURT

Rule   Include the name of the court in parentheses before the year observing the following rules:

(a)   Federal Courts:

(i)   Supreme Court of the United States

Examples   *Burger King* v. *Rudzewicz*, 471 U.S. 462 (1985).
North Dakota v. *United States*, 58 U.S.L.W. 4574 (**U.S.** May 21, 1990).

Rule   Omit the name of the court unless citing to the *United States Law Week* service (U.S.L.W.), in which case "U.S." is required to indicate the Supreme Court.

(*ii*)   Courts of Appeals

Examples   *United States* v. *Dorsey*, 852 F.2d 1068 (**8th Cir.** 1988).
             Naartex Consulting Corp. v. *Watt*, 722 F.2d 779 (**D.C. Cir.** 1983).
Rules   Refer to the numbered circuit (1st, 2d, 3d, 4th, etc.). The Court of Appeals of the District of Columbia Circuit is referred to as "D.C. Cir." and that of the Federal Circuit as "Fed. Cir."

(*iii*)   District Courts

Examples   *Jackson* v. *People's Republic of China*, 596 F. Supp. 386 (**N.D. Ala.** 1984).
             Callahan v. *Scott Paper Co.*, 541 F. Supp. 550 (**E.D. Pa.** 1982).
Rule   Provide the abbreviated name of the district.

(b)   State Courts:

Examples   *Sucher* v. *Sucher*, 416 N.W.2d 182 (**Minn. Ct. App.** 1987).
             Kelly v. *Mississippi Valley Gas Co.*, 397 So. 2d 874 (**Miss.** 1981).
             Nunes Turfgrass, Inc. v. *Vaughan-Jacklin Seed Co.*, 200 Cal. App. 3d 1518, 246 Cal. Rptr. 823 (**Ct. App.** 1988).
             Chrysler Corp. v. *Wilson Plumbing Co.*, 132 Ga. App. 435, 208 S.E.2d 321 (1974).
Rules   Provide the jurisdiction and court in parentheses.
             Omit the name of the jurisdiction if it is obvious from the name of the reporter.
             Omit the name of the court if it is the highest court of its jurisdiction.
             Omit both if both the above rules apply.

7

7.   **YEAR**

Examples   *Johnson* v. *Mobil Oil Corp.*, 415 F. Supp. 264 (E.D. Mich. **1976**).
Upjohn Co. v. *United States*, 449 U.S. 383 **(1981)**.

Rules   Give the year of the decision.
Indicate the year in parentheses after the name of the court.

For a more comprehensive look at American legal citation, see *The Bluebook: A Uniform System of Citation*, 15th ed. (Cambridge: Harvard Law Review Association, 1991).

8

INTERNATIONAL MATERIALS

A. TREATIES

General Form

Charter of the United Nations, 26 June 1945, Can. T.S. 1945 No. 7, 59 Stat. 1031, 145 U.K.F.S. 805, art. 2(7).

European Convention for the Protection of Human Rights and Fundamental Freedoms, 4 November 1950, Eur. T.S. 5, 213 U.N.T.S. 221 [hereinafter *European Human Rights Convention*].

Charter of the Organization of American States (as amended), 30 April 1948, Can. T.S. 1990 No. 23, 21 U.S.T. 607, T.I.A.S. No. 6847 [hereinafter *OAS Charter*] (entered into force 13 December 1951, signed by Canada 13 November 1989, in force for Canada 8 January 1990).

Exchange of Notes between Canada and the United States concerning the Establishment and Operation of a Temporary Space Tracking Facility in Newfoundland, 20 December 1971, Can. T.S. 1972 No. 4, 23 U.S.T. 2069, T.I.A.S. No. 7246, 829 U.N.T.S. 273.

Elements

1. Title

2.   Date
3.   Parties (if applicable)
4.   Treaty Series Citation
5.   Pinpoint Citation
6.   Parenthetical Information

1.   TITLE

Examples   [*Agreement between the Government of Canada and the Government of the Republic of Poland for the Promotion and Reciprocal Protection of Investments* cited as]
Canada-Poland Agreement for the Promotion and Reciprocal Protection of Investments, 6 April 1990, Can. T.S. 1990 No. 43 [hereinafter *Investment Protection Agreement*].

[*Joint Declaration of the Government of the United Kingdom of Great Britain and Northern Ireland and the Government of the People's Republic of China on the Question of Hong Kong* cited as]
United Kingdom-China Joint Declaration on the Question of Hong Kong, 19 December 1984, U.K.T.S. 1984 No. 26, 23 I.L.M. 1366 [hereinafter *Joint Declaration*].

Rules   Provide the shortened title of the treaty, followed by a comma. Shorten the names of the signatories, if they are included in the title of the treaty, in order to reflect common usage.

Retain the essential elements in the title for sufficient identification.

Capitalize the first letters of all words except prepositions, articles and connectives.

Provide in square brackets a "hereinafter" reference containing the established short title of a treaty or, where it is not available, the author's own short title after the treaty series citation.

2. DATE

Examples   *United States-Switzerland Treaty on Mutual Assistance in Criminal Matters*, **25 May 1973,** 27 U.S.T. 2019, T.I.A.S. No. 8302, 12 I.L.M. 916, art. 15 [hereinafter *Treaty on Mutual Assistance in Criminal Matters*].
Convention on the Elimination of All Forms of Discrimination against Women, **1 March 1980,** Can. T.S. 1982 No. 31, 19 I.L.M. 33.

Rules   Provide the full date upon which the treaty was signed or opened for signature; where applicable, provide only the first date of signature for bilateral treaties.

3. PARTIES (IF APPLICABLE)

Examples   *Treaty relating to Boundary Waters and Questions Arising with Canada*, 11 January 1909, **United States-United Kingdom**, 36 Stat. 2448, U.K.T.S. 1910 No. 23.
Agreement on German External Debts, 27 Feburary 1953, **Canada *et al.*–Federal Germany,** Can. T.S. 1953 No. 2, 4 U.S.T. 443, T.I.A.S. No. 2792, 33 U.N.T.S. 4.

Rules   Cite the state parties to bilateral treaties immediately after the date if they are not mentioned in the title.
Join the parties' names with a hyphen.
State names should not be abbreviated, except for the "U.S.S.R." However, they may be shortened to reflect common usage.
Particular signatories to a multilateral treaty may be included at the end of the citation as parenthetical information (see Rule 6, below).

4. TREATY SERIES CITATION

Examples   *Canada-United States Agreement on Great Lakes Water Quality*, 15 April 1972, **Can. T.S. 1972 No. 12, 23 U.S.T. 301, 837 U.N.T.S. 213, T.I.A.S. No. 7312, 11 I.L.M. 694** [hereinafter *Great Lakes Agreement*].
General Act for the Pacific Settlement of International Disputes, 26 **September 1928, Can. T.S. 1931 No. 4, 93 L.N.T.S. 343.**
Vienna Convention on the Law of Treaties between States and International Organizations or between International Organizations, 20

8

March 1986, **U.N. Doc. A/CONF.129/15 (1986), 25 I.L.M. 543.**

United Nations Convention on International Bills of Exchange and International Promissory Notes, 9 December 1988, **U.N. Doc. A/RES/43/165 (1989), 28 I.L.M. 177.**

Rules   Where applicable, cite the official treaty series in the following order: *Canada Treaty Series,* Official treaty series of the other state involved, primary international treaty series (*e.g.* "U.N.T.S." or "L.N.T.S."), other international treaty series (*e.g.* "Con. T.S." or "Rec. G.T.F.) and parallel citation (*e.g.* "I.L.M.").

See Appendix 8, below, for a list of abbreviation of treaty series.

For those United Nations conventions not yet in effect, cite the U.N. document in which it is adopted, followed by a parallel citation if it is available.

5.   PINPOINT CITATION

Examples   *General Agreement on Tariffs and Trade,* 30 October 1947, Can. T.S. 1947 No. 27, 55 U.N.T.S. 187, T.I.A.S. No. 1700, **art. 23.**

Treaty Establishing a Single Council and a Single Commission of the European Communities, 8 April 1965, U.K.T.S. 15 (1979), 4 I.L.M. 776, **art. 2.**

International Convention on the Elimination of All Forms of Racial Discrimination, 7 March 1966, Can. T.S. 1970 No. 28, 660 U.N.T.S. 195, 5 I.L.M. 352, **art. 3.**

Rule   Place a specific citation to a section, an article or an appendix of a treaty after the treaty series citation.

6.   PARENTHETICAL INFORMATION

Examples   *International Covenant on Civil and Political Rights,* 19 December 1966, Can. T.S. 1976 No. 47, 999 U.N.T.S. 171, 6 I.L.M. 368 **(acceded to by 89 states as of 31 December 1989 but not United States; entered into force 23 March 1976).**

Canada-United States Free Trade Agreement, 22 December 1987, Can. T.S. 1989 No. 3, 27 I.L.M. 281, art. 1806 [hereinafter *Free Trade Agreement*] **(Part A, Schedule to** the *Canada-United States Free Trade Agreement Implementation Act*, S.C. 1988, c. 65).

Rules   Specific information (the date of entry into force, the names of the states which have or have not ratified the treaty, or citation from sources other than the treaty series, etc.) may be included in parentheses at the end of the citation, followed by a period.

B.   CASES

1.   INTERNATIONAL COURT OF JUSTICE

(a)   Judgments

Examples   **Delimitation of the Maritime Boundary in the Gulf of Maine Area (*Canada* v. *United States*), [1984] I.C.J. Rep. 246 at 368, 23 I.L.M. 1197 [hereinafter *Gulf of Maine*].**
Appeal relating to the Jurisdiction of the ICAO Council (*India* v. *Pakistan*), [1972] I.C.J. Rep. 46.

Rules   *Style of cause* (*parties*), [volume] reporter abbreviation page reference pinpoint reference, parallel citation [if applicable] [hereinafter rule].
Cite the official style of cause as provided by the Court; include the names of the states to the dispute in parentheses after the style of cause, followed by a comma; separate the parties' names with a "v.", regardless of whether it is joined with a "/" in the official citation of the Court.
Abbreviate *International Court of Justice: Reports of Judgments, Advisory Opinions and Orders* to "I.C.J. Rep."

(b)   Orders and Advisory Opinions

Examples   **Land, Island and Maritime Frontier Dispute (*El Salvador* v. *Honduras*), Order of 13 December 1989, [1989] I.C.J. Rep. 129.**
Certain Phosphate Lands in Nauru (*Nauru* v. *Australia*), Order of 18 July 1989, [1989] I.C.J. Rep. 12.
Applicability of Article VI, Section 22, of the Convention on the Privileges and Immunities of the United Nations, Advisory Opinion, [1989] I.C.J. Rep. 177.

8

Legal Consequences for States of the Continued Presence of South Africa in Namibia (South West Africa) Notwithstanding Security Council Resolution 276 (1970), Advisory Opinion, [1971] I.C.J. Rep. 16 at 40-41.

Rules

Style of cause (parties [if applicable]), Order of [date]/ Advisory Opinion, [volume] reporter abbreviation page reference pinpoint reference.

Follow the basic rules for citing judgments of the Court, with the following exceptions:

Indicate the source materials as an order or advisory opinion after the title, set off by commas.

When referring to an order, provide the full date.

Parenthetical information may be included at the end of the citation.

(c)   Pleadings

Examples

United States Diplomatic and Consular Staff in Teheran (United States v. Iran), "Memorial of the Government of the United States of America," [1981] I.C.J. Pleadings 123.

Case concerning Right of Passage over Indian Territory (Portugal v. India), Vol. IV, "Oral Argument of Shri M.C. Setalvad" (23 September 1957), [1960] I.C.J. Pleadings 14 at 23.

Fisheries Jurisdiction (Federal Republic of Germany v. Iceland), "Request for the Indication of Interim Measures of Protection Submitted by the Government of the Federal Republic of Germany" (21 July 1972), [1975] I.C.J. Pleadings 23 at 29.

Rules

Style of cause (parties [if applicable]), "title" (date [if applicable]), [volume] reporter abbreviation page reference.

Follow the basic rules for citing judgments of the Court, with the following exceptions:

Provide in quotation marks the title of the specific document as indicated in the reporter, with the date indicated in the parentheses following the title.

If the pleadings relating to a single judgment are published in separate volumes, indicate the number of the volume after the case name.

Cite to the *International Court of Justice: Pleadings, Oral Arguments, Documents*, abbreviated to "I.C.J. Pleadings".

2.   PERMANENT COURT OF INTERNATIONAL JUSTICE

(a)   Judgments

Examples   **Mavrommatis Jerusalem Concessions (Greece v. United States) (1925), P.C.I.J. Ser. A, No. 5 at 3.**
Lighthouses in Crete and Samos (France v. Greece) (1937), P.C.I.J. Ser. A/B, No. 71 at 107.

Rules   *Style of cause (parties)* (year of decision), reporter abbreviation series reference, decision number pinpoint reference.

Follow the basic rules for citing judgments of the International Court of Justice, with the following exceptions:

Provide the year of decision in parentheses, followed by a comma.

Provide the identification of the series after the reporter abbreviation.

Include the decision number after the series reference, preceded by a comma.

Place the pinpoint reference, if any, after the decision number.

Cite to the *Publications of the Permanent Court of International Justice: Series A, Collection of Judgments,* abbreviated to "P.C.I.J. Ser. A"; *Series A/B, Judgments, Orders and Advisory Opinions,* abbreviated to "P.C.I.J. Ser. A/B".

(b)   Orders and Advisory Opinions

Examples   **Electricity Company of Sofia and Bulgaria, Order of 5 December 1939, P.C.I.J. Ser. A/B, No. 79 at 6 (Interim measures of protection).**
Jurisdiction of the Courts of Danzig, Advisory Opinion (1928), P.C.I.J. Ser. B, No. 15.

Rules   *Title of Order/Advisory Opinion (parties* [if applicable]), Order of date/Advisory Opinion (Year [if applicable]), reporter abbreviation series reference, document number pinpoint reference.

Follow the basic rules for citing the judgments of the Court, with the following exceptions:

Identify the decision as an order or advisory opinion after the title of the document, preceded by a comma.

Provide the full date when referring to an order.

8

Cite to P.C.I.J. Ser. A/B and *Series B: Collection of Advisory Opinions*, abbreviated to "P.C.I.J. Ser. B".

Parenthetical information may be included at the end of the citation.

(c)   Pleadings

Examples   **Minority Schools in Albania, "Note from the Albanian Government" (21 June 1921), P.C.I.J. Ser. C, No. 76, 199.**

Rules   *Style of cause*, "title" (date [if applicable]), reporter abbreviation series reference, collection number, page reference.

Follow the basic rules for citing the judgments of the Court, with the following exceptions:

Provide the title of the specific document as indicated in the reporter, with the full date of the document indicated in parentheses following the title.

Cite to *Series C: Pleadings, Oral Statements and Documents*, abbreviated to "P.C.I.J. Ser. C".

Indicate the number that identifies the collection of pleadings after the series reference, set off by commas.

3.   EUROPEAN COURT OF HUMAN RIGHTS

(a)   Judgments

Examples   **Sunday Times Case (1979), Eur. Ct. H.R. Ser. A, No. 30, 22 Yearbook Eur. Conv. H.R. 402, (sub nom. Sunday Times v. United Kingdom) 2 E.H.R.R. 245.**
De Wilde, Ooms and Versyp Cases (1971), Eur. Ct. H.R. Ser. A, No. 12, 14 Y.B. Eur. Conv. H.R. 788, (sub nom. Vagrancy Cases) 1 E.H.R.R. 373.

Rules   *Style of cause* (year of decision), Eur. Ct. H.R. Ser. A, decision number pinpoint reference, parallel citation(s).

Follow the style of cause of the first reporter cited.

Abbreviate "European Court of Human Rights" to "Eur. Ct. H.R."

Cite first to the official *Publications of the European Court of Human Rights: Series A: Judgments and Decisions*, abbreviated to "Eur. Ct. H.R. Ser. A".

Provide at least one parallel citation if available.

Cite to the *Yearbook of the European Convention on Human Rights*, abbreviated to "Y.B. Eur. Conv. H.R."
A second parallel citation may be given to the *European Human Rights Reports*, abbreviated to "E.H.R.R."

(b) Pleadings, Oral Arguments and Documents

Examples   **Case of Kjeldsen, Busk Madsen and Pedersen, "Memorial of the Danish Government Concerning the Merits of the Case" (11 March 1976), Eur. Ct. H.R. Ser. B, No. 21, 123 at 132.**
Golder Case, "Verbatim Report of the Public Hearings Held on 11 and 12 October 1974", Eur. Ct. H.R. Ser. B, No. 16, 161 at 172.

Rules   *Style of cause*, "title" (date [if applicable]), Eur. Ct. H.R. Scr. B, decision number, page reference.
Cite to the official *Publications of the European Court of Human Rights: Series B: Pleadings, Oral Arguments and Documents*, abbreviated to "Eur. Ct. H.R. Ser. B".
Provide the title of the source material in quotations marks.
Provide the complete date in parentheses following the title if the date is not included in the title of the document.

4. EUROPEAN COMMISSION OF HUMAN RIGHTS

Examples   **X v. Federal Republic of Germany (No. 9228/80) (1982), 30 Eur. Comm. H.R. D.R. 132 at 139, (sub nom. Glasenapp v. Federal Republic of Germany) 25 Y.B. Eur. Conv. H.R. 182.**
X v. Norway (No. 867/60) (1961), 6 Eur. Comm. H.R. C.D. 34, 4 Y.B. Eur. Conv. H.R. 270.

Rules   *Style of cause* (decision number) (year of decision), volume reporter identification page reference pinpoint reference, parallel citation(s).
Cite to the official publication of the Commission: *Decisions and Reports* (1975-present), abbreviated to "Eur. Comm. H.R.D.R."; *Collection of Decisions of the European Commission of Human Rights* (1960-74), abbreviated to "Eur. Comm. H.R.C.D."

8

Provide parallel citations, if available, to the *Yearbook of the European Convention on Human Rights* and the *European Human Rights Reports*.

5. COURT OF JUSTICE OF THE EUROPEAN COMMUNITIES

Examples *Einberger* v. *Hauptzollamt Freiburg* (No. 240/81), [1982] C.J.E.C. Rep. 3699 at 3703, (1983) 2 C.M.L.R. 170, (1981-83) C.M.R. 8469.
Bureau national interprofessionnel du cognac v. *Clair* (No. 123/83), [1985] C.J.E.C. Rep. 391, (1985) 2 C.M.L.R. 430, (1983-85) C.M.R. 15938.
Parti Ecologiste "Les Verts" v. *European Parliament* (No. 294/83), [1986] C.J.E.C. Rep. 1357, (1987) 2 C.M.L.R. 343, (1985-86) C.M.R. 14317.

Rules *Style of cause* (decision number), [volume] reporter abbreviation page reference pinpoint reference, parallel citation(s).
Cite to the official publication of the Court: *Reports of Cases before the Court*, abbreviated to "C.J.E.C. Rep."
Provide parallel citations, if available, to the *Common Market Law Reports*, abbreviated to "C.M.L.R.", or the *Common Market Reporter*, abbreviated to "C.M.R."

6. INTER-AMERICAN COURT OF HUMAN RIGHTS

(a) Judgments

Examples *Velásquez Rodríguez Case (Honduras)* (1988), Inter-Am. Ct. H.R. Ser. C No. 4, para. 149, *Annual Report of the Inter-American Court of Human Rights: 1988*, OEA/Ser.L/V/ III.19/ doc.13 (1988) 35 at 66, 28 I.L.M. 321.
Godínez Cruz Case (Honduras) (1989), Inter-Am. Ct. H.R. Ser. C No. 5, para. 197, *Annual Report of the Inter-American Court of Human Rights: 1989*, OEA/ Ser.L/V/III.21/doc.14 (1989) 15 at 58.

Rules *Style of cause* (*state*) (year), Inter-Am. Ct. H.R. Ser. C No., pinpoint paragraph reference, parallel citation(s).
Follow the style of cause as indicated in Ser. C.
Abbreviate "Inter-American Court of Human Rights" to "Inter-Am. Ct. H.R."

Abbreviate *Series C: Decisions and Judgments* to "Ser. C".
Indicate the name of the state if the case involves an individual state.

Provide at least one parallel citation; if a parallel citation is the annual report of the Court, follow the rules of citing the annual report of the Commission, at Rule 7, below.

b. Advisory Opinions

Examples

In the Matter of Viviana Callardo et al (Costa Rica) **(1981), Inter-Am. Ct. H.R. Advisory Opinion No. G. 101/81, Ser. A,** *Annual Report of the Inter-American Court of Human Rights: 1981,* **OEA/Ser.L/ III.5/doc.13 (1981) 13, 20 I.L.M. 1424.**

Compulsory Membership in an Association Prescribed by Law for the Practice of Journalism (Arts. 13 and 29 American Convention on Human Rights) (sub nom. Costa Rican Law for the Practice of Journalism) (Costa Rica) **(1985), Inter-Am. Ct. H.R. Advisory Opinion OC-5/85, Ser. A No. 5, para. 73,** *Annual Report of the Inter-American Court of Human Rights: 1985,* **OEA/Ser.L/V/ III.12/doc.13 (1985) 19 at 42, 25 I.L.M. 142.**

Habeas Corpus in Emergency Situations **(1987), Inter-Am. Ct. H.R. Advisory Opinion OC-8/87, Ser. A No. 8, para. 24,** *Annual Report of the Inter-American Court of Human Rights: 1987,* **OEA/Ser.L/V// III.17/doc.13 (1987) 17 at 24, 27 I.L.M. 519.**

Rules

Style of cause (sub nom [if applicable]) *(state)* (year), Inter-Am. Ct. H.R. Advisory Opinion number, Ser. A No. [if applicable], pinpoint reference, parallel citation(s).

Follow the style of cause as indicated in *Series A: Judgments and Opinions,* abbreviated to "Ser. A".

Follow the rules of parallel citation set out in Rule 6(a) on Judgments, above.

Indicate the name of the state if the case involves an individual state.

8

(c)   Pleadings, Oral Arguments and Documents

Examples   *Restrictions to the Death Penalty [Arts. 4(2) and 4(4) American Convention on Human Rights]* (1983), "Verbatim Record of Public Hearing" (26 July 1983), Inter-Am. Ct. H.R. Advisory Opinion OC-3/83, Ser. B No. 3 192 at 203.

Proposed Amendments to the Naturalization Provisions of the Constitution of Costa Rica (1984), "Observations Received from the Supreme Electoral Tribunal of Costa Rica" (6 September 1983), Inter-Am. Ct. H.R. Advisory Opinion OC-4/84, Ser. B No. 4 at 21.

Rules   *Style of cause* (year), "title" (date [if applicable]), Inter-Am. Ct. H.R. Advisory Opinion number, Ser. B No. page reference pinpoint reference.

Cite the title of the document, in quotation marks, as it appears in the table of contents, making changes if necessary.

Provide the complete date of the document in parentheses if it is not part of the title.

Provide the name of the state involved if it is not indicated in the style of cause.

Cite to *Series B: Pleadings, Oral Arguments and Documents*, abbreviated to "Ser. B".

7.   INTER-AMERICAN COMMISSION ON HUMAN RIGHTS

Examples   *In the Matter of Viviana Gallardo and Others (Costa Rica)* (1983), Inter-Am. Comm. H.R. Res. No. 13/83, *Annual Report of the Inter-American Commission on Human Rights: 1982-1983*, OEA/Ser.L/V/II.61/Doc.22 rev.1 (1983).

Case 9647 (United States) (1987), Inter-Am. Comm. H.R. Res. No. 3/87, para. 46, *Annual Report of the Inter-American Commission on Human Rights: 1986-1987*, OEA/ Ser.L/V/II.71/ Doc.9 rev.1 (1987) 147 at 165.

Case 10.252 (El Salvador) (1989), Inter-Am. Comm. H.R. Res. No. 28/89, *Annual Report of the Inter-American Commission on Human Rights: 1989-1990*, OEA/Ser.L/V/ II.77/Doc.7 rev.1 (1990).

Rules   *Style of cause (state)* (year), Inter-Am. Comm. H.R. Resolution number, pinpoint paragraph reference, *Annual Report of the Inter-American Commission on Human Rights*, document number (year of document) page reference pinpoint reference.

Cite to the annual report of the Commission, include the year(s) covered in the title of the report, set off by a colon;

Cite the style of cause as it appears at the heading of the resolution.

Abbreviate "Inter-American Commission on Human Rights" to "Inter-Am. Comm. H.R."

Abbreviate "Resolution" to "Res."

Note the different rules in citing the annual report and citing OAS documents set out in Part D, Rule 4 on OAS documents, at page 123.

8. GENERAL AGREEMENT ON TARIFFS AND TRADE (GATT) (PANELS)

Examples   **The Australian Subsidy on Ammonium Sulphate (*Chile* v. *Australia*) (1950), GATT Doc. CP.4/39, para. 12, 2 B.I.S.D. (1952) 188 at 193.**

Income Tax Practices Maintained by the Netherlands (*U.S.* v. *Netherlands*) (1976), GATT Doc. L/4425, 23d supp. B.I.S.D. (1977) 137, 20 I.L.M. 856.

EEC – Quantitative Restrictions against Imports of Certain Products from Hong Kong (*United Kingdom* v. *European Community*) (1983), GATT Doc. L/5511, para. 31, 30th supp. B.I.S.D. (1984) 129 at 139.

United States – Taxes on Petroleum and Certain Imported Substances (*Canada et al* v. *U.S.*) (1987), GATT Doc. L/6175, para. 3.1.4, 34th supp. B.I.S.D. (1988) 136 at 141, 27 I.L.M. 1601.

Republic of Korea – Restrictions on Imports of Beef, Complaint by New Zealand (*New Zealand* v. *Republic of Korea*) (1989), GATT Doc. L/6505, 36th supp. B.I.S.D. (1990) 234.

Rules   *Style of cause (parties)* (year), GATT document number, pinpoint paragraph reference [if applicable], volume B.I.S.D. (year) page reference pinpoint reference, parallel citation.

Indicate the names of the parties in parentheses.

8

Where applicable, include pinpoint paragraph reference immediately after the document reference.

Cite to the *Basic Instruments and Selected Documents*, abbreviated to B.I.S.D.

9. CANADA-UNITED STATES FREE TRADE AGREEMENT (PANELS)

Examples   *In the Matter of Canada's Landing Requirement for Pacific Coast Salmon and Herring* (1989), 2 T.C.T. 7162 (Ch. 18 Panel), 1 T.T.R. 237.

In the Matter of Lobsters from Canada (1990), 3 T.C.T. 8182 (Ch. 18 Panel), 2 T.T.R. 72.

In the Matter of Red Raspberries from Canada (Remand Opinion) (1990), 3 T.C.T. 8175 (Ch. 19 Panel), 2 T.T.R. 214.

If unpublished,

In the Matter of Lobsters from Canada (25 May 1990), USA-89-1807-01 (Ch. 18 Panel).

New Steel Rail, except Light Rail, from Canada (30 August 1990), USA-89-1904-08 (Ch. 19 Panel).

In the Matter of Fresh, Chilled or Frozen Pork from Canada (14 June 1991), ECC-91-1904-01 USA (Ex. Chall. Ctee.).

Rules   *Style of cause* (year), volume T.C.T. page reference (arbitrating body), parallel citation.

If unpublished,

Style of cause (date), Secretariat file No. (arbitrating body).

Cite to the first reporter (*Free Trade Law Reports* and *Free Trade Update*).

Abbreviate the "Canada-U.S. Trade Commission Panel" under Chapter 18 to "Ch. 18 Panel", the "Canada-U.S. Binational Panel" under Chapter 19 to "Ch. 19 Panel" and "Extraordinary Challenge Committee" under Chapter 19 to "Ex. Chall. Ctee."

C. UNITED NATIONS DOCUMENTS

In citing the documents of the United Nations, abbreviate the following commonly used words and phrases as follows:

Decision . . . . Dec.

Document	Doc.
Emergency	Emer.
Meeting	Mtg.
Mimeograph(ed)	Mimeo.
Number	No.
Official Record	OR
Paragraph	Para.
Plenary	Plen.
Recommendation	Rec.
Regular	Reg.
Resolution	.Res.
Session	Sess.
Special	Spec.
Supplement	Supp.

1. OFFICIAL RECORDS

(a) Meeting Records

General Form

UNCTAD TDBOR, 14th Sess., 382d Mtg., UN Doc. TD/B/ SR.382 (1974) para. 5 [hereinafter UN Doc. TD/B/SR.382].

Elements

(i) UN body official record
(ii) Session or year
(iii) Meeting
(iv) UN document number, (Sales No. #) [optional]
(v) Year of document
(vi) Pinpoint reference [optional]
(vii) Provisional Documents

8

(i) UN Body Official Record

Examples   **UN ESCOR**, 19th Sess., 839th Mtg., UN Doc. E/SR.839 (1955).
UN GAOR C.2, 20th Mtg., UN Doc. A/C.2/40/SR.20 (1985).

Rules   Identify the official record of the UN body, followed by a comma.

Abbreviate the principal UN bodies as follows:

Economic and Social Council . . . . **ESC**
First Committee, Second Committee,
    etc . . . . **C.1, C.2,** etc.
General Assembly . . . . **GA**
General Committee . . . . **GC**
Security Council . . . . **SC**
Trade and Development Board . . . . **TDB**
Trusteeship Council . . . . **TC**
United Nations Conference on Trade
    and Development . . . . **UNCTAD**

For abbreviations of other UN bodies, see *Lexique général anglais-français,* UN Doc. ST/DCS/1/Rev.2 (1982) and *Terminology Bulletin No. 311/Rev.1,* UN Doc. ST/CS/ SER.F/311/Rev.1 (1981).

For those UN bodies which have no official acronyms or abbreviations, cite the full name, followed by OR.

(*ii*) Session or Year

Examples   UN GAOR, **13th Spec. Sess.,** 7th Plen. Mtg., Annexes, UN Doc. A/S-13/PV.7 (1986).

UN GAOR, **8th Emer. Spec. Sess.,** 6th Plen. Mtg., Annexes, UN Doc. A/ES-8/PV.6 (1981).

UN SCOR, **33d Year,** 2092d Mtg., UN Doc. S/PV.2092 (1978).

Rule   Indicate the session number, the year of the UN body or the calendar year immediately after the official record designation, followed by a comma.

(*iii*) Meeting

Examples   UN GAOR, 13th Spec. Sess., **7th Plen. Mtg.,** Annexes, UN Doc. A/S-13/PV.7 (1986).

UN GAOR C.2, 40th Sess., **20th Mtg.,** UN Doc. A/ C.2/40/ SR.20 (1985).

Rules   Place the meeting number after the session or year indication, followed by a comma.

Where the document has no session or year, place the meeting number after the official record designation.

(*iv*) UN Document Number

Examples   UN GAOR, 13th Spec. Sess., 7th Plen. Mtg., Annexes, **UN Doc. A/S-13/PV.7** (1986).

UN SCOR, 33d Year, 2092d Mtg., **UN Doc. S/PV.2092** (1978).

Rules   Place the UN document number after the meeting number.

If a document has two UN document numbers, include both in the citation, separated by a hyphen.

The sales number of the document may be included at the author's discretion, indicated by "Sales No. #".

Place the sales number in parentheses following the UN document number.

(*v*) Year of Document

Examples   UN ESCOR, 19th Sess., 835th Mtg., UN Doc. E/SR.835 **(1955).**

UN GAOR C.2, 40th Sess., 20th Mtg., UN Doc. A/C.2/40/ SR.20 **(1985).**

UN ESCOR, 1978, 5th Plen. Mtg., UN Doc. E/1978/SR.5.

Rules   Indicate the year of the document in parentheses after the UN document number, followed by a period, if there is no pinpoint reference.

Where the volume of the official record is indicated by calendar year rather than by session or year of the body, omit the calendar year at the end of the reference.

The year is that of the document which is often found under the UN Document number, or the year of the event in question but not that of the publication.

8

(vi) Pinpoint Reference

Examples   UN SCOR, 33d Year, 2092d Mtg., UN Doc. S/PV.2092 (1978) **at 2**.
UN ESCOR, 19th Sess., 835th Mtg., UN Doc. E/ SR.835 (1955) **para. 12**.

Rules   Place the pinpoint reference after the year of document or the UN document number, as the case may be, followed by a period.
The author may refer to page numbers or to paragraph numbers.

(vii) Provisional Documents

Example   UN GAOR, 17th Spec. Sess., 8th Mtg., UN Doc. A/ S-17/ PV.8 (1990) **[provisional]**.

Rules   Refer to an official document before a provisional one. Where the official document is not available, indicate the provisional nature of the document by placing the word "provisional" enclosed in square brackets after the year.

(b) Supplements

(i) Reports

Examples   **Commission on Human Rights, *Report on the Thirty-Sixth Session*, UN ESCOR, 1980, Supp. No. 3, UN Doc. E/1980/13-E/CN.4/1408 and Corr.1 para. 118.**
***Report of the UN High Commissioner for Refugees*, UN GAOR, 15th Sess., Supp. No. 11, UN Doc. A/4378/Rev.1 (1960) at 13.**
***Report of the Security Council Commission of Inquiry Established under Resolution 496 (1981)*, UN SCOR, 37th Year, Spec. Supp. No. 2, UN Doc. S/14905/Rev.1 (1982).**
***Report of the Committee on Shipping*, UNCTAD TDBOR, 25th Sess., Supp. No. 4., UN Doc. TD/B/921-TD/B/ C.4/254 (1982) [hereinafter *Shipping Report*].**

Rules   Authoring body [if applicable], *title*, UN body official record designation, session or year, supplement number, UN document number (Sales No. # [optional]) (year of document) pinpoint reference [optional].

Where applicable, provide the authoring body of the document, followed by a comma, if it is not indicated in the title.

The title may be abbreviated at the author's discretion but must be easily identifiable.

The short form used in the "hereinafter" rule may be the UN Document number or an abbreviated form of the title.

(*ii*)   Resolutions and Decisions

Examples   *Ad hoc Intergovernmental Committee for the Integrated Programme for Commodities*, UNCTAD TDB Dec. 140 (XVI), UNCTAD TDBOR, 16th Sess., Supp. No. 1, UN Doc. TD/B/638 (1976) 4, para. 4.

United Nations conferences to conclude a code of conduct on transnational corporations, ESC Dec. 1980/174, UN ESCOR, 1980, Supp. No. 1A, UN Doc. E/1980/80/ Add.1 30.

Effects of Atomic Radiation, GA Res. 34/12, UN GAOR, 34th Sess., Supp. No. 46, UN Doc. A/34/626 (1979) 79 [hereinafter *Effects of Atomic Radiation*]

Rules   *Title*, resolution/decision number, UN body official record and session or year, supplement number [if available], UN document number (year of document) first page of document, pinpoint reference.

Where the document is part of a consecutively paginated collection, indicate the first page of the document after the year of document.

The short form used in the "hereinafter" rule may be the UN Document number or an abbreviated form of the title.

8

(c) Annexes

Examples *USSR: draft resolution*, UN ESCOR, 3d year, 7th Sess., Annex, Agenda Item 7, UN Doc. E/884/Rev.1 (1948) para. 3.
UNCTAD Trade Projections for 1975 and 1980, UNCTAD TDBOR, 9th Sess., Annexes, Agenda Item 3, UN Doc. TD/B/264/Rev.1 (1969) at 5.

Rules *Title*, UN body official record designation, session or year, annex(es), agenda item #, UN document number (or Sales No. # [optional]) (year of document) pinpoint reference.
Identify the series as "Annex(es)", as it appears on the title page of the document, followed by a comma and the agenda item number.
Refer to the document as "Agenda Item #".

2. MIMEOGRAPHED DOCUMENTS

Examples UN ESC, Commission on Human Rights, 24th Sess. *Questions of the Violation of Human Rights and Fundamental Freedoms, including Policies of Racial Discrimination and Segregation and of Apartheid, in All Countries, with Particular Reference to Colonial and Other Dependent Countries and Territories*, UN Doc. E/CN.4/ L.1001/Rev.1 (February 1968) (Mimeo., Limited).
UN GA, Disarmament Commission, *Verbatim Record of the Fortieth Meeting*, UN Doc. A/CN.10/PV.40 (June 1980) (Mimeo.).

Rules UN authoring body, session or year [if applicable], *title*, UN Doc. No. (full date) (Mimeo., distribution information [if applicable]).
If the mimeographed version is the only version available, cite it according to the same rules as the corresponding official document of publication.
Where applicable, indicate in parentheses other nature of document, i.e., "Limited", "Restricted" or "Provisional", in addition to "Mimeo."

3. PERIODICALS AND YEARBOOKS

(a) Periodicals

Examples "Human Rights Commission Accepts Cuba's Invitation to Observe Its Human Rights Situation, Considers First Report on Mercenaries" (1988) 25:2 *UN Chronicle* 65.

C.P. Romulo, "Why Sanctions Would Work" (1982) 14:1 *Objective: Justice* 7 (United Nations, Department of Public Information).

Rules Cite UN periodicals as any other journals, according to the rules set out in Chapter 3, with the following modifications:

Italicize the title of the journal.

Provide the author (corporate or otherwise) if it is available.

If it is not clear from the title that the periodical is from the UN add, in parentheses, at the end of the citation, United Nations and the issuing department, separated by a comma.

Include the document number in parentheses if it is available.

In citing from tables of data, the author may cite the title of the table.

(b) Yearbooks

Examples "Legal Questions: International Organizations and International Law" in *Yearbook of the United Nations 1984* (New York: UN Department of Public Information, 1988) (Sales No E.87.I.1).

"Report of the Commission to the General Assembly on the work of its thirty-ninth Session" (UN Doc. A/42/10) in *Yearbook of the International Law Commission 1987*, vol. II, Part 2 (New York, 1989) at 50 (UN Doc. A/CN.4/SER.A/1987/Add.1 (Part 2), Sales No.E.88.V.7 (Part II)).

United Nations Juridical Yearbook 1982 (New York, 1989) (UN Doc. ST/LEG/SER.C/20, Sales No.E.89.V.1)

8

Rules   Cite articles in yearbooks as monographs according to the rules set out in Chapter 3 of the *Guide* on citing collections of essays, omitting the elements of author and/ or editor if they are not available.

Where applicable, include UN document number and sales number in parentheses.

4. SALES PUBLICATIONS

Examples   UNCTAD, *The Least Developed Countries 1988 Report* (New York, 1989) at 16 (UN Doc. TD/B/1202, Sales No. E.89.II.D.3)

United Nations, *Recommendations on the Transport of Dangerous Goods*, 5th rev'd ed. (New York, 1988) at 139 (UN Doc. ST/SG/AC.10/1/Rev.5, Sales No. E.87.VIII.1)

Rules   Cite sales publications as monographs according to the rules set out in Chapter 3 of the *Guide*, with the UN body as the corporate author.

Where applicable, include UN document number and sales number in parentheses.

D. DOCUMENTS OF OTHER INTERNATIONAL ORGANIZATIONS

In citing the documents of other international organizations, abbreviate the following commonly used words and phrases as follows:

Decision . . . . Dec.
Document . . . . Doc.
Emergency . . . . Emer.
Meeting . . . . Mtg.
Mimeograph(ed) . . . . Mimeo.
Number . . . . No.
Official Record . . . . OR
Paragraph . . . . Para.
Plenary . . . . Plen.
Recommendation . . . . Rec.
Regular . . . . Reg.
Resolution . . . . .Res.
Session . . . . Sess.

Special . . . . Spec.

Supplement . . . . Supp.

1.   EUROPEAN COMMUNITY

(a)   Official Journals

Examples   EC, *Single Market and Its Implication for Women*, O.J. Debates (1991) No 398 at 303.

EC, *Statement by Alliot-Marie*, O.J. Debates (1989) No 279 at 46.

EC, *Commission Regulation (EEC) No 2045/73 of 27 July 1973*, O.J. Legislation (1973) No L207 at 38.

EC, *Council Regulation No 2299/89 of 27 July 1989 concerning rules of conduct for computerized reservation systems*, O.J. Legislation (1989) No L220 at 1.

EC, *Commission Directive 70/50/EEC of 22 December 1969*, O.J. Special Edition (1970) at 17.

EC, *Written Question No 194/75: Misleading advertising in the member states*, O.J. Information (1975) No C292 at 1.

EC, *Amended proposal for a Council decision adopting a specific research and technological development programme in the field of agriculture and agro-industry (1990 to 1994)*, O.J. Information (1991) No 91/C77/05 at 6.

Rules   EC, *Title*, series title (year) document number pinpoint page reference.

Long title may be shortened.

Abbreviate *Official Journal of the European Communities: Information and Notices* to "O.J. Information"; *Official Journal of the European Communities: Legislation* to "O.J. Legislation"; *Official Journal of the European Communities: Debates of the European Parliament* to "O.J. Debates"; *Official Journal of the European Communities: English Special Edition* to "O.J. Special Edition".

8

(b)   Series

Examples   EC, Commission, *The European Community and the Environment*, European Documentation 3/1987 (Luxembourg: EC, 1987).
EC, Commission, *The Special Training Needs of Immigrant Women*, Commission Document Series (Luxembourg: EC, 1987).

Rule   EC, authoring body, *title*, series title (publication information).

(c)   Periodicals

Examples   EC, *External Trade Monthly Statistics (4-6, 1988)*, 1988.
EC, *Industrial Trends: Monthly Statistics (1-3, 1989)*, 1989.

Rule   EC, *title*, year.
Where applicable, after the title include in parentheses the period covered, as indicated on the title page of the periodical.

(d)   General Publications

Examples   EC, Commission, *Investment Laws of ACP Countries* (Luxembourg: EC, 1979).
EC, Council, *European Educational Policy Statements*, 2d ed. (Luxembourg: EC, 1986).

Rule   EC, authoring body, *title* (publication information).

2.   GENERAL AGREEMENT ON TARIFFS AND TRADE (GATT)

(a)   Decisions, Recommendations, etc.

Examples   *Freedom of Contract in Transport Insurance*, GATT C.P. Rec. (27 May 1959), 15th sess., 8th supp. B.I.S.D. (1960) 26.
Ministerial Declaration (29 November 1982), 38th sess. at Ministerial Level, GATT Doc. L/5424, para. 6, 29th supp. B.I.S.D. (1983) 9 at 11.

Agreement on ASEAN Preferential Trading Arrangements, GATT C.P. Dec. (29 January 1979), 35th sess., GATT Doc. L/4768, 26th supp. B.I.S.D. (1980) 224.
Uruguay–Import Surcharges: Extension of Time Limit, GATT C.P. Dec. L/6207, 43d sess., 34th supp. B.I.S.D. (1988) 37.
Improvements to the GATT Dispute Settlement Rules and Procedures. GATT C.P. Dec. L/6489, 45th sess., 36th supp. B.I.S.D. (1990) 61.

Rules   *Title*, GATT body decision/recommendation, session or meeting, GATT Doc. number, volume B.I.S.D. (year) first page of document.

If the decision or recommendation has no GATT document number, indicate the full date in parentheses after the GATT body designation.

Wherever possible, cite to the supplements to B.I.S.D.

Abbreviate "Contracting Parties" to "C.P."

Abbreviate *Basic Instruments and Selected Documents* to "B.I.S.D."

(b) Reports

Examples   GATT, Committee on Tariff Concessions, *Report Presented to the Council on 7 November 1989*, GATT Doc. TAR/177, 36th supp. B.I.S.D. (1990) 47.

GATT, *Trade Liberalization, Protectionism and Interdependence*, GATT Studies in International Trade, No. 5 (Geneva: GATT, 1977).

GATT, *Trade Relations Under Flexible Exchange Rates*, GATT Studies in International Trade, No. 8 (Geneva: GATT, 1980).

GATT, *The International Markets for Meat: 1990/91* (Geneva: GATT, 1991).

Rules   GATT, authoring body [if applicable], *title*, GATT Doc. number, volume B.I.S.D. (year) first page of document. Wherever possible, cite to B.I.S.D. or its supplements. If the report has no document number or if it is published as a monograph, cite it according to the rule for secondary materials:

Authoring body, *title* (publication information).

3.   ORGANIZATION OF ECONOMIC COOPERATION AND DEVELOPMENT

(a)   Series

Examples   OECD, *Austria (1990/1991)*, OECD Economic Surveys (Paris: OECD, 1991).

OECD, Nuclear Energy Agency, *Feasibility of Disposal of High-Level Radioactive Waste into the Seabed*, Geoscience Characterization Studies (Paris: OECD, 1988).

OECD, *Reforming Public Pensions*, Social Policy Studies No. 5 (Paris: OECD, 1988).

OECD, *International Subcontracting: A New Form of Investment*, Development Centre Studies (Paris: OECD, 1980).

For working papers:

OECD, Department of Economics and Statistics, *Tax Reform in OECD Countries: Economic Rationale and Consequences*, Working Paper No. 40, August 1987.

OECD, Department of Economics and Statistics, *Deregulation, Credit Rationing, Financial Fragility and Economic Performance*, Working Paper No. 97, OECD/GD/(91) 68, February 1991.

Rules   OECD, authoring body [if applicable], *title*, series title number [if applicable] (publication information).

Do not underline the series title.

For working papers:

OECD, authoring body [if applicable], *title*, working paper number, document number [if applicable], month year.

(b)   Periodicals and Annual Publications

Examples   OECD, *Monthly Statistics of Foreign Trade, Series A*, March 1985.

OECD, *Foreign Trade by Commodities: Series C, Vol. 2: Imports 1985*, 1987.

OECD, *Financial Accounts of OECD Countries*, 1988.

OECD, *Financial Statistics Monthly*, March 1991.

Rules   OECD, *title*, year.
Cite the full title of the periodical, including the series number.
Where applicable, provide the month of the publication.

4.   ORGANIZATION OF AMERICAN STATES

General Form

OAS, General Assembly, 2d Reg. Sess., *Draft Standards Regarding the Formulation of Reservations to Multilateral Treaties*, OR OEA/Ser.P/AG/doc.202 (1972) at 1.
OAS, Inter-American Judicial Committee, *Working Document on Revision of the Bustamante Code or the Code of Private International Law*, OR OEA/Ser.I/VI.2/CIJ-72 (1964) at 7.
OAS, Meeting of Consultation of Ministers of Foreign Affairs, 12th Mtg., *Report of Committee I of the Twelfth Meeting of Consultation of Ministers of Foreign Affairs*, OR OEA/Ser.F/II.12/Doc.22 Corr.2 (1967).
OAS, Inter-American Commission on Human Rights, *Report on the Situation of Human Rights in Chile*, OR OEA/Ser.L/V/II.66/doc.17 (1985) at 208.

Elements

(a)   OAS, Issuing Organ
(b)   Session or Meeting (if applicable)
(c)   Title
(d)   Official Records Designation with Document Number
(e)   Year of Document
(f)   Pinpoint Reference

(a)   OAS, Issuing Organ

8

Example   **OAS, General Assembly, Preparatory Committee**, *Summary of the Meeting of the Preparatory Committee on October 25, 1984*, OR OEA/Ser.P/AG/CP/SA.184/84 (1984).

Rule   Identify the Organization of American States by "OAS", followed by a comma and the name of the issuing organ, if any, set off by commas, as they are indicated on the title page of the document.

(b) Session or Meeting

Example OAS, Meeting of Consultation of Ministers of Foreign Affairs, **20th Mtg.**, *Note from the Permanent Mission of Argentina Enclosing its Government's Press Release of January 3, 1987 on the Malvinas Islands*, OR OEA/Ser.F/ II.20/Doc.124/87 (1987).

Rule Where applicable, indicate the session or meeting number after the name of the issuing organ, followed by a comma.

(c) Title

Example OAS, Inter-American Commission on Human Rights, **Report on the Work Accomplished by the Inter-American Commission on Human Rights at its Thirty-Second Session**, OR OEA/Ser.L/V/ II.32/doc.31 rev.1 (1975) at 35.

Rule Cite the title of the document as indicated on the title page, followed by a comma.

(d) Official Record Designation with Document Number

Example OAS, Permanent Council, *Summary of the Permanent Council Meeting on July 26, 1989*, **OR OEA/Ser.G/CP/ SA.782/89** (1989).

Rules Cite the full document number as indicated on the title page, preceded by "OR"; if the document number consists of more than one part, join the number with "/". Use the Spanish "OEA/..." designation even if the document number is indicated in "OAS/..."

(e) Year of Document

Example OAS, General Secretariat, *Agreement Between the General Secretariat of the Organization of American States and the International Reading Association*, OR OEA/Ser.D/V.11/80 **(1980).**

Rule Cite in parentheses the year of the document as indicated on the title page, followed by a period if there is no pinpoint reference.

(f)   Pinpoint Reference

Example   OAS, Inter-American Committee on the Alliance for Progress, Subcommittee on Peru, *Domestic Efforts and the Needs for External Financing for the Development of Peru*, OR OEA/Ser.H/XIV/CIAP/336 (1969) **at 53.**

Rule   Place the pinpoint reference after the year, followed by a period.

5.   COUNCIL OF EUROPE

(a)   Official Report of Debates

Examples   **Council of Europe, P.A., 29th Sess., Debates, vol. I (1977) at 94.**

Rules   Council of Europe, P.A./C.A., session number, Debates, volume (year) pinpoint reference.
Abbreviate "Parliamentary Assembly" to "P.A."
For documents before 1974, abbreviate "Consultative Assembly" to "C.A."
Abbreviate the *Official Report of Debates* as "Debates".

(b)   Texts Adopted

Examples   **Council of Europe, C.A., 21st Sess., Part III, Texts Adopted, Rec. 585 (1970) at 1.**

Rules   Council of Europe, P.A./C.A., session number, session part, Texts Adopted, recommendation, resolution, opinion or order number (year) descriptive title [optional], pinpoint reference.
Abbrevicate *Texts Adopted by the Assembly* to "Texts Adopted".

(c)   Documents (Working Papers)

Examples   **Council of Europe, C.A., 21st Sess., Documents, vol. III, Doc. 2573 (1969) at 3.**
Council of Europe, P.A., 38th Sess., *Written Declaration No. 150 on the protection of the archaeological site of Pompeii* (1987), Documents, vol. VII, Doc. 5700 at 1.

8

Rules Council of Europe, P.A./C.A., session number, title [optional] (year), Documents, volume, document number pinpoint reference.
Abbreviate *Documents (Working Papers)* to "Documents".

(d) Orders of the Day and Minutes of Proceedings

Example **Council of Europe, C.A., 21st Sess., Part II, Orders, 10th Sitting (1969) at 20.**

Rules Council of Europe, P.A./C.A., session number, session part, Orders, sitting number (year) pinpoint reference.
Abbreviate *Orders of the Day and Minutes of Proceedings* to "Orders".

(e) Documents in Series

Examples **Council of Europe, *New Trends in European Mortality*, Population Studies No. 5 (Strasbourg: Council of Europe, 1981) at 46.**
For *Information Bulletin on Legal Affairs*:
Council of Europe, Committee of Ministers, Rec. No. R(82)1 (1980) 12 Inf. Bull. 58.

Rules Council of Europe, *title of document*, series title number (publication information).
For *Information Bulletin on Legal Affairs*:
Council of Europe, Committee of Ministers, recommendation number descriptive title [optional] (year) issue # Inf. Bull. first page of reference pinpoint reference.
Abbreviate *Information Bulletin on Legal Affairs* to "Inf. Bull."

APPENDIX 1

STATUS OF REPORTERS

According to Chapter 2, Rule A 8(a), official and semi-official reporters are to be cited before unofficial reporters. Official reporters are those published by the Queen's Printer; semi-official reporters are those published under the auspices of a provincial or territorial bar association. All reporters not listed here are unofficial.

A. CANADA

Official   Canada Supreme Court Reports
[1970-date] .... S.C.R.

Official   Canada Law Reports, Supreme Court of
Canada [1963-69] .... S.C.R.

Official   Canada Law Reports, Supreme Court of
Canada [1923-62] .... S.C.R.

Official   Canada Supreme Court Reports (1876-1922),
vols. 1-64 .... S.C.R.

Official   Canada Federal Court Reports [1971-date] .....F.C.

Official   Canada Law Reports, Exchequer Court
of Canada [1963-70] ....Ex. C.R.

Official   Canada Law Reports, Exchequer Court
of Canada [1923-62] .... Ex. C.R.

Official   Reports of the Exchequer Court of Canada
(1881-1922), vols. 1-21 .... Ex. C.R.

B. ALBERTA

Semi-official Alberta Reports (1976-date), vols. 1-date ..... A.R.

Unofficial   Alberta Law Reports (2d) (1976-date),
vols. 1-date .... Alta. L.R. (2d)

Semi-official Alberta Law Reports (1907-32),
vols. 1-26 .... Alta. L.R.

C. BRITISH COLUMBIA

Unofficial   British Columbia Law Reports (1976-date),
vols. 1-date .... B.C.L.R.

Semi-official British Columbia Reports (1867-1947),
vols. 1-63 .... B.C.R.

D. MANITOBA

Unofficial   Manitoba Reports (2d) (1979-date),
vols. 1-date .... Man. R. (2d)

Semi-official Manitoba Reports (1883-1961),
vols. 1-67 .... Man. R.

Unofficial   Manitoba Law Reports [1875-83] .... Man. L.R.

E. NEW BRUNSWICK

Semi-official New Brunswick Reports (2d) (1984-date),
vols. 44-date .... N.B.R. (2d)

Semi-official New Brunswick Reports (2d) (1968-83),
vols. 1-43 .... N.B.R. (2d)

Unofficial   New Brunswick Reports (1825-1929),
vols. 1-54 .... N.B.R.

F. NEWFOUNDLAND & PRINCE EDWARD ISLAND

Semi-official Newfoundland & Prince Edward Island Reports
(1970-date), vols. 1-date . . . . Nfld. & P.E.I.R.

Unofficial Newfoundland Law Reports (1817-1946),
vols. 1-15 . . . . Nfld. L.R.

G. NORTHWEST TERRITORIES

Semi-official Northwest Territories Reports
[1983-date] . . . . .N.W.T.R.

Semi-official Territories Law Reports (1885-1907),
vols. 1-7 . . . . .Terr. L.R.

H. NOVA SCOTIA

Semi-official Nova Scotia Reports (2d) (1969-date),
vols. 1-date . . . . N.S.R. (2d)

Semi-official Nova Scotia Reports (1965-69), vols. 1-5 . . . .N.S.R.

Unofficial Nova Scotia Reports (1834-1929),
vols. 1-60 . . . . .N.S.R.

I. ONTARIO

Unofficial Ontario Appeal Cases (1983-date),
vols. 1-date . . . . O.A.C.

Semi-official Ontario Reports (2d) (1973-date),
vols. 1-date . . . . .O.R. (2d)

Semi-official Ontario Reports [1931-73] . . . . O.R.

Semi-official Ontario Law Reports (1900-31), vols. 1-66 . . .O.L.R.

Unofficial Ontario Reports (1882-1900), vols. 1-32 . . . . . . O.R.

Unofficial Ontario Appeal Reports (1876-1900),
vols. 1-27 . . . . O.A.R.

Semi-official Ontario Weekly Notes . . . . .O.W.N.

J. QUEBEC

Semi-official Recueils de jurisprudence du Québec
[1986-date] . . . . R.J.Q.

Semi-official Recueils de jurisprudence du Québec, Cour d'appel
[1970-85] . . . . C.A.

Semi-official Recueils de jurisprudence du Québec, Cour du Banc de
la Reine/du Roi [1942-69] . . . . B.R.

Semi-official Rapports judiciaires officiels de Québec, Cour du Banc
de la Reine/du Roi (1892-1941), vols. 1-71 . . . B.R.

Semi-official Recueils de jurisprudence du Québec, Cour supérieure
[1967-85] . . . . C.S.

Semi-official Rapports judiciaires officiels de Québec, Cour supérieure [1942-66] . . . . C.S.

Semi-official Rapports judiciaires officiels de Québec, Cour supérieure (1892-1941), vols. 1-79 . . . . C.S.

Semi-official Recueils de jurisprudence du Québec, Cour provinciale,
Cour des Sessions de la paix, Cour du bien-être social
[1975-85] . . . . C.P./C.S.P./C.B.E.S.

K. SASKATCHEWAN

Unofficial Saskatchewan Reports (1979-date),
vols. 1-date . . . . Sask. R.

Semi-official Saskatchewan Law Reports (1907-31),
vols. 1-25 . . . . Sask. L.R.

L. YUKON

Semi-official Yukon Reports . . . . Y.R.

APPENDIX 2

LAW REPORTERS

Canadian Human Rights Reporter . . . . C.H.R.R.
Canadian Insurance Law Reporter . . . . .I.L.R.
Canadian Intellectual Property Reports . . . . C.I.P.R.
Canadian Labour Law Cases . . . . .C.L.L.C.
Canadian Labour Law Reporter .C.L.L.R.
Canadian Labour Relations Boards Reports . . . . .Can. L.R.B.R.
Canadian Native Law Cases . . . . C.N.L.C.
Canadian Native Law Reporter . . . . C.N.L.R.
Canadian Patent Reporter . . . . C.P.R.
Canadian Radio-television and Telecommunications
      Decision and Policy Statements . . . . C.R.T.
Canadian Railway Cases . . . . .C.R.C.
Canadian Railway and Transport Cases . . . . C.R.T.C.
Canadian Rights Reporter . . . . .C.R.R.
Canadian Transport Cases . . . . .C. Trans. C.
Carswell's Practice Cases . . . . C.P.C.
Causes en appel au Québec . . . . Q.A.C.
Charter of Rights Decisions . . . . .C.R.D.
Construction Law Reports . . . . C.L.R.
Criminal Reports . . . . C.R.
Décisions de la Commission des Affaires sociales . . . . C.A.S.
Décisions des Tribunaux du Bas-Canada (1851-1867) . . . Déc. B.-C.
Décisions et énoncés de pratique sur la
      radiodiffusion et les télécommunications
      canadiennes . . . . R.T.C.
Dominion Law Reports . . . . D.L.R.
Dominion Tax Cases . . . . .D.T.C.
Eastern Law Reporter (1906-1914) . . . . E.L.R.
Estates and Trusts Reports . . . . E.T.R.
Exchequer Court of Canada Reports . . . . .Ex. C.R.
Family Law Reform Act Cases . . . . F.L.R.A.C.
Federal Court Reports (see Canada Federal Court Reports)
Fox's Patent, Trademark, Design and
      Copyright Cases . . . . Fox Pat. C.
Immigration Appeal Cases . . . . I.A.C.
Jurisprudence Express . . . . J.E.
Labour Arbitration Cases . . . . L.A.C.
Land Compensation Reports . . . . L.C.R.
Lower Canada Reports (1851-1867) . . . . L.C. Rep.
Manitoba Reports . . . . .Man. R.
Maritime Provinces Reports . . . . .M.P.R.
Motor Vehicle Reports . . . . M.V.R.
Municipal and Planning Law Reports . . . . M.P.L.R.

Reports of Patent Cases . . . . R.P.C.
Revue de droit du travail . . . . .R.D.T.
Revue de droit judiciaire . . . . R.D.J.
Revue légale . . . . .R.L.
Saskatchewan Reports . . . . .Sask. R.
Sentences arbitrales de griefs . . . . S.A.G.
Supreme Court Reports (see Canada Supreme Court Reports)
Tariff Board Reports . . . . T.B.R.
Tax Appeal Board Cases Tax . . . . A.B.C.
Tribunal du travail (Jurisprudence en droit du travail) . . . . .T.T.
Upper Canada Common Pleas Reports (1850-1882) . . . . . . U.C.C.P.
Upper Canada King's Bench Reports (1831-1844) . . . . U.C.K.B.
Upper Canada Queen's Bench Reports (1844-1882) . . . . . U.C.Q.B.
Weekly Digest of Civil Procedure . . . . .W.D.C.P.
Western Labour Arbitration Cases . . . . .W.L.A.C.
Western Law Reporter (1905-1916) . . . . W.L.R.
Western Weekly Reports . . . . .W.W.R.
Yukon Reports . . . . Y.R.

A.C.W.S. All Canada Weekly Summaries
Admin. L.R. Administrative Law Reports
A.I.A. . . . . .Affaires d'immigration en appel
Alta. L.R. . . . . .Alberta Law Reports
A.R. . . . . Alberta Reports
A.P.R. . . . . Atlantic Provinces Reports
B.C.L.R. . . . . .British Columbia Law Reports
B.C.L.R.B. Dec. . . . . .British Columbia Labour
                                                    Relations Board Decisions
B.C.R. . . . . British Columbia Reports
B.L.R. . . . . .Business Law Reports
B.R. . . . . .Rapports judiciaires officiels de Québec:
                                            Cour du banc du roi (de la reine)
Can. L.R.B.R. . . . . Canadian Labour Relations Board Reports
C.A. . . . . Recueils de jurisprudence du Québec:
                                                        Cour d'appel (1970-1985)
C.A.S. . . . . Décisions de la Commission des Affaires sociales
C.B.E.S. . . .Recueils de jurisprudence du Québec: Cour de Bien-être
                                                            social (1975-1985)
C.B.R. . . . . .Canadian Bankruptcy Reports
C.E.R. . . . . .Canadian Customs and Excise Reports
C.C.C. . . . . Canadian Criminal Cases
C.C.E.L. . . . . .Canadian Cases on Employment Law
C.C.L. . . . . Canadian Current Law

C.C.L.I. . . . . Canadian Cases on the Law of Insurance
C.C.L.R. . . . . Canadian Computer Law Reporter
C.C.L.T. . . . . Canadian Cases on the Law of Torts
C.E.B. & P.G.R. . . . . Canadian Employment Benefits
and Pension Guide Reports
C.E.L.R. . . . . Canadian Environmental Law Reports
C.F. . . . . Recueils des arrêts de la Cour fédérale du Canada
C.H.R.R. . . . . Canadian Human Rights Reporter
C.I.L.R. . . . . Canadian Insurance Law Reports
C.I.P.R. . . . . Canadian Intellectual Property Reports
C.L.L.C. . . . . Canadian Labour Law Cases
C.L.L.R. Canadian Labour Law Reports
C.L.R. . . . . Construction Law Reports
C.N.L.C. Canadian Native Law Cases
C.N.L.R. . . . . Canadian Native Law Reporter
C.P. . . . . Recueils de jurisprudence du Québec:
Cour provinciale (1975-1985)
C.P.C. . . . . Carswell's Practice Cases
C.P.R. . . . . Canadian Patent Reporter
C.R. . . . . Criminal Reports
C.R.C. . . . . Canadian Railway Cases
C.R.D. . . . . Charter of Rights Decisions
C.R.R. . . . . Canadian Rights Reporter
C.R.T. . . . . Canadian Radio-television and Telecommunications
Decisions and Policy Statements
C.R.T.C. . . . . Canadian Railway and Transport Cases
C.S. . . . . Recueils de jurisprudence du Québec:
Cour supérieure (1970-1985)
C.S. . . . . Rapports judiciaires officiels de Québec:
Cour supérieure
C.S.P. . . . . Recueils de jurisprudence du Québec:
Cour des Sessions de la paix (1975-1985)
C.T.C. . . . . Canada Tax Cases
C. Trans. C. . . . . Canadian Transport Cases
Déc. B.-C. . . . Décisions des Tribunaux du Bas-Canada (1851-1867)
D.L.R. . . . . Dominion Law Reports
D.T.C. . . . . Dominion Tax Cases
E.T.R. . . . . Estates and Trusts Reports
E.L.R. . . . . Eastern Law Reporter (1906-1914)
Ex. C.R. . . . . Exchequer Court of Canada Reports
F.C. . . . . Canada Federal Court Reports
F.L.R.A.C. . . . . Family Law Reform Act Cases

Fox Pat. C. . . . . Fox's Patent, Trademark, Design
and Copyright Cases
I.A.C. . . . . Immigration Appeal Cases
I.L.R. . . . . .Canadian Insurance Law Reports
J.E. . . . . .Jurisprudence Express
L.A.C. . . . . Labour Arbitration Cases
L.C.R. . . . . Land Compensation Reports
L.C. Rep. . . . . Lower Canada Reports
Man. R. . . . . .Manitoba Reports
M.P.L.R. . . . . Municipal and Planning Law Reports
M.P.R. . . . . Maritime Provinces Reports
M.V.R. . . . . Motor Vehicle Reports
N.B.R. . . . . New Brunswick Reports
Nfld. & P.E.I.R. . . . . . Newfoundland & Prince Edward Island Reports
Nfld. R. . . . . .Newfoundland Reports
N.R. . . . . .National Reporter
N.S.R. . . . . .Nova Scotia Reports
N.W.T.R. . . . . Northwest Territories Reports
O.A.C. . . . . .Ontario Appeal Cases
O.L.R. . . . . Ontario Law Reports
O.L.R.B. Rep. . . . . Ontario Labour Relations Board Reports
O.M.B.R. . . . . Ontario Municipal Board Reports
O.R. . . . . .Ontario Reports
O.W.N. . . . . Ontario Weekly Notes
O.W.R. . . . . Ontario Weekly Reporter
P.P.S.A.C. . . . . .Personal Property Security Act Cases
Q.A.C. . . . . Quebec Appeal Cases/Causes en appel au Québec
Que. P.R. . . . . .Quebec Practice Reports
Que. Q.B. . . . . . . .Quebec Court of Queen's (King's) Bench Reports
R.C. de l'É. . . . . Recueils de jurisprudence de la Cour de l'Échiquier
R.C.S. . . . . Recueils des arrêts de la Cour suprême du Canada
R.D.F. . . . . Recueil de droit de la famille
R.D.F.Q. . . . . Recueil de droit fiscal québécois
R.D.J. . . . . .Revue de droit judiciaire
R.D.T. . . . . Revue de droit du travail
R.F.L. . . . . Reports of Family Law
R.J.Q. . . . . Recueils de jurisprudence du Québec (1986-to date)
R.L. . . . . Revue légale
R.P.C. . . . . Reports of Patent Cases
R.P. Qué. . . . . Rapports de Pratique de Québec
R.P.R. . . . . .Real Property Reports
R.T.C. . . . . . . .Décisions et énoncés de pratique sur la radiodiffusion
et les télécommunications canadiennes

APPENDIX 3

JURISDICTIONS

APPENDIX 4

COURTS

Admiralty Court . . . . Adm. Ct.
County Court . . . . Co. Ct.
Circuit Court . . . . Circ. Ct.
Cour canadienne de l'impôt . . . . C.C.I.
Cour d'appel . . . . C.A.
Cour de circuit . . . . C. circ.
Cour de district . . . . C. dist.
Cour de magistrat . . . . C. mag.
Cour de révision . . . . C. rév.
Cour de l'Échiquier . . . . C. de l'É.
Cour des Sessions de la paix . . . . C.S.P.
Cour divisionnaire . . . . C. div.
Cour du Banc de la Reine (du Roi) . . . . B.R.
Cour du Québec . . . . C.Q.
Cour fédérale d'appel . . . . C.F.A.
Cour fédérale, premiere instance . . . . C.F. (1re inst.)
Cour municipale . . . . C. mun.
Cour provinciale . . . . C.P.
    Division civile . . . . Div. civ.
    Division criminelle . . . . Div. crim.
    Division de la famille . . . . Div. fam.
Cour supérieure . . . . C.S.
Cour suprême (provinciale) . . . . C.S.
Cour suprême du Canada . . . . C.S.C.
Court of Appeal . . . . C.A.

Court of Criminal Appeals ....Ct. Crim. App.
Court of King's Bench ...........................K.B.
Court of Queen's Bench .........................Q.B.
Court of Review ....Ct. Rev.
Court of Sessions of the Peace ....Ct. Sess. P.
District Court ....Dist. Ct.
Divisional Court ....Div. Ct.
Divorce and Matrimonial Causes Court ...Div. & Matr. Causes Ct.
Exchequer Court ....Ex. Ct.
Family Court ....Fam. Ct.
Federal Court Appeal Division .....................F.C.A.
Federal Court Trial Division ....................F.C.T.D.
General Division ....Gen. Div.
Haute Cour ....................................H.C.
High Court of Justice ..........................H.C.J.
Justice of the Peace Court ....Just. of Peace Ct.
Juvenile Court ....Juv. Ct.
Magistrate's Court ....Mag. Ct.
Municipal Court ....Mun. Ct.
Petites créances ....Pet. cré.
Probate court ....Prob. Ct.
Provincial Court ....Prov. Ct.
        Civil Division ....Civ. Div.
        Family Division ....Fam. Div.
        Criminal Division ....Crim. Div.
        Youth Division ....Youth Div.
        Small Claims Division ....Sm. Cl. Div.
Provincial Division ....Prov. Div.
Small Claims ....Sm. Claims
Superior Court ....Sup. Ct.
Supreme Court (provincial) ......................S.C.
        Appellate Division ...................A.D.
        Trial Division ......................T.D.
Supreme Court of Canada ........................S.C.C.
Surrogate Court ....Surr. Ct.
Tax Court of Canada ..........................T.C.C.
Territorial Court ....Terr. Ct.
Tribunal de la jeunesse ....Trib. jeun.
Unified Family Court ....Unif. Fam. Ct.
Youth Court ....Youth Ct.

APPENDIX 5

ADMINISTRATIVE BOARDS AND TRIBUNALS

Atomic Energy Control Board .... A.E.C.B.
Canada Labour Relations Board .... .C.L.R.B.
Canadian Human Rights Commission .... C.H.R.C.
Canadian International Trade Tribunal .... C.I.T.T.
Canadian Pension Commission .... C.P.C.
Canadian Radio-Television and Telecommunications
     Commission .... C.R.T.C.
Canadian Transport Commission .... .C.T.C.
Civil Aviation Tribunal .... .C.A.T.
Competition Tribunal .... Comp. Trib.
Human Rights Tribunal .... H.R.T.
Immigration and Refugee Board .... .I.R.B.
National Energy Board .... N.E.B.
National Parole Board .... N.P.B.
Pension Appeals Board .... P.A.B.
Public Service Staff Relations Board .... .P.S.S.R.B.
Veterans Appeal Board .... V.A.B.

APPENDIX 6

PERIODICALS

Current Legal Problems .... Curr. Legal Probs.
Dalhousie Law Journal .... Dalhousie L.J.
Estates and Trusts Quarterly .... Est. & Tr. Q.
Examiner (L'observateur) (1861) .... Examiner (L'obervateur)
Family Law Review .... Fam. L. Rev.
Health Law In Canada .... Health L. Can.
Industrial Law Journal .... Indust. L.J.
Intellectual Property Journal .... I.P.J.
Journal of Business Law .... J. Bus. L.
Journal of Law and Social Policy .... J.L. & Social Pol'y
Journal of Planning and Environmental Law ..... J. Plan. & Env. L.
Journal of Social Welfare Law .... J. Social Welfare L.
Justice Report .... Justice Rep.
Law Librarian .... L. Lib.
Law Quarterly Review .... L.Q. Rev.
Law Society Gazette (Law Society of
    Upper Canada) .... L. Soc. Gaz.
Legal News (1887-1897) .... Legal N.
Local Courts' and Municipal
    Gazette (1865-1872) .... Local Cts. & Mun. Gaz.
Lower Canada Jurist (1848-1891) .... L.C. Jurist
Lower Canada Law Journal (1865-1868) .... L.C.L.J.
Manitoba Bar News .... Man. Bar N.
Manitoba Law Journal .... Man. L.J.
McGill Law Journal .... McGill L.J.
National Banking Law Review .... Nat'l Banking L. Rev.
National Insolvency Review .... Nat'l Insolv. Rev.
National Journal of Constitutional Law .... N.J.C.L.
Osgoode Hall Law Journal .... Osgoode Hall L.J.
Ottawa Law Review .... Ottawa L. Rev.
Provincial Judges Journal .... Prov. Judges J.
Queen's Law Journal .... Queen's L.J.
Revue canadienne de propriété intellectuelle .... R.C.P.I.
Revue canadienne du droit d'auteur .... Rev. Can. D.A.
Revue critique (1870-1875) .... Rev. crit.
Revue critique de législation et
    de jurisprudence du Canada .... R.C.L.J.
Revue de droit, Université de Sherbrooke .... R.D.U.S.
Revue de droit de McGill .... R.D. McGill
Revue de droit d'Ottawa .... R.D. Ottawa
Revue de jurisprudence .... R. de J.
Revue de législation (1845-1848) .... R. de L.
Revue de planification fiscale et successorale .... R.P.F.S.

APPEN-DICES

Revue juridique des étudiants et
    étudiantes de l'Université Laval .... R.J.E.L.
Revue du Barreau .... R. du B.
Revue du Barreau canadien .... R. du B. can.
Revue du droit (1922-1939) .... R. du D.
Revue du Notariat .... R. du N.
Revue générale de droit .... .R.G.D.
Revue juridique "La femme et le droit" .... R.J.F.D.
Revue juridique Thémis .... .R.J.T.
Revue nationale de droit constitutionnel .... N.J.C.L.
Revue québécoise de droit international .... .R.Q.D.I.
Saskatchewan Bar Review .... Sask. Bar Rev.
Saskatchewan Law Review .... Sask. L. Rev.
Special Lectures of the Law Society of
    Upper Canada .... Spec. Lect. L.S.U.C.
Studia Canonica .... Stud. Canon.
Supreme Court Law Review .... Supreme Court L.R.
Trade Law Topics .... Trade L. Topics
Uniform Law Conference of
    Canada, Proceedings .... Unif. L. Conf. Proc.
University of British Columbia Law Review .... U.B.C. L. Rev.
University of New Brunswick Law Journal .... U.N.B.L.J.
University of Toronto Faculty of Law Review .... U.T. Fac. L. Rev.
University of Toronto Law Journal .... U.T.L.J.
University of Western Ontario Law Review ...... U.W.O. L. Rev.
Upper Canada Jurist (1844-1848) .... U.C. Jurist
Upper Canada Law Journal (1855-1864) .... U.C.L.J.
Western Law Review (1961-1966) .... West. L. Rev.
Western Ontario Law Review (1967-1976) ..... West. Ont. L. Rev.
Windsor Yearbook of Access to
    Justice .... Windsor Y.B. Access Just.

A.C.D.I. .... Annuaire canadien de droit international
A.C.D.P. .... Annuaire canadien des droits de la personne
Acta Crim. .... Acta Criminologica
Actualités .... Actualités
Actualités-Justice .... Actualités-Justice
Admin. L.J. .... Administrative Law Journal
Advocate .... Advocate
Advocates' Q. .... Advocates' Quarterly
Advocates' Soc. J. .... Advocates' Society Journal
Alta. L. Rev. .... Alberta Law Review
Anal. de Pol. .... Analyse de Politiques

Ann. Air & Sp. L. . . . . Annals of Air and Space Law
Assurances . . . . .Assurances
Barrister . . . . Barrister (1894-1897)
B.C.L.N. . . . . British Columbia Law Notes
Bus. & L. . . . . .Business and the Law
Bus. Q. . . . . .Business Quarterly
B.C. Br. Lect. . . . . .Canadian Bar Association,
British Columbia Branch Lectures
Can. Bar J. . . . . Canadian Bar Journal
Can. Bar Rev. . . . . Canadian Bar Review
Can. Bus. L.J. . . . . .Canadian Business Law Journal
Can. Communic. L. Rev. . . .Canadian Communications Law Review
Can. Community L.J. . . . . Canadian Community Law Journal
Can. Comp. Pol. Rec. . . . . . . .Canadian Competition Policy Record
Can. Council Int'l L. Proc. . . . . Canadian Council on
International Law, Proceedings
Can. Crim. Forum . . . . Canadian Criminology Forum
Can. Curr. Tax . . . . Canadian Current Tax
Can. Env. L.N. . . . . Canadian Environmental Law News
Can. H.R. Advoc. . . . . Canadian Human Rights Advocate
Can. Hum. Rts. . . . . .Y.B. Canadian Human Rights Yearbook
Can. Intell. Prop. Rev. . . . . . .Canadian Intellectual Property Review
Can. J. Crim. . . . . Canadian Journal of Criminology
Can. J. Crim. & Corr. . . . . Canadian Journal of Criminology
and Corrections
Can. J. Fam. L. . . . . Canadian Journal of Family Law
Can. J. Ins. L. . . . . Canadian Journal of Insurance Law
Can. J. Law & Jur. . . . . . Canadian Journal of Law and Jurisprudence
Can. L.J. . . . . Canada Law Journal
Can. L.T. . . . . Canadian Law Times (1881-1922)
Can. Law. . . . . Canadian Lawyer
Can. Legal Stud. . . . . .Canadian Legal Studies
Can. L. Rev. . . . . Canadian Law Review (1901-1907)
Can. Mun. J. . . . . Canadian Municipal Journal
Can. Pub. Pol. .Canadian Public Policy
Can. Tax Found. . . . .Canadian Tax Foundation (Conference Report)
Can. Tax J. . . . . .Canadian Tax Journal
Can. Tax N. . . . . .Canadian Tax News
Can. Tax'n: J. Tax Pol'y . . . . Canadian Taxation:
A Journal of Tax Policy
Can.-U.S. L.J. . . . . .Canada-United States Law Journal
Can. Y.B. Int'l L. . . . . Canadian Year Book of International Law
C.B.A. Papers . . . . .Canadian Bar Association Papers

C.B.A. Y.B. . . . . Canadian Bar Association Year Book
C. de D. . . . . Cahiers de droit
C. de l'I.Q.A.J. . . . . .Cahiers de l'Institut québécois
d'administration judiciaire
Chitty's L.J. . . . . .Chitty's Law Journal
C.J.W.L. . . . . Canadian Journal of Women and the Law
Computer L. . . . . .Computer Law
Corp. Mgt. Tax Conf. . . . . .Corporate Management Tax Conference
Corr. jud. . . . . .Correspondances judiciaires (1906)
C.P. du N. . . . . Cour de perfectionnement du notariat
Crim. L.Q. . . . . Criminal Law Quarterly
Criminologie . . . . Criminologie
Crown Coun. Rev. . . . . Crown Counsel's Review
Curr. Legal Probs. . . . . Current Legal Problems
Dalhousie L.J. . . . . Dalhousie Law Journal
Est. & Tr. Q. . . . . .Estates and Trusts Quarterly
Examiner (L'observateur) . . . . Examiner (L'observateur) (1861)
Fam. L. Rev. . . . . Family Law Review
Health L. Can. . . . . Health Law in Canada
Indust. L. J. . . . . Industrial Law Journal
I.P.J. . . . . Intellectual Property Journal
J. Bus. L. . . . . Journal of Business Law
J.L. & Social Pol'y . . . . Journal of Law and Social Policy
J. Plan. & Env. L. . . . . .Journal of Planning and Environmental Law
J. Social Welfare L. . . . . .Journal of Social Welfare Law
Justice Rep. . . . . Justice Report
L.C. Jurist . . . . .Lower Canada Jurist (1848-1891)
Legal N. . . . . Legal News (1878-1897)
L.C.L.J. . . . . Lower Canada Law Journal (1865-1868)
L. Lib. . . . . Law Librarian
Local Cts. & Mun. Gaz. . . . . Local Courts' and Municipal
Gazette (1865-1872)
L.Q. Rev. . . . . Law Quarterly Review
L. Soc. Gaz. . . Law Society Gazette (Law Society of Upper Canada)
Man. Bar N. . . . . Manitoba Bar News
Man. L.J. . . . . Manitoba Law Journal
McGill L.J. . . . . McGill Law Journal
Nat'l Banking L. Rev. . . . . National Banking Law Review
Nat'l Insolv. Rev. . . . . National Insolvency Review
N.J.C.L. . . . . National Journal of Constitutional Law
N.J.C.L. . . . . Revue nationale de droit constitutionnel
Osgoode Hall L.J. . . . . Osgoode Hall Law Journal
Ottawa L. Rev. . . . . .Ottawa Law Review

Prov. Judges J. . . . . Provincial Judges Journal
Queen's L.J. . . . . Queen's Law Journal
R.C.L.J. . . . . Revue critique de législation
et de jurisprudence du Canada
R.C.P.I. . . . . .Revue canadienne de propriété intellectuelle
R. de J. . . . . .Revue de jurisprudence
R. de L. . . . . Revue de Législation (1845-1848)
R.D. McGill . . . . Revue de droit de McGill
R.D. Ottawa . . . . Revue de droit d'Ottawa
R. du B. . . . . .Revue du Barreau
R. du B. can. . . . . .Revue du Barreau canadien
R. du D. . . . . .Revue du droit (1922-1939)
R. du N. . . . . Revue du Notariat
R.D.U.S. . . . . Revue de droit, Université de Sherbrooke
R.G.D. . . . . Revue générale de droit
R.J.F.D. . . . . Revue juridique "La femme et le droit"
R.J.T. . . . . Revue juridique Thémis
R.P.F.S. . . . . Revue de planification fiscale et successorale
R.Q.D.I. . . . . .Revue québécoise de droit international
Rev. Can. D.A. . . . . .Revue canadienne du droit d'auteur
Rev. crit. . . . . Revue critique (1870-1875)
Sask. Bar Rev. . . . . .Saskatchewan Bar Review
Sask. L. Rev. . . . . Saskatchewan Law Review
Spec. Lect. L.S.U.C. . . . . .Special Lectures of the Law
Society of Upper Canada
Stud. Canon. . . . . .Studia Canonica
Supreme Court L.R. . . . . Supreme Court Law Review
Trade L. Topics . . . . .Trade Law Topics
U.B.C. L. Rev. . . . . . . .University of British Columbia Law Review
U.C. Jurist . . . . .Upper Canada Jurist (1844-1848)
U.C.L.J. . . . . .Upper Canada Law Journal (1855-1864)
U.N.B.L.J. . . . . .University of New Brunswick Law Journal
Unif. L. Conf. Proc. . . . . Uniform Law Conference
of Canada, Proceedings
U.T. Fac. L. Rev. . . . . University of Toronto Faculty of Law Review
U.T.L.J. . . . . University of Toronto Law Journal
U.W.O. L. Rev. . . . . . . .University of Western Ontario Law Review
West. L. Rev. . . . . Western Law Review (1961-1966)
West. Ont. L. Rev. . . . . .Western Ontario Law Review (1967-1976)
Windsor Y.B. Access Just. . . Windsor Yearbook of Access to Justice

APPENDIX 7

INTERNATIONAL LAW JOURNALS

Harvard International Law Journal . . . . Harv. Int'l L.J.
Human Rights Law Journal . . . . .HRLJ
Human Rights Quarterly . . . . .Hum. Rts. Q.
ICSID Review . . . . ICSID Rev.
International and Comparative Law
    Quarterly . . . . .I.C.L.Q.
International Business Law Journal . . . . IBLJ
International Business Lawyer . . . . IBL
International Commission of Jurists
    Review . . . . Int'l Comm. Jur. Rev.
International Journal of Law and
    Psychiatry . . . . .Int'l J. L. & Psy.
International Journal of Legal Information . . . . Int'l J. L. Inf.
International Lawyer . . . . .Int'l Lawyer
International Legal Materials . . . . I.L.M.
International Legal Practitioner . . . . Int'l L. Pract.
International Review of Criminal Policy . . . . . Int'l Rev. Crim. Pol'y
International Review of Industrial
    Property and Copyright Law IIC
International Review of Law and
    Economics . . . . .Int'l Rev. L. & Econ.
International Tax and Business Lawyer . . . . Int' Tax & Bus. Lawyer
International Trade Law and Practice . . . . . . .Int'l Trade L. & Pract.
Journal du droit international . . . . .J.D.I.
Journal of Comparative Business and
    Capital Market Law . . . . J. Comp. Bus. & Cap. Mkt. L.
Journal of International Arbitration . . . . J. Int'l Arb.
Journal of International Banking Law . . . . J. Int'l Bank. L.
Journal of Maritime Law and Commerce . . . . J. Marit. L. & Comm.
Journal of Space Law . . . . .J. Space L.
Journal of World Trade . . . . J. World T.
Korean Journal of Comparative Law . . . . .Korean J. Comp. L.
Law and Policy in International Business . . . Law & Pol'y Int'l Bus.
Netherlands International Law Review . . . . . . Netherl. Int'l L. Rev.
New York University Journal of International
    Law and Politics . . . . N.Y.U.J. Int'l L. & Pol.
Northwestern Journal of International Law
    and Business . . . . Nw. J. Int'l L. & Bus.
Nordic Journal of International Law . . . . .Nordic J. Int'l L.
Notre Dame International Law Review . . . Notre Dame Int'l L. Rev.
Ocean Development and International Law . . .Ocean Dev. & Int'l L.
Recueil des Cours . . . . .Rec. des Cours

Revue africaine de droit international
et comparé .... RADIC
Revue algérienne des sciences juridiques,
économiques et politiques .... Rev. A.S.J.E.P.
Revue belge de droit international ....Rev. B.D.I.
Revue critique de droit international
privé .... Rev. cri. dr. internat. privé
Revue de droit des affaires internationales .... RDAI
Revue de droit international et
de droit comparé .... Rev. D.I. & D.C.
Revue de droit uniforme .... Rev. D.U.
Revue de l'arbitrage .... Rev. arb.
Revue du droit public et de la science
politique en France et à l'étranger ....Rev. D.P. & S.P.
Revue egyptienne de droit international ....Rev. E.D.I.
Revue générale de droit international public ....Rev. D.I.P.
Revue hellénique de droit international .... Rev. H.D.I.
Revue internationale de droit comparé ................R.I.D.C.
Revue internationale de droit pénal ....Rev. I.D.P.
Revue internationale de politique criminelle ....Rev. I.P.C.
Revue trimestrielle de droit commercial
et de droit économique .... Rev. trim. Droit com.
Revue trimestrielle de droit européen ....Rev. trim. dr. europ.
Stanford Journal of International Law .... Stanf. J. Int'l L.
Texas International Law Journal .... Texas Int'l L.J.
Uniform Law Review .... Unif. L. Rev.
University of Miami Inter-American
Law Review .... U. Miami Inter-Am. L. Rev.
University of Pennsylvania Journal of
International Business Law ....U. Pa. J. Int'l Bus. L.
Vanderbilt Journal of Transnational Law .... Vand. J. Transnat'l L.
Virginia Journal of International Law .... Va. J. Int'l L.
World Trade Materials .........................W.T.M.
Yale Journal of International Law .... Yale J. Int'l L.

APPEN-
DICES

APPENDIX 8

TREATY SERIES

APPENDIX 9

INTERNATIONAL CASE REPORTERS

Reports of Judgments, Advisory Opinions
and Orders (I.C.J.) .... I.C.J. Rep.
Série A : Arrêts et décisions
(Cour Eur. D.H.) .... Cour Eur. D.H. Sér. A
Série A : Recueil des arrêts (C.P.J.I.) .... C.P.J.I. Sér. A
Série A/B: Arrêts, ordonnances et
avis consultatifs (C.P.J.I.) .... C.P.J.I. Sér. A/B
Série B : Recueil des avis consultatifs
(C.P.J.I.) .... C.P.J.I. Sér. B
Série B : Mémoires, plaidoiries et
documents (Cour Eur. D.H.) .... Cour Eur. D.H. Sér. B
Série C : Plaidoiries, exposés oraux
et documents (C.P.J.I.) .... C.P.J.I. Sér. C
Series A, Collection of Judgments
(P.C.I.J.) .... P.C.I.J. Ser. A
Series A: Judgments and Decisions
(Eur. Ct. H.R.) .... Eur. Ct. H.R. Ser. A
Series A: Judgments and Opinions
(Inter-Am. Ct. H.R.) .... Inter-Am. Ct. H.R. Ser. A
Series A/B, Judgments, Orders and Advisory
Opinions (P.C.I.J.) .... P.C.I.J. Ser. A/B
Series B: Collection of Advisory Opinions
(P.C.I.J.) .... P.C.I.J. Ser. B
Series B: Pleadings, Oral Arguments and
Documents (Eur. Ct. H.R.) .... Eur. Ct. H.R. Ser. B
Series B: Pleadings, Oral Arguments and
Documents (Inter-Am. Ct. H.R.) .... Inter-Am. Ct. H.R. Ser. B
Series C: Decisions and Judgments
(Inter-Am. Ct. H.R.) .... Inter-Am. Ct. H.R. Ser. C
Series C: Pleadings, Oral Statements and
Documents (P.C.I.J.) .... P.C.I.J. Ser. C
Trade and Tarrif Reports .... T.T.R.
Yearbook of the European Convention on
Human Rights .... Y.B. Eur. Conv. H.R.

APPENDIX 10

INTERNATIONAL LAW YEARBOOKS

Annuaire canadien de droit international . . . . Ann. can. dr. int.
Annuaire canadien des droits de la personne . . . . . . Ann. can. dr. P.
Annuaire de droit aérien et spatial . . . . Ann. dr. a. s.
Annuaire de droit maritime et aérien . . . . Ann. dr. m. a.
Annuaire de droit maritime et
aéro-spatial . . . . .Ann. dr. m. a.-s.
Annuaire de la Haye de droit
international . . . . Ann. Haye dr. int.
Annuaire de la Société française de droit
aérien et spatial . . . . .Ann. S. fran. dr. A. S.
Annuaire de la Société des Nations . . . . Ann. S.N.
Annuaire de législation étrangère . . . . Ann. lég. étrang.
Annuaire de législation française . . . . Ann. lég. fran.
Annuaire des Nations Unies . . . . Ann. N.U.
Annuaire de l'Institut de droit
international . . . . .Ann. inst. dr. int.
Annuaire français de droit international . . . . .Ann. fran. dr. int.
Annuaire français des Droits de l'Homme . . . . Ann. fran. D.H.
Annuaire français du transport aérien . . . . Ann. fran. transp. A.
Annuaire international de justice
constitutionnelle . . . . Ann. int. j.c.
Annuaire suisse de droit international . . . . .Ann. suisse dr. int.
Annual Survey of American Law . . . . .Ann. Surv. Amer. L.
Annual Survey of Australian Law . . . . .Ann. Surv. Austral. L.

Annual Survey of Commonwealth
    Law . . . . .Ann. Surv. Commonwealth L.
Annual Survey of English Law . . . . .Ann. Surv. Engl. L.
Annual Survey of South African Law . . . . Ann. Surv. S.A.L.
Canadian Human Rights Yearbook . . . . Can. H.R.Y.B.
Canadian Yearbook of International Law . . . . Can. Y.B. Int'l L.
Chinese Yearbook of International
    Law and Affairs . . . . .Chinese Y.B. Int'l L. & Aff.
Current Law Yearbook . . . . .Curr. L.Y.B.
European Environment Yearbook . . . . Eur. Env. Y.B.
Hague Yearbook of International Law . . . . .Hague Y.B. Int'l L.
Harvard Human Rights Yearbook . . . . .Harv. H.R.Y.B.
Scottish Current Law Yearbook . . . . .Scot. Curr. L.Y.B.
Yearbook: Commercial Arbitration . . . . Y.B. Comm. Arb.
Yearbook of Air and Space Law . . . . Y.B. Air & Sp. L.
Yearbook of European Law . . . . Y.B. Eur. L.
Yearbook of Human Rights Committee . . . . Y.B.H.R. Ctee.
Yearbook of International Court of Justice . . . . Y.B.I.C.J.
Yearbook of International Environmental
    Law . . . . Y.B. Int'l Env. L.
Yearbook of Maritime Law . . . . .Y.B. Marit. L.
Yearbook of the Institute of International
    Law . . . . Y.B. Inst. Int'l L.
Yearbook of the United Nations . . . . Y.B.U.N.
Yearbook on Human Rights . . . . Y.B.H.R.

INDEX

Manuel canadien de la RÉFÉRENCE JURIDIQUE

3e édition

Revue de droit de McGill
McGill Law Journal

CARSWELL
Publications spécialisées Thomson

© 1992 Fiduciaires du fonds en fiducie de la Revue de droit de McGill/
Trustees of the McGill Law Journal Trust Fund

Tous droits réservés. Il est interdit de reproduire, enregistrer ou diffuser un
extrait quelconque de cet ouvrage, sous quelque forme ou par quelque procédé
que ce soit, électronique, mécanique, photographique, sonore, magnétique ou
autre, sans avoir obtenu au préalable l'autorisation écrite de l'éditeur.

Données de catalogage avant publication (Canada)
Vedette principale au titre:
  Manuel canadien de la référence juridique

3e éd.
Texte en français et en anglais.
Titre de la p. de t. addit., tête-bêche :
  Canadian guide to uniform legal citation.
«McGill Law Journal = Revue de droit de McGill»
Comprend des références bibliographiques et un index.

ISBN 0-459-55149-3 (rel.) –
ISBN 0-459-55151-5 (br.)

1. Recueils juridiques faisant autorité –
Citation – Canada.   I. Titre : Canadian Guide to Uniform Legal Citation.
KE259.C34 1992   808' .06634   C92-094846-4F

CARSWELL
Publications spécialisées Thomson

One Corporate Plaza   **Service à la clientèle**
2075 Kennedy Road   Toronto 1-416-609-8000
Scarborough, Ontario   Ailleurs au Canada/É.-U. 1-800-387-5164
M1T 3V4   Télécopieur 1-416-298-5094

Officiellement adopté par :

Alberta Law Review
Canadian Journal of Law and Jurisprudence
Revue canadienne de droit et société/Canadian Journal of Law and
Society
Revue de droit de McGill/McGill Law Journal
Manitoba Law Journal
Osgoode Hall Law Journal
Revue de droit d'Ottawa/Ottawa Law Review
Queen's Law Journal
Saskatchewan Law Review
University of British Columbia Law Review
Revue de droit de l'Université du Nouveau-Brunswick/University of
New Brunswick Law Journal
University of Toronto Faculty of Law Review
Colombie-Britannique : Cour d'appel, Cour suprême et Cour de
comté

TABLE DES MATIÈRES

AVANT-PROPOS

Au cours du printemps 1984, les rédacteurs de la Revue de droit de McGill ont entrepris un processus de recherche et de discussion sur la référence juridique qui a débouché sur la publication, deux ans plus tard, de la première édition du *Manuel canadien de la référence juridique/ Canadian Guide to Uniform Legal Citation*. La raison d'être de ce projet reposait sur la constatation que, si plusieurs systèmes de référence avaient été proposés au fil des ans, aucun n'était devenu le modèle standard. Les rédacteurs estimèrent qu'un système de référence reflétant le caractère bilingue et bijuridique de notre pays offrirait mieux que tout autre une norme acceptable pour la nation.

La recherche pour le projet de référence débuta au cours de l'été 1984, alors que la Revue bénéficiait d'une subvention du programme d'emploi «Été Canada» attribuée par le Ministère de l'Emploi et de l'Immigration. Les chercheurs ont procédé à un examen détaillé et à la comparaison des divers modes de référence existants. Plutôt que d'adopter comme modèle le mode de référence d'une revue ou d'un éditeur en particulier, les comités de rédaction de la Revue de l'époque ont choisi les critères de clarté, de simplicité, d'uniformité et de concision pour les guider dans la formulation des règles de base dans les quatre principaux domaines : la législation, la jurisprudence, la doctrine et la documentation gouvernementale.

Afin de réaliser notre objectif d'arriver à un consensus sur un mode de référence uniforme à travers le Canada, nous avons distribué, en mars 1985, un nombre limité de copies de la version préliminaire du *Manuel*, en français et en anglais, en vue de recevoir des commentaires. Nous commençâmes à utiliser le nouveau système à la Revue de droit de McGill en septembre 1984, dans le but d'en éprouver l'applicabilité. Les motifs qui sous-tendent les règles ont été inclus dans la version initiale afin de servir de base à la discussion.

Le projet a reçu un accueil formidable de la part de la communauté juridique. Des directeurs de périodiques, de revues juridiques et de maisons d'édition, des bibliothécaires de facultés de droit, des membres de l'Association canadienne de bibliothèques de droit (A.C.B.D.), des juges de diverses provinces, des conseillers législatifs, des directeurs de recherche de cabinets d'avocats ainsi que de nombreuses autres personnes ont exprimé leur appui au projet et ont fait parvenir au comité des commentaires détaillés.

À l'été 1985, une bourse de recherche octroyée à la Revue de droit de McGill par le Conseil canadien de la documentation juridique (C.C.D.J.) nous a permis de compiler et d'intégrer les commentaires reçus et d'entreprendre la recherche dans de nouveaux domaines : la documentation britannique et internationale et les modes d'abréviation. Le premier chapitre, «Législation», fut retravaillé afin d'y incorporer les commentaires fournis par les conseillers législatifs ainsi que la recherche plus approfondie qui avait été effectuée. Vu la nature de plus en plus interdisciplinaire de la science juridique, les directives publiées par l'Organisation internationale de normalisation (ISO) ont été incorporées au *Manuel*, qui recommande maintenant au chapitre trois, «Doctrine», d'inclure le lieu d'édition et l'éditeur dans une référence à une monographie.

Des copies de ces nouveaux modes de référence avec motifs à l'appui furent distribuées au cours de l'automne 1985, en versions française et anglaise. De plus, un certain nombre de copies du *Manuel* furent imprimées pour l'usage du programme de recherche et de rédaction juridiques et du Tribunal école de McGill. La conférence régionale des revues juridiques, convoquée par le Queen's Law Journal en février 1986, nous donna l'occasion de discuter des modes de référence avec les responsables d'autres revues et de parvenir à un meilleur consensus. Les commentaires concernant les nouvelles parties du *Manuel* furent étudiés et incorporés à la version finale que l'on envoya à Carswell pour publication en avril 1986.

Une deuxième subvention du programme d'emploi «Été Canada» du Ministère de l'Emploi et de l'Immigration nous a permis, durant l'été 1986, de poursuivre la recherche concernant les modes de référence pour la documentation française continentale et pour la documentation internationale. Cette recherche s'est poursuivie jusqu'à l'été 1987, en même temps que la préparation des règles de rédaction plus générales.

Pendant l'été 1987, nous entreprîmes une révision importante du *Manuel*, avec le soutien du Bureau du doyen de la faculté de droit de l'Université McGill. La modification de la règle exigeant la date de la décision dans une référence à la jurisprudence figure parmi les changements les plus importants apportés à la deuxième édition : l'année de la décision n'est plus exigée dans tous les cas. Le mode de référence pour la

jurisprudence est maintenant plus conforme aux normes du Conseil canadien de la documentation juridique pour l'identification des jugements. De plus, nous avons modifié et élargi les chapitres portant sur la législation, la jurisprudence et les documents gouvernementaux canadiens, et les parties du *Manuel* concernant la législation, la jurisprudence et les documents gouvernementaux du Royaume-Uni furent réunies pour former un seul chapitre. Un chapitre présentant un système de référence pour la législation, la jurisprudence et la doctrine de France ainsi qu'une introduction aux notes infra-paginales dans les textes juridiques complètent les parties ajoutées à la deuxième édition. Une version préliminaire de cette édition fut distribuée pour fins de commentaires aux membres de la communauté juridique – publications juridiques, tribunaux, juristes et avocats.

De nouveau avec le soutien du Bureau du doyen et une bourse «Été Canada» du Ministère de l'Emploi et de l'Immigration, nous pûmes commencer le travail de recherche et de révision en vue de cette troisième édition. Une subvention octroyée par le Centre de recherches pour le développement international a permis un remaniement complet du chapitre sur la documentation internationale durant les étés 1990 et 1991, comportant de nouvelles recherches, une révision intégrale et l'ajout de nouvelles sections. Ce chapitre est désormais beaucoup plus complet et énonce des règles de référence pour les documents et les décisions de nombreux organismes et tribunaux, y compris l'Organisation des États américains, l'Accord de libre-échange canado-américain et l'Accord général sur les tarifs douaniers et le commerce (GATT). À cela s'ajoutent quatre nouveaux appendices sur les sources internationales. Plusieurs juristes ont commenté une version annotée de ce chapitre.

Bon nombre des modifications qu'on trouvera dans cette troisième édition reprennent les suggestions que les lecteurs des éditions antérieures ont bien voulu nous transmettre. Suite aux commentaires de nombreux lecteurs, le *Manuel* contient un nouveau chapitre sur les sources américaines (chapitre 7). Les règles générales qui, dans la deuxième édition, se trouvaient à l'introduction, ont été remaniées et systématisées dans une section qui s'intitule «Références et notes infra-paginales : notions de base». À une exception près, les diverses sections dispersées à travers le *Manuel* qui traitaient de l'emploi de «ci-après», «*supra*», «*infra*», etc., ont été réunies ici afin d'éviter les répétitions inutiles et la possibilité de règles contradictoires.

Dans les autres chapitres du *Manuel*, les règles et la structure générale sont celles qui ont fait le succès des éditions précédentes, mais nous avons tenté d'en alléger la présentation. Bon nombre de règles ont été retravaillées afin de les rendre plus parlantes. Le présentation bilingue, en vertu de laquelle quelqu'un qui lisait la partie française du *Manuel* trou-

vait des règles non seulement pour le rédacteur francophone mais aussi pour le rédacteur anglophone, a été abolie : la personne qui rédige en anglais devra désormais consulter la partie anglaise du *Manuel.* Nous avons cru que la présentation des éditions antérieures était non seulement inutile, mais prêtait à confusion car le lecteur francophone serait peut-être porté à croire que les règles «anglaises» s'appliquent aux sources anglaises qu'on veut citer dans un texte écrit en français. Cette dernière question – celle des références aux sources écrites dans une langue autre que celle dans laquelle on rédige – ne fut pas traitée dans les éditions antérieures; dans la troisième édition elle fait l'objet d'une analyse dans la section intitulée «Références et notes infra-paginales : notions de base».

Le comité du *Manuel* reconnaît l'apport de nombreux documents exposant des systèmes de référence juridique qui furent consultés au moment où la recherche débutait. Nous aimerions mentionner en particulier les ouvrages de M. Chin-Shih Tang, et des professeurs Margaret Banks, Douglass T. MacEllven et Ernest Caparros.

Nous sommes très heureux que le *Manuel* continue d'être utilisé par un nombre croissant de juristes – avocats, juges, professeurs, rédacteurs de revues – ainsi que dans les cours de méthodologie de la plupart des facultés de droit. Nous aimerions souligner le fait que le projet de référence est soumis à un processus constant de recherche et de discussion, et nous serions heureux de recevoir toute suggestion ou critique qui nous permettrait d'améliorer le contenu de ce *Manuel.* Tous les commentaires sont les bienvenus. Veuillez les faire parvenir au Rédacteur des références, Revue de droit de McGill, 3644, rue Peel, Montréal (Québec) H3A 1W9.

REMERCIEMENTS

Nous aimerions remercier le Conseil canadien de la documentation juridique (C.C.D.J.) de son appui et son encouragement au cours de la préparation des deux premières éditions du *Manuel*. Nous tenons à exprimer notre dette envers le Centre de recherches pour le développement international pour la bourse qui a permis la révision et l'expansion du chapitre sur la documentation internationale de la troisième édition. Nous reconnaissons aussi l'apport des subventions octroyées par le Ministère de l'Emploi et de l'Immigration. Par son soutien et son encouragement, le Bureau du doyen de la faculté de droit de l'Université McGill a joué un rôle de premier plan tout au long de l'histoire du *Manuel*.

Il importe de souligner le travail de Sonia Struthers et de Robert Metcalfe, premiers coordonnateurs du projet, qui ont eu l'idée de faire ce *Manuel* et l'ont menée à bonne fin dans la première édition. Des recherchistes d'été et des membres des comités de rédaction des volumes 30 à 33 de la Revue de droit de McGill ont fait la recherche de base, la vérification des sources et la révision des premières ébauches. Chantal Roy, Kathryn Sabo, Randall Hofley et Michael Waterston ont coordonné la deuxième édition. Louis Fortier et Nathalie Vézina ont fourni des services de traduction pour la première et la deuxième édition respectivement.

Le travail en vue d'une troisième édition fut entrepris par James W.E. Doris et Timothy M. Egan, Rédacteurs des références du volume 35. La recherche et les révisions débutèrent à l'été 1990, sous la direction de Julia E. Hanigsberg, Rédactrice en chef du volume 36, avec Lisa Yarmoshuk occupant le poste de coordonnatrice du projet. Marie-Claude

Goulet commença alors la recherche pour les nouvelles sections du chapitre sur la documentation internationale. Durant l'été 1991, sous la direction de David Chemla, Rédacteur en chef du volume 37, le chapitre sur la documentation internationale fut complété par Nan Wang, et Mark Phillips a révisé tout le texte du *Manuel* et a ajouté un chapitre sur les sources américaines.

De plus, nous aimerions remercier toutes les personnes – juges, conseillers à la rédaction des lois, directeurs de recherche, professeurs, bibliothécaires, rédacteurs, avocats et étudiants – qui ont si généreusement pris le temps de répondre à nos questions et de nous faire parvenir de très utiles commentaires sur les diverses versions des trois éditions. Nous désirons exprimer notre gratitude aux professeurs J.E.C. Brierley, P.-A. Crépeau, P.G. Jobin, R.A. Macdonald, A.L.C. de Mestral, ainsi qu'à l'ensemble des membres de la faculté de droit de l'Université McGill, qui ont bien voulu nous faire part de leurs commentaires. Nous remercions également les bibliothécaires à la bibliothèque de droit qui nous ont si gentiment aidés au cours de la recherche.

De même, nous aimerions remercier le doyen Y.-M. Morissette et les professeurs G.B. Baker, S.J. Toope et P. Healy, conseillers à la Revue de droit de McGill, ainsi que les fiduciaires de la Revue, de leur apport pendant le processus de publication. Nous tenons à les remercier ainsi que les autres membres, actuellement ou dans le passé, du comité consultatif du *Manuel* – Jill Frank, Daniel Gogek, Jane Graham, Hélène Guay, Randall Hofley, Elizabeth Massey, Grant McCrea, Donald L. Munn, Peter Oliver, Raj Pande, Brian Pel, Chantal Roy, Kathryn Sabo et Henry K. Schultz.

David Chemla	Lisa Yarmoshuk
Rédacteur en chef	Rédactrice des références
Volume 37	Volume 37

RÉFÉRENCES ET NOTES
INFRA-PAGINALES :
NOTIONS DE BASE

INTRODUCTION

Le *Manuel canadien de la référence juridique* a pour but de présenter un système de référence qui réponde aux besoins du juriste canadien. Le *Manuel* cherche à aider l'auteur à structurer ses notes infra-paginales de façon à permettre au lecteur de repérer facilement les sources. Si les modes de référence indiqués pour la législation et la jurisprudence s'appliquent non seulement aux notes infra-paginales, mais également aux tables, bibliographies, etc., les règles relatives à la doctrine ne sauraient être utilisées que dans les notes infra-paginales; pour les références bibliographiques de la doctrine, le lecteur consultera un des nombreux ouvrages de référence qui traitent de cette question.

Ceux et celles qui ont utilisé les versions précédentes de ce manuel constateront un changement majeur dans la présentation. Dans les éditions antérieures, les deux parties s'adressaient tant aux auteurs anglophones que francophones. Dans la présente édition, la partie française du *Manuel* n'énonce que les règles pour les auteurs francophones. La personne qui écrit en anglais devra donc consulter la partie anglaise du *Manuel*. Pour des indications sur la façon de faire référence à une source en langue anglaise lorsqu'on écrit en français, on devra consulter, ci-dessous, la section «Les références aux sources écrites dans une langue autre que le français».

Les écrits savants sont composés de *texte* et de *notes infra-paginales*. Les notes infra-paginales fournissent des renseignements supplémentaires qu'on ne veut pas inclure dans le texte. La note infra-paginale est obligatoire lorsque l'auteur s'inspire d'une autre source, qu'elle soit citée ou non. Dans le domaine juridique, les notes infra-paginales servent le plus souvent à fournir des références : lois, jurisprudence, doctrine, documents gouvernementaux, etc. Les références ne doivent jamais apparaître dans le texte, mais toujours en notes infra-paginales.

Une référence comporte plusieurs éléments qui identifient la source et permettent son repérage dans une bibliothèque. Les éléments sont donnés dans un ordre précis et selon certaines conventions de caractère et de ponctuation. Il peut être exigé, par exemple, qu'un élément de la référence soit mis en italique, entre parenthèses, suivi d'une virgule, etc. Les règles énoncées dans ce manuel visent la clarté, la simplicité, la constance et la concision des références. **N.B. Selon un usage bien établi, le soulignement peut toujours remplacer l'italique.**

Les notes infra-paginales sont numérotées. En général, cette numérotation est consécutive du début du texte jusqu'à la fin. Dans le texte, les numéros se placent au-dessus de la ligne et peuvent suivre n'importe quel mot dans la phrase. Il n'y a pas d'espace entre le mot et le numéro. Si le mot est suivi d'un signe de ponctuation, le numéro se place entre le mot et la ponctuation, sauf s'il s'agit d'une citation placée entre guillemets, auquel cas le numéro se met après le guillemet final.

Les notes elles-mêmes se mettent au bas de la page. Chaque note est précédée de son numéro correspondant. Si possible, la note devrait commencer sur la page où se trouve le numéro correspondant dans le texte.

Un point-virgule sépare deux références dans une même note, et la note se termine toujours par un point. Une note discursive, c'est-à-dire une note contenant des commentaires plus ou moins développés, est composée d'une ou plusieurs phrases complètes.

FORMULES INTRODUCTIVES

Exemples   [25] **Voir** *Ford* c. *Québec (P.G.)*, [1988] 2 R.C.S. 712, 54 D.L.R. (4e) 577. La conclusion de la cour y fut sans équivoque. **Comparer** *Irwin Toy* c. *Québec (P.G.)*, [1989] 1 R.C.S. 927, 58 D.L.R. (4e) 577. **Voir toutefois** *Mahe* c. *Alberta*, [1990] 1 R.C.S. 342, 68 D.L.R. (4e) 69.

Règles   En plus de fournir la référence, l'auteur voudra peut-être l'introduire par une formule indiquant la relation logique entre la source en question et la proposition

énoncée dans le texte. Sans être exhaustive, la liste suivante présente quelques-unes de ces formules :

- **(Aucune formule)** : La source en question est citée dans le texte ou énonce l'idée exprimée dans le texte.
- **Voir** : La source en question appuie la proposition énoncée dans le texte.
- **Par ex.** ou **Voir par ex.** : La source est l'une de celles qui appuient l'idée exprimée dans le texte.
- **Voir surtout** : La source en question est la plus concluante de toutes celles qui soutiennent la proposition énoncée dans le texte.
- **Voir aussi** : La source en question vient s'ajouter à d'autres qui appuient l'idée exprimée dans le texte.
- **Voir généralement** : La source en question fournit des renseignements généraux sur le sujet.
- **Comparer** : La source offre une comparaison intéressante avec l'idée exprimée dans le texte.
- **Voir toutefois** : La source est en désaccord partiel avec la proposition énoncée dans le texte.
- *Contra* : La source en question contredit directement la proposition énoncée dans le texte.

Ne pas mettre les formules introductives en italique (à l'exception de *contra*).

RÉFÉRENCES ULTÉRIEURES

Exemples [2] *Nouvelle-Écosse (P.G.)* c. *Phillips* (1987), 34 D.L.R. (4e) 633 (N.S.S.C. A.D.) [ci-après *Phillips*].
[43] *Phillips, supra* note 2 à la p. 655.

Règles Il arrive souvent qu'une source soit mentionnée plusieurs fois. La référence complète n'apparaît qu'une seule fois, soit dans la note qui accompagne la première mention. Les références ultérieures renvoient à cette première référence.

Si le titre est long, l'auteur doit l'abréger dans les références ultérieures, mais d'une façon qui ne prête à aucune équivoque. Voir ci-dessous la section sur l'emploi de l'expression «ci-après».

L'auteur se servira aussi de renvois (*supra, ibid.*, etc.) pour que le lecteur puisse trouver la note qui contient la référence complète. Voir ci-dessous les règles relatives aux notes contenant des références ultérieures.

Emploi de l'expression «ci-après»

Si le titre de la source est suffisamment court, l'auteur peut l'utiliser tel quel partout dans le texte et les notes infra-paginales. Mais s'il est long, l'auteur doit trouver un titre abrégé qui sera placé entre crochets à la fin de la première référence et introduit par l'expression «ci-après». C'est cette forme abrégée que l'auteur utilisera chaque fois qu'il fait mention de la source, que ce soit dans le texte ou dans les notes.

Les titres s'abrègent selon certaines règles pour chaque catégorie de source :

Législation

Exemples
[3] *Loi sur les musées*, L.C. 1990, c. 3.

[8] *Loi autorisant l'aliénation de Nordion et de Theratronics*, L.C. 1990, c. 4 **[ci-après *Loi sur Nordion*]**.

[10] *Charte canadienne des droits et libertés*, Partie I de la *Loi constitutionnelle de 1982*, constituant l'annexe B de la *Loi de 1982 sur le Canada* (R.-U.), 1982, c. 11 **[ci-après la Charte]**.

[12] *Charte de la langue française*, L.R.Q. c. C-11 **[ci-après la Loi 101]**.

Règles
Si la loi a un titre abrégé officiel, on se sert toujours de celui-ci dans la première référence. Si ce titre abrégé est suffisamment court, on peut l'employer dans les références ultérieures aussi, auquel cas point n'est besoin d'utiliser l'expression «ci-après». Si la loi n'a pas de titre abrégé ou si l'auteur ne veut pas s'en servir dans les références ultérieures, la meilleure solution consiste à choisir un titre court mais distinctif, introduit par l'expression «ci-après».

Jurisprudence

Exemples
[15] *R. c. Lavallée*, [1990] 1 R.C.S. 852, 76 C.R. (3e) 329 **[ci-après *Lavallée* avec renvois aux R.C.S.]**.

[23] Voir *Société des Acadiens du Nouveau-Brunswick Inc. c. Association of Parents for Fairness in Education*, [1986] 1 R.C.S. 549, 27 D.L.R. (4e) 406 **[ci-après *Société des Acadiens* avec renvois aux R.C.S.]** pour un examen de cette question.

NOTIONS DE BASE

Règles On prend le nom d'une des parties ou une partie distinctive de celui-ci.

Si la référence mentionne plusieurs recueils, l'auteur doit indiquer celui dans lequel il faut chercher les références précises subséquentes («avec renvois à ...»). À cette fin, l'auteur devrait choisir le recueil le plus officiel.

Doctrine

Exemples [3] G. Massol, *La lésion entre majeurs en droit québécois*, Cowansville (Qué.), Yvon Blais, 1989.

[6] Massol, *supra* note 3 à la p. 25.

OU

[3] G. Massol, *La lésion entre majeurs en droit québécois*, Cowansville (Qué.), Yvon Blais, 1989 **[ci-après *La lésion entre majeurs*]**.

[6] *La lésion entre majeurs*, *supra* note 3 à la p. 25.

[10] A. Lajoie, «De l'interventionnisme judiciaire comme apport à l'émergence des droits sociaux» (1991) 36 R.D. McGill 1338 **[ci-après «Interventionnisme judiciaire»]**.

[15] «Interventionnisme judiciaire», *supra* note 10 à la p. 1341.

[25] J. Darbelnet, «Niveaux et réalisations du discours juridique» dans J.-C. Gémar, dir., *Langage du droit et traduction : Essais de jurilinguistique*, Montréal, Linguatech/ Conseil de la langue française, 1982, 51.

[31] G. Cornu, «Les définitions dans la loi» **dans J.-C. Gémar, dir., *supra* note 25**, 15 à la p. 21.

Règles Pour la doctrine, il est toujours possible d'utiliser le nom de l'auteur, sans qu'il soit nécessaire d'employer l'expression «ci-après».

Si on veut faire référence à plusieurs ouvrages d'un même auteur, il faut recourir à une forme abrégée du titre dans les références ultérieures. Dans ce cas, il importe d'indiquer quelle est cette forme abrégée à la fin de la première référence avec l'expression «ci-après». Le titre abrégé suivra la forme typographique du titre complet : en italiques pour un livre, et en caractères romains entre guillemets pour un article.

Si on a fait référence à un essai qui fait partie d'un ouvrage collectif, il suffit, dans le cas de références à d'au-

tres essais dans le même ouvrage, de renvoyer à la référence complète en mentionnant le nom du directeur.

Documents gouvernementaux

Exemple 25 Canada, *Rapport de la Commission royale d'enquête sur le bilinguisme et le biculturalisme*, livres 1, 2, Ottawa, Imprimeur de la Reine, 8 octobre 1967, 23 mai (Présidents : A. Laurendeau et A.D. Dunton) **[ci-après Commission Laurendeau-Dunton]** ou **[ci-après *Commission royale*]**.

Règle On peut reprendre soit le nom du président de la commission, soit une forme abrégée du titre.

Royaume-Uni

Exemple 45 *Woolmington* c. *D.P.P.*, [1935] A.C. 462 (H.L.) **[ci-après *Woolmington*]**.

Règle Les règles énoncées ci-dessus pour les sources canadiennes s'appliquent également aux sources du Royaume-Uni.

France

Exemples *Loi nº 78-23 du 10 janvier 1978 sur la protection et l'information des consommateurs de produits et de services*, J.O., 11 janvier 1978, 301, D.1978.Lég.86 **[ci-après *Loi du 10 janvier 1978*]**.
Décret nº 84-854 du 21 septembre 1984, J.O., 23 septembre 1984, 2977, D.1984.Lég.538 **[ci-après *Décret du 21 septembre 1984*]**.
Cass. Ch. réun., 13 février 1930, *Jeand'heur*, S.1930.I.121 (note Esmein), D.P.1930.I.57 (note Ripert) **[ci-après *Jeand'heur*]**.

Règles Pour la législation française, la forme abrégée est constituée du nom de la législation («Loi», «Arrêté», «Ordonnance», «Décret») et de la date à laquelle elle fut adoptée.
Si, dans un même article, on fait référence à deux législations adoptées le même jour, on ajoute, dans les références ultérieures, le numéro de la législation ou une version abrégée du titre.

Dans le cas de la jurisprudence, le plus simple est d'utiliser le nom d'une des parties. Autrement, il suffit de mentionner le nom du tribunal et la date, auquel cas l'indication «ci-après» n'est pas nécessaire.

Pour des renseignements sur les encyclopédies françaises, se reporter au chapitre 6.

États-Unis

Exemples [12] 42 U.S.C. 1983 (1988).
[13] 42 U.S.C. 1985(3) (1988).
[15] *Griggs* c. *Duke Power Company*, 401 U.S. 424 (1971) **[ci-après *Griggs*]**.

Règle Les règles sont les mêmes que pour les sources canadiennes. Toutefois, pour la législation codifiée, il est souvent plus simple de donner la référence complète à chaque fois.

Documentation internationale

Exemples *Accord entre le gouvernement du Canada et le gouvernement de la République de Pologne sur l'encouragement et la protection réciproque des investissements*, 6 avril 1990, R.T. Can. 1990 n° 43 **[ci-après *Accord sur la protection des investissements*]**.
Doc. off. AG NU, 36ᵉ sess., 78ᵉ séance plén., Doc. NU A/36/PV.78 (1981) **[ci-après Doc. NU A/36/PV.78]**.

Règles Pour les traités, employer une forme abrégée du titre. Pour les autres documents, utiliser soit un titre abrégé, soit le numéro.

Notes contenant des références ultérieures

Exemple [10] *Sansregret, supra* note 3 à la p. 502.
Règles Il n'est pas nécessaire d'inclure une note infra-paginale chaque fois qu'une source est mentionnée. La note ne devient nécessaire que lorsqu'on cite ou fait allusion à une section particulière, la référence précise étant donc obligatoire. Pour la législation, les références précises (article, alinéa, etc.) peuvent être mentionnées dans le

texte, la note étant donc superflue.

Lorsqu'il faut recourir à une note infra-paginale pour une référence ultérieure, elle peut contenir jusqu'à quatre éléments :

1. L'identification de la source;
2. Le renvoi (*supra*, *ibid.*, etc.);
3. Le numéro de la note à laquelle on renvoie;
4. La référence précise.

Mettre une virgule après l'identification de la source.

Selon les règles énoncées ci-dessous, les quatre éléments ne sont pas tous nécessaires dans certains cas.

Supra (Latin – ci-dessus)

Exemples

[1] *Reference re Education Act of Ontario and Minority Language Education Rights* (1984), 47 O.R. (2e) 1, 10 D.L.R. (4e) 491 (Ont. C.A.) [ci-après *Renvoi de l'Ontario* avec renvois aux O.R.].

[32] *Renvoi de l'Ontario*, **supra** note 1 à la p. 13.

[37] Voir aussi **supra** note 28 et texte correspondant.

Règles

Si la source est clairement identifiée dans le texte, il n'est pas nécessaire de l'identifier dans la note.

«*Supra* note n^o» dirige le lecteur à la note qui contient la première référence à la source en question. **«Supra» doit toujours renvoyer à la référence complète.**

La mention «*supra* note n^o et texte correspondant» renvoie d'abord à la note en question, puis au texte que cette note accompagne.

Ibid. (Latin «ibidem» – ici même)

Exemples

[12] Voir *Commission des Écoles Fransaskoises Inc.* c. *Saskatchewan*, [1988] 3 W.W.R. 354, 48 D.L.R. (4e) 315, 64 Sask. R. 123 (Sask. Q.B.) [ci-après *Écoles Fransaskoises* avec renvois aux W.W.R.].

[13] **Ibid.** à la p. 358. Voir aussi *R.* c. *Big M Drug Mart*, [1985] 1 R.C.S. 295 à la p. 326, 18 D.L.R. (4e) 321 [ci-après *Big M* avec renvois aux R.C.S.].

[14] *Big M*, **ibid.** à la p. 330.

[15] **Ibid.**

[16] **Ibid.** à la p. 331.

[41] Comparer *R. c. Oakes*, [1986] 1 R.C.S. 103, 26 D.L.R. (4e) 200 [ci-après *Oakes* avec renvois aux R.C.S.]. Dans la même décision il fut question du test relatif à l'article premier de la *Charte* (**ibid.** aux pp. 135-142).

Règles

«*Ibid.*» renvoie à la note précédente; il n'est donc jamais suivi du numéro de celle-ci.

L'identification de la source n'est nécessaire que si plusieurs sources sont mentionnées dans la note précédente.

On peut recourir à «*ibid.*» soit dans la note suivant la référence complète, soit dans la note suivant une note qui renvoie à la référence complète au moyen de «*supra*», soit dans la note suivant un autre «*ibid.*»

Lorsque «*ibid.*» est employé sans référence précise, il est entendu que la référence précise contenue dans la note précédente continue de s'appliquer.

«*Ibid.*» est également employé lorsqu'on mentionne la même source plus d'une fois dans la même note.

Infra (Latin – ci-dessous)

Exemples

[10] Pour d'autres exemples de restrictions sur la publicité, voir **infra** note 53.

[53] En 1988, le gouvernement fédéral a interdit la publicité sur le tabac avec la *Loi réglementant les produits du tabac*, L.C. 1988, c. 20.

Règles

En général la référence complète se trouve dans la note qui accompagne la première mention de la source. Il est donc rare que l'auteur doive renvoyer le lecteur à une note ultérieure. Il arrive cependant que cela se fasse, par exemple s'il y a des remarques pertinentes dans cette note. La référence dans un tel cas s'effectue au moyen de «*infra* note no», ou bien à une note ultérieure et au texte qui l'accompagne au moyen de «*infra* note no et texte correspondant».

Ci-dessus, ci-dessous

Exemples

[23] Voir la partie II, **ci-dessus**, pour une analyse de cette question.

[43] Aux pp. 405-410, **ci-dessous**, le lecteur trouvera les statistiques pertinentes.

xxxii RÉFÉRENCES ET NOTES INFRA-PAGINALES

[51] Au sujet de la conclusion de la cour dans l'arrêt *Bernard*, voir le texte correspondant à la note 72.

Règles   Les mots français «ci-dessus» et «ci-dessous» renvoient non pas aux notes infra-paginales, mais au *texte*. Si le texte n'est pas divisé en paragraphes ou sections numérotés, et que la pagination finale n'est pas claire au moment de la rédaction, l'auteur peut guider le lecteur au moyen des notes infra-paginales : «voir le texte correspondant à la note n°».

LES RÉFÉRENCES AUX SOURCES ÉCRITES DANS UNE LANGUE AUTRE QUE LE FRANÇAIS

Lorsqu'il faut mentionner une source écrite dans une langue autre que le français, il faut tenir compte de certains principes :

Premièrement, quelle que soit la langue de la source, il faut toujours suivre les règles énoncées dans la partie française du *Manuel*. Si, par exemple, on a à citer un livre anglais dans un article écrit en français, il ne faut pas consulter la partie anglaise du *Manuel*; les règles qui se trouvent dans la partie anglaise ne s'appliquent que lorsqu'on écrit en anglais.

Deuxièmement, il importe de savoir ce qui peut être traduit et ce qui doit rester dans la langue originale. À ce sujet, il faut s'attarder brièvement sur chacune des principales catégories de sources.

En matière de législation, il faut souligner d'abord qu'au Canada les lois des juridictions suivantes sont adoptées en français : Canada, Québec, Nouveau-Brunswick, Ontario, Manitoba, les Territoires du Nord-Ouest et le Territoire du Yukon; cependant, il se peut que, dans certains cas, les lois antérieures à une certaine date n'existent qu'en version anglaise. D'autres provinces adoptent de temps à autre des lois en français.

Pour toute loi adoptée en français, on tâchera d'en donner le titre en français dans la référence et de toujours citer la version française, à moins qu'il ne s'agisse de comparer les versions française et anglaise. Pour les lois adoptées en anglais seulement, il faudra bien sûr donner le titre anglais dans la référence.

Exemple   **Livestock Brand Act**, R.S.N.S. 1989, c. 261, art. 3.

Pour ce qui est de la jurisprudence, il faut tenir compte des principes suivants. Dans l'intitulé, on utilise toujours le «c.» (jamais «v.») pour séparer les noms des parties. Le titre du recueil et le nom du tribunal doivent rester dans la langue originale, à moins qu'il n'en existe une version officielle française.

Exemple   **Lightburn c. *Belmont Sales Ltd.* (1969), 6 D.L.R. (3e) 692 (B.C.S.C.)**

En matière de doctrine, le titre de l'ouvrage ne peut évidemment être traduit. Les autres éléments de la référence qui n'ont pas le caractère d'un titre ou d'un nom propre apparaissent en français.

Exemple   **J.G. Fleming, *The Law of Torts*, 7e éd., Sydney, Law Book, 1987 à la p. 17.**

CITATIONS

Les règles suivantes s'appliquent à toutes les citations, que ce soit dans le texte ou dans une note infra-paginale :

Les citations brèves (c'est-à-dire de quatre lignes ou moins) s'insèrent dans le texte, placées entre guillemets. Le numéro qui renvoie à la note infra-paginale se place à l'extérieur des guillemets. Les citations plus longues (de plus de quatre lignes) sont mises en retrait des deux marges, à simple interligne et sans guillemets. Les citations de dispositions législatives, bien que de moins de quatre lignes, peuvent aussi être mises en relief de cette façon.

Une citation doit respecter intégralement l'original, y compris pour ce qui est de l'orthographe, l'emploi de majuscules et la ponctuation interne. Tout changement doit être signalé. Les points de suspension entre crochets («[...]») indiquent qu'une partie du passage a été supprimée. On se sert de crochets lorsqu'il s'agit d'indiquer un changement quelconque : orthographe, ponctuation, emploi de majuscules, ou la correction d'une faute. Dans le cas d'une faute, on met soit la correction, soit «*sic*» entre crochets. Les expressions telles que «c'est nous qui soulignons», «italiques de l'original», «notes omises», etc. se mettent entre crochets après la citation.

Lorsque la citation est insérée dans une phrase, la première lettre, si elle était une majuscule, devient une minuscule, le changement se mettant entre crochets. Lorsqu'une phrase débute par une citation qui, elle, ne commence pas par une majuscule dans l'original, il faut y mettre une majuscule. Cette modification se met entre crochets.

Exemples   Le juge a déclaré qu'«[i]l s'agit d'une obligation de résultat»[7].

«[F]aute lourde»[13] était l'expression qu'employait la doctrine.

1

LÉGISLATION

A. LOIS

Modèle de base

Loi sur les juges,	L. R.	C.	1985,	c. J-1,	art. 4.
titre	recueil	législature	année	chapitre	référence précise

Éléments

1. Titre
2. Recueil
3. Législature
4. Année
5. Chapitre
6. Référence précise (article, alinéa, etc.)
7. Modifications et abrogations
8. Appendice
9. Loi contenue dans une autre loi

1. TITRE

Exemples   *Loi sur les Indiens*, L.R.C. 1985, c. I-5, art. 19(a).
Loi de 1990 sur le régime de retraite de la cité de Moncton, L.N.-B. 1990, c. 69.
The Emergency Planning Act, S.S. 1989-90, c. E-8.1.
Archives Act, L.T.N.-O. 1981 (3e sess.), c. 2.

Règles   Le titre de la loi se met en italique et est suivi d'une virgule.

Employer le titre abrégé lorsque le texte de loi en fait mention. S'il n'y a pas de titre abrégé, utiliser le titre qui se trouve au début de la loi.

Si l'année fait partie du titre, il faut l'inclure.

On ne met l'article défini que s'il fait partie intégrante du titre.

Pour les lois dont le titre est en français, mettre en majuscules la première lettre du premier mot du titre, ainsi que la première lettre de chaque nom propre; si le titre de la loi contient un autre titre, le premier mot de ce titre porte une majuscule. Si la loi n'existe qu'en langue anglaise, on met en majuscules la première lettre du premier mot du titre, ainsi que la première lettre de tous les mots sauf les articles («the», «a», «an»), les conjonctions («and») et les prépositions.

Si le titre de la loi apparaît dans le texte, on l'omet dans la note infra-paginale.

Note   Pour la législation des Territoires du Nord-Ouest et du Yukon, remplacer le mot «Ordinance» par le mot «Act» dans le titre de la loi.

2. RECUEIL

(a) Lois révisées et refondues

Exemples   *Loi sur les tribunaux judiciaires*, **L.R.O.** 1990, c. C.43.
Loi d'interprétation, **L.R.C.** 1985, c. I-21.
Loi sur la preuve au Manitoba, **L.R.M.** 1987, c. E150.

Règle   Lorsque les lois ont été révisées, refondues ou réadoptées, on fait référence à ces recueils de préférence aux recueils sessionnels ou annuels.

Note   Au Québec, la référence habituelle est à l'édition sur feuilles mobiles (voir la règle 2(c) (viii) (ci-dessous). Employer les abréviations suivantes : «L.R.» pour «Lois révisées» (Canada, Nouveau-Brunswick, Territoires du Nord-Ouest), «Lois refondues» (Québec, Ontario) et «Lois réadoptées» (Manitoba); «R.S.» pour «Revised Statutes» (Terre-Neuve, Nouvelle-Écosse, Île-du-Prince-Édouard, Saskatchewan, Alberta, Colombie-Britannique, Yukon).

(b) Recueils sessionnels ou annuels

Exemples   *Police Act,* **S.B.C.** 1988, c. 53.
The Public Utilities Act, **S.N.** 1989, c. 37, art. 4.
Transportation of Dangerous Goods Act, 1990, **L.T.N.-O.** 1990, c. 36.

Règles   Les lois qui n'ont pas fait l'objet d'une révision ou d'une refonte se trouvent dans les recueils sessionels ou annuels.

Employer les abréviations suivantes : «L.» pour «Lois» (Canada, Québec, Nouveau-Brunswick, Manitoba, Ontario, Territoires du Nord-Ouest, Territoire du Yukon); «S.» pour «Statutes» (Alberta, Colombie-Britannique, Saskatchewan, Nouvelle-Écosse, Île-du-Prince-Édouard, Terre-Neuve). L'abréviation «S.» s'emploie aussi pour les recueils intitulés «Statuts», anglicisme critiqué et rejeté de nos jours.

Note   On n'utilise plus la désignation «O.» («Ordinance») pour les recueils des Territoires du Nord-Ouest et du Yukon. Toujours utiliser «L.», quelle que soit la date du recueil.

(c) Lois sur feuilles mobiles

(*i*) Canada

Règle   Ne pas renvoyer à l'édition sur feuilles mobiles.

(*ii*) Alberta

Règle   Ne pas renvoyer à l'édition sur feuilles mobiles.

(iii) Colombie-Britannique

Règle   On fait référence aux recueils à feuilles mobiles de la même façon qu'aux recueils reliés.

(iv) Île-du-Prince-Édouard

Exemples   *Emergency Measures Act*, S.P.E.I. 1990, c. 60, **R.S.P.E.I. 1988, c. E-6.1.**
Agricultural Development Corporation Act, S.P.E.I. 1990, c. 11, **R.S.P.E.I. 1988, c. A-8.1.**
Règles   La référence à l'édition sur feuilles mobiles est facultative et doit toujours être précédée de la référence au recueil relié.
La mention «R.S.P.E.I. 1988» suivie du chapitre renvoie à l'édition sur feuilles mobiles.

(v) Manitoba

Exemples   *Code de la route*, L.M. 1985-86, c. 3, **C.P.L.M. c. H60.**
Loi sur l'évaluation municipale, S.M. 1989-90, c. 24, **C.P.L.M. c. M226.**
Règles   La référence à l'édition à feuilles mobiles (la Codification permanente des lois du Manitoba) est facultative. L'abréviation «C.P.L.M.» est suivie du numéro de chapitre, sans mention de l'année.
Note   Les lois incluses dans les Lois réadoptées du Manitoba portent le même numéro de chapitre dans l'édition à feuilles mobiles.

(vi) Nouveau-Brunswick

Règle   On fait référence aux recueils à feuilles mobiles de la même façon qu'aux recueils reliés.

(vii) Nouvelle-Écosse

Règle   On fait référence aux recueils à feuilles mobiles de la même façon qu'aux recueils reliés.

(*viii*) Québec

Exemples	*Loi sur les actions pénales,* **L.R.Q. c. A-5.**
	Loi sur les biens culturels, **L.R.Q. c. B-4, art. 26.**
Règles	Pour les lois québécoises actuellement en vigueur, on utilise toujours la référence à l'édition sur feuilles mobiles.
	La référence «L.R.Q.» suivie du chapitre – sans indication de l'année – renvoie à l'édition sur feuilles mobiles. Par contre, la référence «L.R.Q. 1977» renvoie à l'édition reliée de 1977 et ne tient donc pas compte des modifications subséquentes.

(*ix*) Saskatchewan

Règle	Ne pas renvoyer à l'édition sur feuilles mobiles.

(*x*)   Autres provinces et territoires

À l'heure actuelle, Terre-Neuve, l'Ontario, les Territoires du Nord-Ouest et le Territoire du Yukon ne publient pas d'édition sur feuilles mobiles de leurs lois.

3.   LÉGISLATURE

Exemples	*Code canadien du travail,* **L.R.C.** 1985, c. L-2, art. 14.
	The Co-operatives Act, 1989, **S.S.** 1989-90, c. C-37.2, art. 3.
	Livestock Brands Act, **R.S.N.S.** 1989, c. 261.
Règles	L'indication de la législature se place immédiatement après celle du recueil.
	Il n'y a pas de virgule après l'indication de la législature.
	Employer les abréviations suivantes :

Canada . . . . **C.**
Province du Canada . . . . **Prov. C.**
Bas-Canada . . . . **B.-C.**
Haut-Canada (Upper Canada) . . . . **U.C.**
Alberta . . . . **A.**
Colombie-Britannique . . . . **B.C.**
Île-du-Prince-Édouard . . . . **P.E.I.**
Manitoba . . . . **M.**
Nouveau-Brunswick . . . . **N.-B.**
Nouvelle-Écosse . . . . **N.S.**

Ontario . . . . O.
Québec . . . . Q.
Saskatchewan . . . . S.
Terre-Neuve . . . . N.
Territoires du Nord-Ouest . . . . T.N.-O.
Territoire du Yukon . . . . Y.

4.   ANNÉE

Exemples   *Loi sur le privilège dans l'industrie de la construction*, L.R.O.
1990, c. C.30.
Motor Transport Act, S.Y. **1988**, c. 18.
MAIS
Loi sur les bureaux d'enregistrement, L.R.Q. c. B-9, art. 19.
Loi sur la vente internationale de marchandises, S.M. 1989-90, c.
18, C.P.L.M. c. S11.

Règles   On met l'année après la mention de la législature.
L'année n'est pas mentionnée dans le cas des éditions
sur feuilles mobiles du Québec («L.R.Q.») ou du Manitoba («C.P.L.M.») (voir la règle 2(c) ci-dessus).
Une virgule suit l'année, ou, le cas échéant, l'indication
de la session ou du supplément (voir les règles 4(c) et (d)
ci-dessous).

(a)   **Année civile**

Exemple   *Freedom of Information Act*, S.N.S. **1990**, c. 11.
ET NON
Freedom of Information Act, S.N.S. **39 Eliz. II**, c. 11.

Règle   Toujours mettre l'année civile et non l'année du règne.

(b)   **Lorsque la session parlementaire s'étend sur plus d'une année**

Exemples   *Loi sur les textes réglementaires*, S.C. **1970-71-72**, c. 38.
The Agrologists Act, S.S. **1984-85-86**, c. 57, art. 7.

Règle   Indiquer l'étendue complète de la session.

(c)   **Lorsqu'il y a plus d'une session dans une même année**

Exemple   *An Act to amend the Business Licence Act*, L.T.N.-O. 1985 (**3e
sess.**), c. 1.

Règles   Si le recueil se divise en plusieurs sessions pour une même année, il faut indiquer la session si la numérotation des chapitres recommence lors de chaque session. Le numéro de la session et l'abréviation «sess.» se placent entre parenthèses après l'année. Cette indication est suivie d'une virgule.

1

(d)   Supplément

Exemples   *Loi sur les douanes*, L.R.C. 1985 **(2ᵉ supp.)**, c. 1.
Gas Burning Devices Act, R.S.Y. 1986 **(supp.)**, c. 9.

Règles   Il faut renvoyer au supplément dans les références aux lois adoptées pendant l'année d'une révision ou d'une refonte, mais qui ne furent pas incluses dans celle-ci. Le numéro du supplément et l'abréviation «supp.» se placent entre parenthèses après l'année. Cette indication est suivie d'une virgule.

5.   CHAPITRE

Exemples   *Loan Companies Act*, R.S.N.S. 1989, **c. 264**.
Loi sur le comté d'Oxford, L.R.O. 1990, **c. C.42**.
Loi sur les eaux souterraines et les puits, L.R.M. 1987, **c. G110**, art. 11.
Loi sur l'administration financière, L.R.Q. **c. A-6**, art. 12.

Règle   Le chapitre, dont l'abréviation est «c.», est indiqué selon la désignation numérique ou alphanumérique qui se trouve dans le recueil.

Exception   Les lois de Terre-Neuve qui se trouvent dans les recueils sessionnels de 1934 à 1975-76 ne sont pas identifiées par chapitre, mais par numéro (abrégé «nᵒ»).

Exemple   *The Development Areas (Lands) (Amendment) Act, 1976*, S.N. 1975-76, **nᵒ 18**.

6.   RÉFÉRENCE PRÉCISE (ARTICLE, ALINÉA, ETC.)

Exemples   *Election Act*, R.S.P.E.I. 1988, c. E-1, **art. 3(2)(h)**.
Loi modifiant la Loi sur les langues officielles, L.T.N.-O. 1990, c. 7, **art. 2-3, 8, 10-14**.
Loi sur le droit d'auteur, L.R.C. 1985, c. C-42, **art. 2, al. 4**.

Loi sur les compagnies d'assurance canadiennes et britanniques, L.R.C. 1985, c. I-12, **préambule**.

Appropriation (Interim Supply) Act, 1988, S.A. 1988, c. 13, **ann. A**.

Règles   La référence précise se place après le numéro du chapitre, précédée d'une virgule.

«Article» s'abrège «art.» au singulier comme au pluriel. Si on veut mentionner plusieurs articles consécutifs, il suffit d'en indiquer le premier et le dernier joints par un trait d'union. S'il s'agit de plusieurs articles non consécutifs, ils sont séparés par des virgules.

Pour les paragraphes désignés par un chiffre ou une lettre, il suffit d'inscrire le chiffre ou la lettre entre parenthèses après le numéro de l'article. Pour les alinéas qui ne sont pas désignés par un chiffre ou une lettre, on se sert de l'abréviation «al.» suivie du numéro de l'alinéa.

Le mot «préambule» s'écrit au long.

«Annexe» s'abrège «ann.»

7. MODIFICATIONS ET ABROGATIONS

(a) Lois modifiées

(i) Modifications sous-entendues

Exemple   **Loi sur les chemins de fer, L.R.C. 1985, c. R-3.**
ET NON
Loi sur les chemins de fer, L.R.C. 1985, c. R-3, telle que modifiée.

Règle   En général, il est sous-entendu qu'on fait référence à la loi telle que modifiée.

Note   Dans le cas des lois québécoises, la référence «L.R.Q. 1977» renvoie aux recueils reliés et ne tient donc pas compte des modifications survenues après 1977. Pour citer une loi dans sa forme actuelle, la référence «L.R.Q.» (sans mention de l'année de la refonte) s'impose; elle renvoie le lecteur à l'édition sur feuilles mobiles (voir la règle 2(c) ci-dessus).

(ii)   Modifications mentionnées

Exemples   *Social Services Tax Act*, R.S.B.C. 1979, c. 388, **mod. par S.B.C. 1988, c. 25.**
Municipal Taxation Act, R.S.A. 1980, c. M-31, art. 24, **mod. par *School Act*, S.A. 1988, c. S-3.1, art. 249(a).**

Règles   Si l'indication de la modification s'avère pertinente, on peut la mentionner.
On donne d'abord la référence à la loi originale, suivie de «mod. par» et la référence à la nouvelle loi.
N'inclure le titre de la loi modificatrice que si elle porte un titre autre que «Loi modifiant ...»

(b)   Loi modifiant une loi antérieure

Exemple   *Loi modifiant la Loi sur l'assurance automobile et d'autres dispositions législatives*, L.Q. 1989, c. 15, **modifiant R.S.Q. 1977, c. A-25.**

Règles   Lorsqu'il s'agit d'une loi qui modifie une loi antérieure, on ajoute le mot «modifiant» suivi de la référence à la loi modifiée.
Le titre de la loi modifiée peut être omis s'il est inclus dans le titre de la loi modificatrice.

(c)   Lois abrogées

Exemple   *Loi sur les mesures de guerre*, L.R.C. 1985, c. W-2, **abr. par la *Loi sur les mesures d'urgence*, L.C. 1988, c. 29, art. 80.**

Règles   Dans le cas d'une loi abrogée, il importe d'inclure la référence à la loi abrogative, introduite par la mention «abr. par».
Le titre de la loi abrogative peut être omis s'il contient le titre de la loi abrogée ou est semblable à celui-ci.

(d)   Loi abrogeant une loi antérieure

Exemple   *Loi scolaire*, L.N.-B. 1990, c. S-5.1, art. 83, **abrogeant L.R.N.-B. 1973, c. S-5.**

Règles Si on mentionne une loi qui abroge une loi antérieure, on ajoute le mot «abrogeant» suivi de la référence à la loi abrogée.

Le titre de la loi abrogée peut être omis s'il est inclus dans le titre de la loi abrogative ou est semblable à celui-ci.

8. APPENDICE

Exemple *Déclaration canadienne des droits*, L.C. 1960, c. 44, **reproduite dans L.R.C. 1985, app. III.**

Règles La référence à l'appendice n'est pas suffisante à elle seule; elle doit toujours être précédée de la référence officielle.

La référence à l'appendice est introduite par l'expression «reproduit(e) dans».

Indiquer la refonte ou le recueil dont l'appendice en question fait partie, suivi d'une virgule.

«Appendice» s'abrège «app.»

9. LOI CONTENUE DANS UNE AUTRE LOI

Exemple **Loi sur la Société d'expansion du Cap-Breton (étant la partie II de la *Loi organique de 1987 sur le Canada atlantique*, L.C. 1988, c. 50), art. 27.**

Règles Donner le titre de la loi contenue dans l'autre loi.

Entre parenthèses, il faut indiquer la partie pertinente de la loi principale et la référence complète de celle-ci. Toute référence précise (article, alinéa, etc.) se met après les parenthèses, et est précédée d'une virgule.

B. LOIS CONSTITUTIONNELLES

1. LOI DE 1982 SUR LE CANADA

Exemple **Loi de 1982 sur le Canada (R.-U.), 1982, c. 11.**

Règle Cette référence suit les règles pour les lois du Royaume-Uni (voir le chapitre 5).

2. *LOI CONSTITUTIONNELLE DE 1982*

Exemple   **Loi constitutionnelle de 1982, constituant l'annexe B de la Loi de 1982 sur le Canada (R.-U.), 1982, c. 11.**

Règle   Suivre l'exemple.

3. *CHARTE CANADIENNE DES DROITS ET LIBERTÉS*

Exemple   **Charte canadienne des droits et libertés, Partie I de la Loi constitutionnelle de 1982, constituant l'annexe B de la Loi de 1982 sur le Canada (R.-U.), 1982, c. 11.**

Règle   La *Charte* n'ayant pas été promulguée indépendamment, on renvoie à la Partie I de la *Loi constitutionnelle de 1982*.

4. AUTRES LOIS CONSTITUTIONNELLES

Exemples   **Loi constitutionnelle de 1867 (R.-U.), 30 & 31 Vict., c. 3.**

Loi constitutionnelle nº 2 de 1975, S.C. 1974-75-76, c. 53.

Loi sur Terre-Neuve (R.-U.), 12 & 13 Geo. 6, c. 22 (antérieurement appelée British North America Act, 1949).

Statute of Westminster, 1931 (R.-U.), 22 & 23 Geo. 5, c. 4, reproduit dans L.R.C. 1985, app. II, nº 27.

Règles   On suit les règles de base pour les lois canadiennes et du Royaume-Uni (les règles relatives au Royaume-Uni se trouvent au chapitre 5).

Utiliser le nouveau titre qui se trouve à l'annexe de la *Loi constitutionnelle de 1982* tout en conservant le reste de la référence. On peut ajouter l'ancien titre entre parenthèses («antérieurement appelée ...»).

L'auteur peut également fournir la référence à l'appendice II des L.R.C. 1985 après la référence officielle.

5. RÉFÉRENCE PRÉCISE

Exemples   *Charte canadienne des droits et libertés*, **art. 33**, Partie I de la *Loi constitutionnelle de 1982*, constituant l'annexe B de la *Loi de 1982 sur le Canada* (R.-U.), 1982, c. 11.

Loi constitutionnelle de 1982, **art. 52**, constituant l'annexe B de la *Loi de 1982 sur le Canada* (R.-U.), 1982, c. 11.

Loi de 1982 sur le Canada (R.-U.), 1982, c. 11, **art. 4.**

Règles   Dans le cas de la *Charte* et de la *Loi constitutionelle de 1982*, la référence précise vient immédiatement après le titre. Pour la *Loi de 1982 sur le Canada* et les autres lois constitutionnelles, la référence précise se place après le numéro du chapitre.

C.   CODES DU QUÉBEC

1.   CODE CIVIL DU BAS-CANADA (1866)

Exemples   **Art. 1024 C.c.B.-C.**
Art. 1053-1057 C.c.B.-C.

Règles   L'indication de l'article précède le titre du code.
«Article» s'abrège «art.» au singulier comme au pluriel.
«*Code civil du Bas-Canada*» s'abrège C.c.B.-C.

2.   CODE CIVIL DU QUÉBEC

Exemple   **Art. 435 C.c.Q.**

Règle   L'expression *Code civil du Québec*, abrégée C.c.Q., renvoie à la *Loi instituant un nouveau Code civil et portant réforme du droit de la famille*, L.Q. 1980, c. 39.

3.   CODE DE PROCÉDURE CIVILE

Exemple   **Art. 710 C.p.c.**

Règle   Le *Code de procédure civile du Québec*, L.R.Q. c. C-25, s'abrège C.p.c.

4.   CODE DE PROCÉDURE PÉNALE

Exemple   **Art. 210 C.p.p.**

Règle   Employer l'abréviation C.p.p. pour le *Code de procédure pénale*.

D.   PROJETS DE LOI

(a)   Modèle de base

P.L. 125,	*Code civil du Québec,*	1re sess.,	34e lég.,	Québec,	1990.
numéro	titre	session	législature	province	année

Exemples   P.L. 49, *Loi concernant la réglementation de la profession de dentiste*, 1re sess., 35e lég., Ontario, 1991, art. 3.

P.L. C-231, *Loi modifiant la Loi sur les allocations familiales*, 3e sess., 34e Parl., 1991.

P.L. S-5, *Loi modifiant certaines lois fédérales pour reconnaître le service en temps de guerre des anciens marins de la marine marchande du Canada*, 3e sess., 34e Parl., 1991.

P.L. 15, *Alberta Foundation for the Arts Act*, 3e sess., 22e lég., Alberta, 1991.

Règles   Des virgules séparent les éléments de la référence.

Au niveau fédéral, le numéro des projets de loi émanant de la Chambre des communes est précédé d'un «C» et ceux qui émanent du Sénat d'un «S».

Le titre se met en italique.

On met toujours le titre complet d'un projet de loi.

Indiquer la province pour les projets de loi provinciaux; point n'est besoin d'indiquer «Canada» pour les projets de loi fédéraux.

Ne pas inclure l'année du règne.

(b)   Renseignements supplémentaires

Exemples   P.L. C-208, *Loi modifiant la Loi sur le ministère de l'Agriculture*, 3e sess., 34e Parl., 1991 **(1re lecture 27 mai 1991)**.

P.L. 81, *Loi autorisant des emprunts garantis par le Trésor*, 1re sess., 35e lég., Ontario, 1991 **(sanction royale le 19 juin 1991, L.O. 1991, c. 8)**.

Règles   Les renseignements supplémentaires se placent entre parenthèses à la fin de la référence. On peut y mentionner, par exemple, l'étape franchie dans l'adoption du projet de loi, le fait qu'une fois sanctionnée, la loi n'entrera en vigueur qu'à une date fixée par proclamation, etc.

Dans le cas d'une loi dûment adoptée, mais qui n'a pas encore été publiée dans un recueil, il faut faire référence au projet de loi, en ajoutant entre parenthèses la date où la loi a été sanctionnée. Si possible, on ajoute aussi entre parenthèses, après la date de la sanction, le numéro de chapitre que portera la loi dans le futur recueil.

E. RÈGLEMENTS

1. RÈGLEMENTS FÉDÉRAUX

(a) Non refondus

Exemples   DORS/90-822.
Règlement sur l'écluse St. Andrew's, DORS/91-144, art. 6.
Règlement sur les frais, droits et taxes (TPS), DORS/91-34.

Règles   [*Titre* facultatif], DORS/deux derniers chiffres de l'année-numéro.

L'abréviation de «Décrets, ordonnances et règlements» est «DORS».

Les règlements fédéraux adoptés après la refonte se trouvent dans la partie II de la Gazette du Canada.

Il n'est pas nécessaire d'inclure la référence à la Gazette.

(b) Refondus

Exemples   *Règlement sur les corporations canadiennes*, C.R.C., c. 424, art. 23.
Règlement sur la voie maritime, C.R.C., c. 1379.

Règles   *Titre*, C.R.C., chapitre.

«Codification des règlements du Canada» s'abrège «C.R.C.».

La mention de l'année est facultative. À moins d'indication contraire, on présume que les références renvoient à la dernière refonte.

2. RÈGLEMENTS DES PROVINCES ET DES TERRITOIRES

(a) Alberta

(i) Non refondus

Exemples   Alta. Reg. 312/90.
Alta. Reg. 207/91.

Règle   Alta. Reg. numéro/deux derniers chiffres de l'année.

(ii) **Refondus**

> *Exemples* **Alta. Reg. 77/91.**
> **Alta. Reg. 254/90.**
> *Règle* Les règlements refondus suivent le même modèle que les règlements non refondus.

(b) **Colombie-Britannique**

(i) **Non refondus**

> *Exemples* **B.C. Reg. 154/91.**
> **B.C. Reg. 210/88.**
> *Règle* B.C. Reg. numéro/deux derniers chiffres de l'année.

(ii) **Refondus**

> *Règle* À l'heure actuelle, il n'y a pas d'édition refondue. On fait référence à l'édition sur feuilles mobiles de la même manière qu'aux règlements non refondus.

(c) **Île-du-Prince-Édouard**

(i) **Non refondus**

> *Exemples* **EC346/89.**
> ***Environmental Protection Act Water Well Regulations* (EC188/90).**
> ***Natural Areas Protection Act Regulations* (EC54/89).**
> *Règles* [*Titre* facultatif mais généralement inclus] (EC numéro/ deux derniers chiffres de l'année).
> Si le titre n'est pas mentionné, on omet les parenthèses.

(ii) **Refondus**

> *Règle* L'édition sur feuilles mobiles n'est pas une refonte officielle. On en donne la référence de la même façon que pour les règlements non refondus.

(d) Manitoba

(i) **Non réadoptés**

Exemples **Règl. du Man. 84/90.**
Règl. du Man. 285/89.
Règle Règl. du Man. numéro/deux derniers chiffres de l'année.

(ii) **Réadoptés**

Exemples **Règl. du Man. 203/87 R.**
Règl. du Man. 75/88 R.
Règle Règl. du Man. numéro/deux derniers chiffres de l'année R.
Note La plupart des règlements du Manitoba furent réadoptés en français et en anglais en 1987 et 1988. Il n'y a pas eu de refonte depuis.

(e) Nouveau-Brunswick

(i) **Non refondus**

Exemples **Règl. du N.-B. 90-119.**
Règl. du N.-B. 89-104, art. 10.
Règle Règl. du N.-B. deux derniers chiffres de l'année-numéro.

(ii) **Refondus**

Règle La dernière refonte des règlements du Nouveau-Brunswick date de 1963. On en donne la référence de la même façon que pour les règlements non refondus.
Note L'édition sur feuilles mobiles n'est pas une refonte officielle.

(f) Nouvelle-Écosse

(i) **Non refondus**

Exemples **N.S. Reg. 211/90.**
N.S. Reg. 131/91, art. 10.

Règle   N.S. Reg. numéro/deux derniers chiffres de l'année.

(g)   Ontario

(*i*)   Non refondus

Exemples   O. Reg. 45/91.
              O. Reg. 10/91.
Règle   O. Reg. numéro/deux derniers chiffres de l'année.

(*ii*)   Refondus

Exemples   R.R.O. 1990, Reg. 71.
              R.R.O. 1990, Reg. 105.
Règle   R.R.O. 1990, Reg. numéro.

(h)   Québec

(*i*)   Non refondus

Exemples   D. 646-91, 8 mai 1991, G.O.Q. 1991.II.1695.
              D. 826-90, 13 juin 1990, G.O.Q. 1990.II.2445.
Règles   D. numéro-deux derniers chiffres de l'année, date au
              complet, référence à la Gazette.
              «Décret» s'abrège «D.».
              La référence à la Gazette officielle du Québec se fait se-
              lon le modèle de base pour les gazettes (voir la partie F
              ci-dessous).

(*ii*)   Refondus

Exemples   *Règlement sur la qualité de l'atmosphère*, R.R.Q.
              1981, c. Q-2, r. 20.
              Règlement sur l'administration fiscale, R.R.Q. 1981,
              c. M-31, r. 1.
Règles   [*Titre* facultatif mais recommandé], R.R.Q. 1981, c. nu-
              méro, r. numéro.
              «Règlements refondus du Québec» s'abrège «R.R.Q.».

(i)   Saskatchewan

(i)   **Non refondus**

Exemples	**Sask. Reg. 49/91.**
	Sask. Reg. 66/90.
Règle	Sask. Reg. numéro/deux derniers chiffres de l'année.

(ii)   **Refondus**

Exemples	**R.R.S. c. W-13.1, Reg. 49, Sask. Gaz. 1991.II.423.**
	R.R.S. c. E-0.1, Reg. 10, Sask. Gaz. 1990.II.563.
Règles	R.R.S. c. numéro, Reg. numéro, référence à la gazette. Voir la partie F, ci-dessous, pour les règles relatives aux gazettes.
Note	Les modifications aux règlements refondus sont citées comme les règlements non refondus (ci-dessus).

(j)   Terre-Neuve

(i)   **Non refondus**

Exemples	**Nfld. Reg. 112/90.**
	Nfld. Reg. 256/90, art. 5.
Règle	Nfld. Reg. numéro/deux derniers chiffres de l'année.

(k)   Territoires du Nord-Ouest

(i)   **Non refondus**

Exemples	**R.T.N.-O. 063-91.**
	R.T.N.-O. 031-91.
Règle	R.T.N.-O. numéro à trois chiffres – deux derniers chiffres de l'année.

(ii)   **Refondus**

Exemple	**R.R.T.N.-O. 1990, c. A-10.**
Règle	R.R.T.N.-O. 1990, numéro de chapitre.

(l)   Yukon

(i)   Non refondus

Exemples	**Yukon D. 1991/141.**
	Yukon O.I.C. 1984/171.
Règles	Yukon O.I.C. année au complet/numéro.
	Employer les abréviations «O.I.C.» et «D.» pour «Order in Council» et «Décret».

1

F.   INFORMATIONS PUBLIÉES DANS LES GAZETTES (AUTRES QUE RÈGLEMENTS)

1.   MODÈLE DE BASE

Avis	,	Gaz. C.	1991	.	I	.	2337.
Titre		Gazette	année		partie de la Gazette		page

Exemples	**Arrêté ministériel 90-023, G.O.Q. 1990.II.675.**
	Ministerial Order 36/91, A. Gaz. 1991.I.1609.
	Avis, Gaz. N.-B. 1990.I.946.
	Ministerial Order, SI-004-90, Gaz. T.N.-O. 1990.I.77.
Règles	En général, on inclut le titre.
	Inclure avec le titre toute forme de numérotation.
	Si la Gazette en question n'est pas publiée en plusieurs parties, l'indication de la page se met immédiatement après l'année.
	Employer les abréviations suivantes :

Canada : La Gazette du Canada . . . . **Gaz. C.**
Alberta : The Alberta Gazette . . . . **A. Gaz.**
Colombie-Britannique :
    The British Columbia Gazette . . . . . . **B.C. Gaz.**
Île-du-Prince-Édouard :
    Royal Gazette . . . . **P.E.I. Gaz.**
Manitoba : Gazette du Manitoba . . . . **Gaz. M.**
Nouveau-Brunswick : La Gazette
    Royale . . . . **Gaz. N.-B.**
Nouvelle-Écosse : Royal Gazette . . . . **N.S. Gaz.**
Ontario : Gazette de l'Ontario . . . . **Gaz. O.**
Québec : Gazette officiel du Québec . . . . **G.O.Q.**

Saskatchewan : The Saskatchewan
Gazette .... **S. Gaz.**
Terre-Neuve : The Newfoundland
Gazette .... **N. Gaz.**
Territoires du Nord-Ouest : Gazette des
Territoires du Nord-Ouest ...... **Gaz. T.N.-O.**
Territoire du Yukon : Gazette du Yukon ... **Gaz. Y.**

2. PROCLAMATIONS

Exemples *Loi sur L'Agence spatiale canadienne*, L.C. 1990, c. 13, **entrée en vigueur le 14 décembre 1990, TR 91-5, Gaz. C. 1991.I.74.**
Proclamation, 9 août 1969, Gaz. C. 1969.I.1998.
Proclamation, 1er avril 1991, S. Gaz. 1991.I.1174.
Règles Inclure la date et la référence à la Gazette.
Pour les proclamations fédérales depuis 1972, inclure aussi le numéro du texte réglementaire («TR»).
Le mot «Proclamation» peut servir de titre si le contexte l'exige.

3. DÉCRETS

(a) Décrets fédéraux

Exemples **C.P. 1979-1823, Gaz. C. 1979.I.4610.**
***Décret de remise de la taxe des services CFR*, TR/90-104, Gaz. C. 1990.II.3526.**
Règles C.P. année-numéro, référence à la Gazette selon les règles ci-dessus.
Mentionner le titre s'il y en a un.
Si le décret porte un numéro de texte réglementaire («TR»), il faut l'inclure.

(b) Décrets provinciaux

Exemples **D. 31-90, G.O.Q. 1990.II.611.**
***The Municipal Government Act, Annexation of Lands*, O.C. 164/80, A. Gaz. 1980.I.759.**

Règles   Numéro, référence à la Gazette selon les règles ci-dessus.

«Décret» s'abrège «D.» Dans le cas d'une publication unilingue anglaise, utiliser «O.C.» ou bien «O.I.C.», selon l'usage de la Gazette en question, pour «Order in Council».

Donner le numéro tel qu'il apparaît dans la Gazette; ce numéro comprend parfois l'année ou les deux derniers chiffres de l'année.

On peut également inclure des informations supplémentaires, tel le titre de la loi en vertu de laquelle le décret est promulgué.

G.   RÈGLEMENTS MUNICIPAUX

Exemples   **Ville de Sherbrooke, Règlement n° 2900-22, *Modifiant le règlement n° 2900* (2 juin 1986).**

Cité de Québec, Règlement n° 1365, *Concernant la prévention des incendies* (6 février 1964), art. 14.

Règles   Ville, Règlement n°, *titre complet* (date au complet), référence précise.

Si le règlement porte un numéro, il faut en faire mention.

Inclure le titre complet s'il n'y a pas de titre abrégé.

H.   RÈGLES DE PRATIQUE

Modèle de base

Manitoba,	Règles de la Cour du Banc de la Reine,	r. 275(2).
province	titre	règle

Exemples   **Règles de la Cour fédérale, r. 41(1).**
Alberta Rules of Court, r. 154.
Ontario, Règles de procédure civile, r. 70.26(3)(b).

Règles   Indiquer la province ou le territoire en question, sauf si le titre des règles en fait mention. Il n'est pas nécessaire d'indiquer «Canada» lorsqu'il s'agit des règles de pratique de la Cour suprême du Canada ou de la Cour fédérale.

La mention de la province est suivie d'une virgule.

Indiquer le titre officiel des règles (voir ci-dessous), suivi d'une virgule.

«Règle» s'abrège «r.».

Note Pour le *Code de procédure civile du Québec* et le *Code de procédure pénale*, voir la partie C ci-dessus.

Titres des règles

Canada
- Règles de la Cour suprême du Canada
- Règles de la Cour fédérale

Alberta
- Alberta Rules of Court

Colombie-Britannique
- Rules of Court
- Court of Appeal Rules
- Family Relations Act Rules and Regulations
- British Columbia Court of Appeal Criminal Appeal Rules, 1986
- Small Claims Rules

Île-du-Prince-Édouard
- Civil Procedure Rules

Manitoba
- Règles de la Cour d'appel
- Règlement de la Cour provinciale (Division de la famille)
- Règles de la Cour du Banc de la Reine

Nouveau-Brunswick
- Règles de Procédure

Nouvelle-Écosse
- Civil Procedure Rules

Ontario
- Règles de procédure civile

Québec
- Règles de procédure de la Cour d'appel en matière civile
- Règles de pratique de la Cour supérieure du Québec en matières civiles
- Règles de pratique de la Cour supérieure du district de Montréal en matières civiles et familiales
- Règles de pratique de la Cour supérieure du district de Québec en matières civiles et familiales
- Règles de pratique de la Cour supérieure du Québec en matière familiale
- Règles de pratique de la Cour du Québec (Chambre civile)

Saskatchewan
- Rules of Court

Terre-Neuve
- Rules of the Supreme Court, 1986

Territoires du Nord-Ouest
- The Supreme Court Rules
- Probate Rules
- Rules of the Court of Appeal Respecting Civil Appeals
- Summary Conviction Appeal Rules of the Supreme Court of the Northwest Territories
- Règles de la Cour d'appel des Territoires du Nord-Ouest concernant A. les appels au criminel B. cautionnement en cas d'appel
- Règles de la Cour suprême des Territoires du Nord-Ouest concernant les conférences préparatoires au procès

Territoire du Yukon
- Rules of Court
- Court of Appeal Rules, Yukon Territory, 1974
- Criminal Appeal Rules, 1973
- Small Claims Court Regulations

2

JURISPRUDENCE

A. MODÈLE DE BASE POUR LA JURISPRUDENCE CANADIENNE

Masson c. Kelly	(1991),	85	D.L.R.	(4e)	214	(C.A. Ont.).
intitulé	année	volume	recueil	série	page	tribunal

R. c. Landry, [1991] 1 R.C.S. 99	à la p. 110,	62 C.C.C. (3e) 117,	M. le juge en chef Lamer.
première référence	référence précise	référence parallèle	juge

Éléments

1. Intitulé
2. Année de la décision
3. Volume
4. Recueil
5. Série
6. Page
7. Référence précise
8. Référence parallèle
9. Tribunal
10. Juge
11. Étapes successives de la cause

1. INTITULÉ

(a) Omission de l'intitulé

Exemple   **[1953] 2 R.C.S. 107 aux pp. 109-10, 107 C.C.C. 93.**
Règle   Omettre l'intitulé dans la note infra-paginale s'il est déjà mentionné dans le texte.

(b) «c.»

Exemple   *Canuel* **c.** *Fournier*, [1990] R.J.Q. 2253 (C.S.).
            ET NON
            Canuel c. Fournier, [1990] R.J.Q. 2253 (C.S.).
Règles   Un «c.» sépare les noms des parties.
            Mettre les noms des parties en italique.
            Ne pas mettre le «c.» en italique.
            Ne jamais écrire «v.» en français.

(c) Majuscules

Exemples ***Beaulieu Électrique Ltée* c. *Letellier*, [1990] R.L. 179 (C.A. Qué.).**
            ***Renvoi relatif à la Loi sur l'instruction publique, L.Q. 1988, c. 84*, [1990] R.J.Q. 2498 (C.A.).**
Règle   Écrire en majuscules seulement la première lettre du nom d'une partie, les majuscules des noms propres et des raisons sociales, et la première lettre d'une appellation comprise dans l'intitulé (par ex. : Loi, Règlements, etc.).

(d) Ponctuation

Exemples *R.* c. *Kumar* (1990), 80 C.R. (3e) 204 (B.C.S.C.).
            MAIS
            Poiré c. *Laflamme*, [1990] R.J.Q. 2703 (C.S.).
Règle   L'intitulé n'est pas suivi d'une virgule si l'année de la décision est indiquée. Toutefois, si l'année de la décision est omise (voir la règle 2 ci-dessous), l'intitulé est suivi d'une virgule.

(e)   Choix de l'intitulé et emploi de «sub nom.»

Exemples   **Laliberté c. Larue** (1930), [1931] S.C.R. 7, (**sub nom. Lafontaine Apts. c. Larue**) [1931] 2 D.L.R. 12.
Martineau c. Matsqui Institution Disciplinary Board (1979), [1980] 1 R.C.S. 602, (**sub nom. Martineau c. Matsqui Institution Disciplinary Board No. 2**) 106 D.L.R. (3ᵉ) 385.

Règles   Les noms des parties utilisés sont ceux qu'on trouve dans le premier recueil auquel on fait référence.
Si, dans une référence parallèle, il y a un intitulé différent, il faut le mettre entre parenthèses, introduit par l'expression «*sub nom.*».

(f)   Jonction d'instances

Exemples   *Syndicat des fonctionnaires provinciaux Inc.* c. **Cour provinciale**
Vanier c. **Rioux**
ET NON
Syndicat des fonctionnaires provinciaux Inc. c. *Cour provinciale et Son Honneur le juge André Desjardins*
Vanier c. *Rioux et al.*
MAIS
Léger, Léger & Léger c. Lemieux

Règles   Si la décision résulte de la jonction de deux ou de plusieurs instances, on mentionne seulement la première qui est inscrite.
Omettre toute expression, telle que «et al.», qui indique qu'il y a plusieurs parties.
Inclure, cependant, le nom complet d'une société de personnes.

(g)   Indications de la qualité d'une partie

Exemples   **McGill** c. *Shea*
A.G. Canada ex rel. McWhirter c. *Independent Broadcasting Authority*
ET NON
Doe dem. McGill c. *Shea*
McWhirter c. *Independent Broadcasting Authority*

Règle   On omet toute indication de la qualité en vertu de laquelle les parties agissent. On donne cependant le nom du premier informateur mentionné introduit par l'expression «ex rel.»

(h) Expressions procédurales

Exemples   **Re** *Guérin*
Ex parte *Delhasse :* **Re** *Megevand*
Perkins c. *Perkins*
ET NON
Dans l'affaire de Guérin
Ex. p. Delhasse : In Re Megevand
Re Perkins c. Perkins

Règles   Le simple «Re» remplace les expressions procédurales telles que «Dans l'affaire de», «In re», «In the matter of». On écrit «Ex parte» au long.

On omet le «Re» qui apparaît devant le nom de la première partie mentionnée dans une décision impliquant un conflit entre deux parties.

(i) Renvois constitutionnels

Exemple   **Renvoi relatif au paragraphe 94(2) de la Motor Vehicle Act, R.S.B.C. 1979**, [1985] 2 R.C.S. 486 , [1986] 1 W.W.R. 481.

Règle   Employer l'expression «Renvoi relatif à».

(j) Prénoms et raisons sociales

Exemples   **Roncarelli** c. **Duplessis**
Smith c. **Jones**
ET NON
Frank Roncarelli c. *L'Honorable Maurice Duplessis*
Bob Smith c. *Martha Jones*
MAIS
Conseil canadien des relations du travail c. **Paul L'Anglais Inc.**

Règle   On omet les prénoms et les initiales sauf s'ils font partie intégrante d'une raison sociale.

(k) Noms composés

Exemples Richard c. **Beaudoin-Daigneault**
Cannon-Callaghan c. *Mercier*
Règle Indiquer les noms composés au complet.

(l) Noms protégés

Exemples **Droit de la famille – 871**, [1990] R.J.Q. 2107 (C.A.).
D.L. c. M.L., [1990] R.L. 566 (C.A. Qué.)
Règles Lorsque les noms des parties ne sont pas divulgués, y substituer le titre et le numéro qui se trouvent dans le recueil.
Employer les initiales si possible.

(m) Omission de l'article défini

Exemples **Société de développement de la Baie James** c. *Kanatewat*
ET NON
La société de développement de la Baie James c. Kanatewat
MAIS
The Mihalis Angelos
Règles Omettre l'article défini («Le», «La», «L'», «Les», «The») même s'il fait partie d'une raison sociale.
Cependant, on garde l'article défini lorsqu'il fait partie du nom d'une chose contre laquelle on a institué une action *in rem* (par ex. : un navire).

(n) La Couronne

Exemples **R.** c. *Romeo*, [1991] 1 R.C.S. 86, 62 C.C.C. (3e) 1.
Doyle c. **M.R.N.** (1989), [1990] 1 C.F. 94.
Québec (P.G.) c. *Lippé*, [1990] R.J.Q. 2200 (C.A.).
Caron c. **Canada (Commission de l'emploi et de l'immigration)**, [1991] 1 R.C.S. 48, 77 D.L.R. (4e) 172.
Ontario (Employment Standards Officer) c. *Equitable Management Ltd.* (1990), 75 O.R. (2e) 506 (Ont. Ct. (Gen. Div.) Div. Ct.).
Règles Utiliser l'abréviation «R.» dans les causes criminelles.
La mention «M.R.N.» s'impose lorsqu'il s'agit du Ministre du revenu national.

Dans les autres cas, il suffit d'indiquer la juridiction, suivie, entre parenthèses, du nom de l'organe gouvernemental en question. On se sert de l'abréviation «P.G.» pour désigner le Procureur général.

Ne jamais écrire «La Reine», «La Couronne», «La Reine du chef de», etc.

Omettre aussi les expressions telles que «Province de».

(o)   Noms de lieux

(i)   Pays, provinces, etc.

Exemple	***Italy*** c. *Piperno* ET NON *Gouvernement de la République d'Italie* c. *Piperno*
Règles	Omettre les expressions «État de», «Peuple de», «Gouvernement de», etc., en gardant seulement le nom du pays ou de la province qui est partie à l'action. Pour le Canada et les provinces canadiennes, voir les règles énoncées sous la rubrique «Couronne» (règle 1(n) ci-dessus).

(ii)   Municipalités

Exemples	*Séminaire de Chicoutimi* c. ***Chicoutimi (Cité de)*** ***St-Denis de Brompton (Municipalité de)*** c. *Filteau*
Règle	Dans le cas de municipalités, on met les indications telles que «Ville de», «Cité de», «Municipalité de», etc., entre parenthèses après le nom.

(iii)   Compléments de lieu

Exemples	*Société de développement **de la Baie James*** c. *Kanatewat* *Roman Catholic Separate Schools **of Ottawa*** c. *Mackell* *Phillips* c. *Blue Cross **of Atlantic Canada*** ET NON *Société de développement* c. *Kanatewat* *Roman Catholic Separate Schools* c. *Mackell* *Phillips* c. *Blue Cross*
Règle	Inclure tous les compléments de lieu.

(p) **Statut corporatif**

Exemples **Cie Immobilière Viger** c. *Lauréat Giguère Inc.*
International Nickel Co. of Canada c. *Smith*
ET NON
Cie Immobilière Viger Ltée c. *Lauréat Giguère Inc.*
International Nickel Co. of Canada Ltd. c. *Smith*
MAIS
Phillips & Wang Associés Inc. c. *R.*
ET NON
Phillips & Wang Associés c. *R.*

Règles On omet «Inc.», «Ltée» ou «Ltd.» lorsque le nom de la partie porte déjà la mention «Cie» ou «Co.», qui indique le statut corporatif de la partie.
Cependant, on doit conserver «Inc.», «Ltée» ou «Ltd.» après «& frères», «Associés», et d'autres expressions qui n'indiquent pas le statut corporatif de la partie.

(q) **Institutions**

Exemples *Damus* c. **St. Boniface School Division No. 4**
McBeth c. **Dalhousie College & University**
ET NON
Damus c. *Board of Trustees of St. Boniface School Division No. 4*
McBeth c. *Governors of Dalhousie College & University*

Règle Omettre les expressions «Gouverneurs de», «Board of Trustees of», «Governors of», etc., et laisser seulement le nom de l'institution.

(r) **Noms de syndicats**

Exemples *Boisvert* c. **A.E.C.R.**
Premier Cable Systems Ltd. c. **I.B.E.W., Local 213**
ET NON
Boisvert c. *Association des employés du Conseil de recherches*
Premier Cable Systems Ltd. c. *International Brotherhood of Electrical Workers, Local 213*

Règle Si possible, utiliser les abréviations du *Répertoire des organisations des travailleurs au Canada* de Travail Canada.

2.   ANNÉE DE LA DÉCISION

Exemples   *Kruger* c. *R.* **(1977)**, [1978] 1 R.C.S. 104, [1977] 4 W.W.R.
300, 34 C.C.C. (2ᵉ) 377.
R. c. *Cooper* **(1981)**, 49 N.S.R. (2ᵉ) 221, 96 A.P.R. 221, 65
C.C.C. (2ᵉ) 254 (S.C.A.D.).
MAIS
R. c. *Keegstra*, [1990] 3 R.C.S. 697.
ET NON
R. c. *Keegstra* (1990), [1990] 3 R.C.S. 697.

Règles   On indique l'année de la décision entre parenthèses,
suivie d'une virgule.

Omettre l'année de la décision lorsque le volume du
premier recueil mentionné est identifié par l'année de
publication (voir la règle 3(a) ci-dessous) et que cette
année est la même que l'année de la décision.

3.   VOLUME

(a)   Les volumes sont identifiés par l'année de publication

Exemples   *Côté* c. *Proulx*, **[1990]** R.L. 191.
R. c. *Landry*, **[1991]** 1 R.C.S. 99.
Canada (P.G.) c. *Lavell* (1973), **[1974]** R.C.S. 1349.

Règles   Les volumes de nombreux recueils sont identifiés par
l'année de publication. Cette indication se met entre
crochets. Dans le cas de quelques-uns de ces recueils
(R.C.S. et C.F., par exemple), cette indication peut être
suivie d'un numéro de volume.

Tel qu'indiqué dans la règle 2, ci-dessus, la mention de
l'année de la décision est omise lorsque le volume du
premier recueil mentionné est identifié par l'année de
publication et que cette année est la même que l'année
de la décision.

(b)   Les volumes sont identifiés par un numéro de volume

Exemples   *Rocheleau* c. *Laberge* (1930), **68** C.S. 202.
Cardinal Construction Ltd. c. *R.* (1981), **38** O.R. (2ᵉ) 161, **128**
D.L.R. (3ᵉ) 662 (C.A.).

Règles   Les volumes d'autres recueils sont identifiés par un numéro.

Ce numéro est placé entre l'année de la décision et l'abréviation du titre du recueil.

4.   RECUEIL

Exemple   *Beauregard* c. *R.*, [1981] 2 **C.F.** 543, 130 **D.L.R.** (3e) 433 (1re inst.).

Règle   On met l'abréviation du titre du recueil (voir appendice 2).

5.   SÉRIE

Exemples   *Re Children's Aid Society of Western Manitoba and Corrigan* (1983), 148 D.L.R. **(3e)** 114 (Man. C.A.).

R. c. *Andrushko* (1977), 40 C.R.**(n.s.)** 216 (Man. C.A.).

Règle   Si le recueil est publié en plusieurs séries, l'indication du rang de la série se met entre parenthèses (1re, 2e, 3e, 4e, etc.; «nouvelle série» s'abrège «n.s.»).

6.   PAGE

Exemple   *Ford* c. *Québec (P.G.)*, [1988] 2 R.C.S. **712**.

Règle   Indiquer le numéro de la première page du jugement.

7.   RÉFÉRENCE PRÉCISE

Exemples   *Canada (P.G.)* c. *Lavell* (1973), [1974] R.C.S. 1349 **à la p. 1388**, 38 D.L.R. (3e) 481.

Doyle c. *Sparling*, [1986] R.D.J. 585 **à la p. 587 et s.** (C.A.).

R. c. *Big M Drug Mart Ltd.*, [1985] 1 R.C.S. 295 **aux pp. 351-53**, 18 D.L.R. (4e) 321.

Règles   La référence précise s'effectue au moyen des expressions «à la p.», «aux pp.» et «à la p. et s.»

Il n'y a pas de virgule entre l'indication de la première page du jugement et la référence précise.

La référence précise renvoie au premier recueil mentionné dans la référence. Les références précises aux autres recueils sont facultatives.

8. RÉFÉRENCES PARALLÈLES

(a) Ordre des recueils

Exemples　*General Motors Products of Canada Ltd.* c. *Kravitz*, [1979] 1 **R.C.S.** 790, 93 **D.L.R.** (3ᵉ) 481.
R. c. *Kulbacki* (1965), 52 **D.L.R.** (2ᵉ) 283, [1966] 1 **C.C.C.** 167 (Man. C.A.).
Sealand of the Pacific Ltd. c. *Robert C. McHaffie Ltd.* (1974), 51 **D.L.R.** (3ᵉ) 702, [1974] 6 **W.W.R.** 724 (B.C.C.A.).

Règles　Si possible, il convient de donner au moins une référence parallèle.
La référence à un recueil officiel ou semi-officiel (voir appendice 1) précède celle qui renvoie à un recueil non officiel.
Les recueils généraux précèdent les recueils spécialisés.
Les recueils couvrant un plus grand territoire géographique précèdent ceux couvrant un territoire plus petit.
Les trois dernières règles sont facultatives.

(b) L'expression «*sub nom.*»

Exemples　***Laliberté* c. *Larue*** (1930), [1931] **S.C.R.** 7, (***sub nom.* Lafontaine Apts. c. *Larue*)** [1931] 2 **D.L.R.** 12.
Martineau* c. *Matsqui Institution Disciplinary Board (1979), [1980] 1 **R.C.S.** 602, (***sub nom. Martineau* c. *Matsqui Institution Disciplinary Board No. 2*)** 106 **D.L.R.** (3ᵉ) 385.

Règle　Si une référence parallèle utilise un intitulé différent, il faut l'inclure entre parenthèses au début de la référence parallèle, introduit par l'expression «*sub nom.*» (voir, ci-dessus, la règle 1(e)).

9. TRIBUNAL

Exemples　*Canadian Imperial Back of Commerce* c. *Otto Timm Enterprises Ltd.* (1991), 79 D.L.R. (4ᵉ) **(Ont. Ct. (Gen. Div.))**.
Murphy c. *Penney Motors Ltd.* (1979), 23 Nfld. & P.E.I.R. 152 **(Nfld. S.C.T.D.)**.
MAIS
Lasby c. *Walsh* (1920), 13 **Sask.** L.R. 201 **(C.A.)**.
Faubert c. *Brown* (1938), 76 **C.S.** 328.

Field c. *Zien*, [1963] R.C.S. 632.
ET NON
Lasby c. *Walsh* (1920), 13 Sask. L.R. 201 (Sask. C.A.).
Faubert c. *Brown* (1938), 76 C.S. 328 (C.S. Qué.).
Field c. *Zien*, [1963] R.C.S. 632 (C.S.C.).

Règles Le nom du tribunal en question, y compris l'indication géographique, se met entre parenthèses après la page. Les abréviations pertinentes se trouvent aux appendices 3 et 4.
Omettre l'indication géographique si elle se déduit aisément du titre du recueil. Si la cour elle-même est évidente, elle aussi se passe de mention.

2

10. JUGE

Exemples *R.* c. *Landry*, [1991] 1 R.C.S. 99 à la p. 110, **M. le juge en chef Lamer**.
Laferrière c. *Lawson*, [1989] R.J.Q. 27 à la p. 28 (C.A.), **M. le juge Vallerand**.

Règle Lorsqu'on mentionne le nom du juge, on le met à la fin de la référence, précédé d'une virgule, introduit par l'expression «M. le juge», «Mme le juge», «M. le juge en chef» ou «Mme le juge en chef».

11. ÉTAPES SUCCESSIVES DE LA CAUSE

(a) Étapes postérieures

Exemples *Gay Alliance Toward Equality* c. *Vancouver Sun* (1975), Report of a Board of Inquiry under the *Human Rights Code of British Columbia*, **conf. par [1976] W.W.D. 160 (B.C.S.C.), inf. par (1977), 77 D.L.R. (3e) 487 (B.C.C.A.), inf. par [1979] 2 R.C.S. 435.**
Asselin c. *Davidson* (1912), 13 R.P. Qué. 423 (C.S.), **conf. par (1914), 23 B.R. 274.**

Règles Si elles sont pertinentes, les étapes postérieures d'une cause constituent le dernier élément de la référence.
On utilise les indications «conf. par» (confirmé par) et «inf. par» (infirmé par).
Ces indications renvoient toujours à la référence principale. Dans le premier exemple ci-dessus, par exemple, la Cour suprême du Canada a décidé, tout comme la Cour

d'appel de la Colombie-Britannique, que la décision originale devait être infirmée; elle n'a pas infirmé la décision de la Cour d'appel.

Les références parallèles sont facultatives lorsqu'on donne les étapes successives d'une cause.

(b)   Étapes antérieures

Exemples   *Multiple Access Ltd.* c. *McCutcheon*, [1982] 2 R.C.S. 161, 138 D.L.R. (3e) 1, 44 N.R. 181, **infirmant (1978), 19 O.R. (2e) 516, 86 D.L.R. (3e) 160 (C.A.).**
Lapierre c. *Québec (P.G.)*, [1985] 1 R.C.S. 241, 58 N.R. 161, **confirmant [1983] C.A. 631.**

Règles   Si cela est pertinent, on ajoute les étapes antérieures d'une cause.

Dans ce cas, il y a lieu d'utiliser les indications «confirmant» et «infirmant».

(c)   Étapes antérieures et postérieures

Exemples   *Luddit* c. *Ginger Coote Airways Ltd.*, [1942] S.C.R. 406, [1942] 4 D.L.R. 353, **infirmant (1942) B.C.R. 176 (C.A.) (infirmant (1941), 56 B.C.R. 401 (S.C.)), conf. par [1947] A.C. 233 (P.C.).**
National Drying Machinery Co. c. *Wabasso Ltd.* (1978), [1979] C.A. 279, **infirmant [1977] C.S. 782, inf. par [1981] 1 R.C.S. 578, 38 N.R. 224.**

Règles   Si on ajoute à la fois les étapes antérieures et postérieures, il convient de mettre les étapes antérieures avant les étapes postérieures.

On met entre parenthèses toute décision qui n'est pas reliée directement au jugement principal.

(d)   Intitulé différent

Exemples   *Oakwood Development Ltd.* c. *St-François Xavier (Municipalité rurale de)*, [1985] 2 R.C.S. 164, 20 D.L.R. (4e) 641, confirmant (**sub nom. Oakwood Development Ltd. c. St-François Xavier (Rural Municipality of)**) (1982), 17

Man. R. (2e) 241 (C.A.).
Glover c. *Glover* (No. 1) (1980), 29 O.R. (2e) 392, 113 D.L.R. (3e) 161 (C.A.), conf. par (*sub nom. Glover* c. *M.R.N.*) [1981] 2 R.C.S. 561.

Règle   Si une affaire porte un intitulé différent à une certaine étape, on le met entre parenthèses introduit par l'expression «*sub nom.*»

B. JUGEMENTS NON PUBLIÉS

1. MODÈLE DE BASE

(a) Québec

Exemples   **St-Pierre c. Services des affaires sociales de la Ville de Montréal (12 mars 1982), Montréal 500-05-006810-806, J.E. 82-371 (C.S.).**
Fredette c. Montreal Dress and Sportswear Manufacturers' Guild (15 décembre 1977), Montréal 500-09-001461-771, J.E. 78-14 (C.A.).

Règles   Inclure la date de la décision au complet entre parenthèses suivie d'une virgule.
Mentionner ensuite le nom du district judiciaire, le numéro de greffe et la référence au Jurisprudence Express. Le nom du tribunal se place entre parenthèses à la fin de la référence.

(b) Provinces de common law et territoires

Exemples   **Stephenson c. Stephenson (6 décembre 1984), Nanaimo 5920/004143 (B.C.S.C.).**
R. c. Rao (24 novembre 1983), (Ont. C.A.) [non publié].

Règles   Suivre les règles ci-dessus, sauf en ce qui concerne la référence au Jurisprudence Express.
Si le numéro de greffe n'apparaît pas sur la page titre d'un jugement de common law non publié, la mention «non publié» se place à la fin de la référence entre crochets.

2. BANQUES DE DONNÉES

Règle   Il ne faut renvoyer à une banque de données que dans le cas où il n'existe pas de version imprimée. Noter les règles suivantes.

(a) QL

Exemples   ***R. c. Butler***, [1992] A.C.S. n° 15 (QL).
R. c. Howard, [1991] A.J. n° 1025 (QL).
Atlas Copco Aktiebolag c. CIL Inc., [1986] A.C.F. n° 987 (QL).

Règles   Placer la référence à QL après l'intitulé. Cette référence comprend l'année entre crochets telle qu'elle apparaît à l'écran, le nom abrégé de la banque de données en question et le numéro de la décision.

La mention «QL» se met entre parenthèses à la fin de la référence.

Note   Il faut éviter les références précises car elles risquent d'induire en erreur. Les numéros qui apparaissent à l'écran peuvent varier selon le choix des modalités de présentation.

(b) SOQUIJ

Règle   La plupart des jugements répertoriés dans les banques de données de SOQUIJ sont publiés. Pour ceux qui ne le sont pas, on suit les règles ci-dessus relatives aux jugements non publiés, en donnant, si possible, le numéro du Jurisprudence Express.

(c) CAN/LAW

Règle   La plupart des décisions saisies dans les banques de données de CAN/LAW sont publiées. Pour celles qui ne le sont pas, suivre les règles énoncées ci-dessus pour les jugements non publiés.

C. TRIBUNAUX ADMINISTRATIFS

1. DÉCISIONS PUBLIÉES

Exemples *Assurance-automobile – 19*, [1989] C.A.S. 558.
Wilpark Farms Ltd. c. *Manitoba (Department of Highways)* (1990), 44 L.C.R. 130 (Manitoba Land Value Appraisal Commission).

Règles Suivre le modèle de base pour la jurisprudence.

Indiquer l'intitulé de la décision tel qu'il apparaît dans le recueil en question, qu'il s'agisse ou non d'un litige opposant deux parties. Faute d'intitulé, y substituer le numéro de la décision.

Mettre le nom du tribunal entre parenthèses à la fin de la référence, à moins qu'il ne se déduise du titre du recueil.

Fournir si possible une ou plusieurs références parallèles.

L'inclusion d'autres renseignements, tels que le numéro de la décision ou le nom du comité qui a rendu la décision, est au choix de l'auteur. Ces informations se placent entre parenthèses à la fin de la référence.

2. DÉCISIONS NON PUBLIÉES

Exemples *Relative à une demande présentée en vertu de la Loi sur l'Office national de l'énergie par Ontario Hydro* (avril 1991), no EW-3-90 (O.N.E.).
James B. Lansing Sound Canada Ltd. c. *Sous-Ministre du Revenu national pour les douanes et l'accise* (9 avril 1979), Appel no 1383 (C.T.).

Règles Indiquer la date de la décision avec le plus de précision possible. Elle se met entre parenthèses après l'intitulé, suivie d'une virgule.

Suivent le numéro de la décision et, entre parenthèses, le nom abrégé du tribunal.

Tout autre renseignement qui faciliterait le repérage de la source peut être inclus au choix de l'auteur.

LA DOCTRINE

A.   LES MONOGRAPHIES

Modèle de base

J.-L. Baudouin,	*Les obligations*,	3e éd.,	Cowansville, Yvon Blais, 1989	à la p. 27.
Auteur	Titre	Édition	Renseignements sur l'édition	Référence précise

Éléments

1.   Auteur
2.   Titre
3.   Volume (si l'ouvrage est publié en plusieurs volumes)
4.   Édition
5.   Renseignements sur l'édition
6.   Référence précise

1.   AUTEUR

(a)   Un seul auteur

Exemples   **R.M. Beaupré**, *Interprétation de la législation bilingue*, Montréal, Wilson et Lafleur, 1986.

M. Ouellette, *Droit de la famille*, Montréal, Thémis, 1984.

Lord A.T. Denning, *What Next in the Law*, Londres, Butterworths, 1982.

Règles   Les initiales précèdent le nom de famille.

On inclut également les titres honorifiques.

(b)   Coauteurs

Exemples   **M. Bolduc, M. Lavigne et J. Giroux**, *Guide du propriétaire et du locataire*, Montréal, Éditions de l'homme, 1977.

MAIS

J. Goulet *et al.*, *Théorie générale du domaine privé*, 2e éd., Montréal, Wilson et Lafleur, 1986.

ET NON

J. Goulet, A. Robinson, D. Shelton et F. Marchand, *Théorie générale du domaine privé*, 2e éd., Montréal, Wilson et Lafleur, 1986.

Règles   Lorsqu'un ouvrage est l'oeuvre de trois auteurs ou moins, on indique le nom et les initiales de chaque auteur.

S'il y a plus de trois auteurs, on indique le nom d'un seul d'entre eux suivi de l'expression «*et al.*».

Ne pas mettre de virgule entre le nom et «*et al.*».

On met une virgule après «*et al.*».

(c)   Directeur d'un ouvrage collectif

Exemples   **R.-P. Barbe, dir.**, *Droit administratif : canadien et québécois*, Ottawa, Université d'Ottawa, 1969.

G.A. Beaudouin et D. Turp, dir., *Perspectives canadiennes et européennes des droits de la personne*, Cowansville (Qué.), Yvon Blais, 1986.

Règles   On nomme jusqu'à trois directeurs; s'il y en a plus, on n'indique que le premier suivi de l'expression «*et al.*». «Directeur» s'abrège «dir.» au singulier comme au pluriel, cette abréviation étant précédée et suivie d'une virgule.

(d)   Directeur ou correcteur d'un ouvrage classique

(*i*)   Le nom de l'auteur original fait partie du titre

Exemple   G. Ripert, dir., *Traité élémentaire de droit civil de Marcel Planiol*, t. 1, 3e éd., Paris, Libraire générale de droit et de jurisprudence, 1946.

Règles   Si le nom de l'auteur original est devenu partie intégrante du titre, le nom du directeur apparaît là où se trouverait normalement celui de l'auteur.
Inclure les initiales du directeur, ainsi que la mention «dir.».

(*ii*)   Le nom de l'auteur original ne fait pas partie du titre

Exemple   H., J. et L. Mazeaud, *Leçons de droit civil*, 6e **éd. par M. de Juglart**, Paris, Montchrestien, 1976.

Règles   Si le nom de l'auteur original ne fait pas partie du titre, le nom du directeur se met après la mention de l'édition : auteur, *titre*, n^o éd. par directeur, etc.
Inclure les initiales complètes de l'auteur et du directeur.

(e)   Traducteur

Exemple   B.P. Archibald, «Le droit relatif à l'arrestation» dans V.M. Del Buono, dir., *Procédure pénale au Canada*, **trad. par E. Groffier**, Montréal, Wilson et Lafleur/Sorej, 1983, 143.

Règles   Auteur, *titre*, édition trad. par nom du traducteur (renseignements sur l'édition).
La mention du traducteur est au choix de l'auteur.

2.   TITRE

Exemple   L. Potvin, **La personne et la protection de son image :**
Étude comparée des droits québécois, français et de la
common law anglaise, Cowansville (Québec), Yvon
Blais, 1991.

Règles   Auteur, *titre*, etc.
On donne, en italique, le principal titre au complet.
Ne pas employer d'abréviation.
On peut inclure le sous-titre, introduit par un deux-points, s'il aide à identifier l'ouvrage.
Mettre en majuscules seulement la première lettre du premier mot, ainsi que la première lettre des noms propres.

3.   NUMÉRO DE TOME ET DE VOLUME

(a)   Livres en français

Exemples   F. Laurent, *Principes de droit civil*, **t. 10**, 5e éd., Bruxelles,
Bruylant-Christophe, 1893.
H., L. et J. Mazeaud, *Leçons de droit civil*, **t. 3, vol. 2**, 6e éd.
par M. de Juglart, Paris, Montchrestien, 1984 à la p. 94
et s., n° 814.

Règles   Les abréviations de «tome» et «volume» sont «t.» et
«vol.» respectivement.
Tomes et volumes peuvent être soit des livres distincts,
soit les divisions d'un seul livre.
Ces indications, toujours précédées et suivies d'une virgule, se placent après le titre.

(b)   Livres en anglais

(i)   Le volume constitue un livre distinct

Exemple   S.A. Schiff, *Evidence in the Litigation Process*, **vol. 1**, Toronto,
Carswell, 1978 aux pp. 69-70.

Règles   Auteur, *titre*, vol. n°, renseignements sur l'édition, etc.
L'indication du numéro du volume se place *avant* les renseignements sur l'édition si le volume constitue un livre distinct.
Utiliser des chiffres arabes.

«Volume» s'abrège «vol.» au singulier comme au pluriel.
Mettre une virgule entre le titre et la mention du volume.

(*ii*)   Les volumes se trouvent dans un seul livre

Exemple   K. Marx, *Capital*, New York : International, 1967, **vol. 1** à
la p. 15.

Règles   Auteur, *titre*, renseignements sur l'édition, vol. n°, etc.
Le numéro du volume se place *après* l'année de publication si le volume est relié avec les autres dans un même
livre.

4.   ÉDITION

(a)   Plusieurs éditions

Exemples   M.A. Tancelin, *Jurisprudence sur les obligations*, **2ᵉ éd.**, Québec, Presses de l'Université Laval, 1981 à la p. 7.
J.G. Fleming, *The Law of Torts*, **7ᵉ éd.**, Sydney, Law Book,
1987 à la p. 104.

Règle   S'il existe plusieurs éditions d'un ouvrage, il faut indiquer le numéro en question (1ʳᵉ, 2ᵉ, 3ᵉ, etc.) après le titre.

(b)   Édition révisée sans numéro

Exemple   M. Tancelin, *Des obligations : Contrat et responsabilité*, **éd.
rév.**, Montréal, Wilson et Lafleur, 1986.

Règle   La mention «éd. rév.» indique une édition révisée qui ne
porte pas de numéro.

5.   RENSEIGNEMENTS SUR L'ÉDITION

(a)   Lieu d'édition

Exemples   P. Lemieux, *Les contrats de l'administration fédérale, provinciale
et municipale*, **Sherbrooke (Québec)**, R.D.U.S., 1981.
M. Jackson, *Prisoners of Isolation : Solitary Confinement in Canada*, **Toronto**, University of Toronto Press, 1983.

Règles   Indiquer le lieu d'édition, tel qu'il apparaît sur la page titre ou au verso de la page titre. Si plusieurs villes y sont énumérées, ne mentionner que la première.

Si la seule mention du nom de la ville est insuffisante, on peut y ajouter d'autres informations géographiques : province, état ou pays.

Mettre une virgule après le lieu d'édition.

(b)   Maison d'édition

Exemples   P. Garant, *Droit administratif*, 2ᵉ éd., Montréal, **Yvon Blais**, 1985.

S.A. Schiff, *Evidence in the Litigation Process*, vol. 1, Toronto, **Carswell**, 1978.

ET NON

P. Garant, *Droit administratif*, 2ᵉ éd., Montréal, Les Éditions Yvon Blais Inc., 1985.

S.A. Schiff, *Evidence in the Litigation Process*, vol. 1, Toronto, The Carswell Co. Ltd, 1978.

MAIS

J.-L. Baudouin, *Les obligations*, 1ʳᵉ éd., Montréal, **Presses de l'Université de Montréal**, 1970.

R. St. J. MacDonald, G.L. Morris et D.M. Johnston, dir., *Canadian Perspectives on International Law and Organisation*, Toronto, **University of Toronto Press**, 1974.

Règles   On indique le nom de l'éditeur commercial tel qu'il apparaît sur la page titre ou au verso de la page titre, suivi d'une virgule.

Omettre l'article défini («Le», «La», «L'», «Les», «The») même s'il constitue le premier mot du nom de la maison d'édition.

Omettre les expressions qui indiquent le statut corporatif comme «Ltée», «Ltd.» ou «Inc.»

Omettre aussi le mot «Éditions» à moins qu'il ne fasse partie d'un syntagme inséparable (on écrit «Yvon Blais» ET NON «Éditions Yvon Blais», MAIS il faut écrire «Éditions de l'homme»). Pour ce qui est des éditeurs de langue anglaise, omettre le mot «Publishing» ou «Publishers».

Conserver le mot «Presses» en français et «Press» en anglais.

(c)   Année de publication

Exemple   P.-A. Crépeau, *L'intensité de l'obligation juridique*, Cowansville (Qué.), Yvon Blais, **1989**.

Règle   On mentionne l'année de l'édition et non celle de l'impression.

6.   RÉFÉRENCE PRÉCISE

Exemples   M. Ouellette, *Droit de la famille*, Montréal, Thémis, 1984 **à la p. 38**.
D. Turp et J. Leavy, *Sources et méthodologie du droit québécois et canadien : Notes et documents*, Montréal, Thémis, 1981 **aux pp. 484-88**.
R. Dussault et L. Borgeat, *Traité de droit administratif*, 2ᵉ éd., Québec, Presses de l'Université Laval, 1984 **à la p. 162 et s.**
M.A. Tancelin, *Des obligations : Contrat et responsabilité*, éd. rév., Montréal, Wilson & Lafleur, 1986 **au nᵒ 708**.
D. Bradet *et al.*, *Droit de la santé et de la sécurité du travail*, Cowansville (Qué.), Yvon Blais, 1986 **au c. 3, nᵒ 3**.

Règles   La référence précise suit les renseignements sur l'édition.
Se servir des indications «à la p.» et «aux pp.» pour renvoyer à une ou plusieurs pages.
Dans le cas de pages consécutives, l'usage du trait d'union s'impose, tout comme le maintien d'au moins les deux derniers chiffres (par ex. : «aux pp. 30-33» ET NON «aux pp. 30-3»).
La mention «et s.» veut dire «et suivantes».
«Chapitre» s'abrège «c.» au singulier comme au pluriel.
La référence au chapitre se donne en chiffres arabes peu importe la forme utilisée dans le texte.
Lorsque les paragraphes sont numérotés, on y renvoie à l'aide du symbole «nᵒ».

3

B.   PÉRIODIQUES

Modèle de base

S. Goyard-Fabre,	«Montesquieu entre Domat et Portalis»	(1990)	35	R.D. McGill	715	à la p. 731.
Auteur	Titre de l'article	Année	Volume	Périodique	Page	Référence précise

Éléments

1. Auteur
2. Titre de l'article
3. Année de publication
4. Volume
5. Titre du périodique
6. Première page de l'article
7. Référence précise

1.   AUTEUR

(a)   Un seul auteur

Exemples   **A.L.C. de Mestral**, «Le rôle de la pratique dans la formation du droit international public» (1984) 14 R.D.U.S. 441.
M. Meltsner, «Feeling Like a Lawyer» (1983) 33 J. Legal Educ. 624.

Règles   Initiale(s) et nom de famille, «titre» etc.
On mentionne les initiales et les titres honorifiques.

(b)   Coauteurs

Exemple   **C. Fabien et A.-M. Morel**, «Le mandat apparent» (1980-81) 15 R.J.T. 319.

Règles   On peut mentionner jusqu'à trois auteurs, toujours avec les initiales.
S'il y a plus de trois auteurs, on n'indique que le premier suivi de l'indication «*et al.*».
Il n'y a pas de virgule entre le nom de l'auteur et «*et al.*».
On met une virgule après «*et al.*».

2.   TITRE

Exemples   A. Popovici, **«De la mutabilité du régime matrimonial étranger»** (1975) 35 R. du B. 77.
I. Hunter, **«Liberty and Equality : A Tale of Two Codes»** (1983) 29 R.D. McGill 1.

Règles   Auteur, «titre» etc.
Le titre se met entre guillemets.
Ne pas mettre de virgule après le titre.

3.   ANNÉE DE PUBLICATION

Exemples   M. Grandbois, «Le droit fédéral et québécois de la conservation de la faune» **(1985)** 16 R.D.U.S. 261.
J. Thilmany, «Fonctions et révisibilité des clauses pénales en droit comparé» **[1980]** R.I.D.C. 17.

Règles   Si une revue est divisée en volumes numérotés, on ajoute l'année de publication de l'article en la mettant entre parenthèses.
Si les volumes ne sont pas numérotés mais s'identifient uniquement par l'année de publication, cette indication – l'année indiqué au dos du volume – se met entre crochets.

4.   VOLUME

Exemples   P.-A. Côté, «L'interprétation de la loi par le législateur» (1980-81) **15** R.J.T. 29.
J. Powis, «The Quiet Revolution» (1981) **77 :2** The Canadian Nurse 26.

Règles   On place le numéro du volume entre l'année de publication et le titre du périodique.
Lorsque les numéros d'un même volume ne sont pas paginés de façon consécutive, il faut indiquer le numéro après le volume, en le faisant précéder d'un deux-points.

5. TITRE DU PÉRIODIQUE

Exemples   Madeleine Caron, «L'égalité sous le Code civil : l'incidence des Chartes» (1990) 24 **R.J.T.** 433.
Madame le juge B.M. McLachlin, «Crime and Women – Feminine Equality and the Criminal Law» (1991) 25 **U.B.C. L. Rev.** 1.

Règles   Auteur, «titre» (année) volume titre du périodique, etc.
Le titre du périodique s'abrège (voir l'appendice 6).
Ne pas mettre l'abréviation en italique.

6. PREMIÈRE PAGE DE L'ARTICLE

(a) Modèle de base

Exemple   F. DePauw, «La Belgique et la compétence obligatoire de la cour internationale» (1965) 1 R.B.D.I. **49**.

Règle   Indiquer la première page de l'article après le titre du périodique.

(b) Lorsque l'article est publié en parties

Exemples   R.A. Macdonald, «Enforcing Rights in Corporeal Moveables : Revendication and Its Surrogates» (1986) 31 R.D. McGill **573**, (1986) 32 R.D. McGill **1**.
S. Massé, «Les régimes matrimoniaux au Canada – Analyse comparative des législations provinciales» (1985-86) 88 R. du N. **103, 223**.

Règles   Lorsque les parties de l'article sont publiées dans différents volumes, on indique le nom de l'auteur et le titre selon les règles énoncées ci-dessus, suivis de la référence complète pour chaque partie.
Lorsque les parties de l'article sont publiées dans le même volume, on donne la référence complète en incluant la première page de chaque partie, une virgule séparant les numéros.

7. RÉFÉRENCE PRÉCISE

Exemple   S. Goyard-Fabre, «De la légitimité du pouvoir» (1989) 35 R.D. McGill 1 **à la p. 12**.

Règle   La référence précise s'effectue au moyen des expressions «à la p.» et «aux pp.».

C.   ENCYCLOPÉDIES

Exemples   *Halsbury's Laws of England*, vol. 34, 4ᵉ éd., Londres, Butterworths, 1980 à la p. 60, para. 71.
American Jurisprudence, vol. 17A, 2ᵉ éd., Rochester, Lawyers Cooperative, 1991 au titre «Contracts», § 97.
Corpus Juris Secundum, vol. 96, Brooklyn, American Law Book, 1957 à la p. 397, § 934.

Règles   Suivre les règles énoncées pour les monographies, en omettant le premier élément (l'auteur).
Les références précises renvoient à la page et/ou au paragraphe (dont l'abréviation est «para.» ou «§»). On peut également mentionner le titre de la partie en question. Pour les encyclopédies françaises, voir le chapitre 6 – France.

D.   OUVRAGES COLLECTIFS

Exemples   W.S. Tarnopolsky, «Les droits à l'égalité» dans G.-A. Beaudouin et W.S. Tarnopolsky, dir., *Charte canadienne des droits et libertés*, Wilson et Lafleur/Sorej, 1982, 497 à la p. 532.
R. Veinott, «Child Custody and Divorce : A Nova Scotia Study, 1866-1910» dans P. Girard et J. Phillips, dir., *Essays in the History of Canadian Law*, vol. 3, *Nova Scotia*, Toronto, University of Toronto Press, 1990, 273.

Règles   Les initiales et le nom de l'auteur de l'article ainsi que le titre de celui-ci précède la référence complète de l'ouvrage collectif, laquelle comprend les initiales et le nom du directeur.
La première page de l'article, ainsi que toute référence précise, suit la référence à l'ouvrage collectif.
Le titre de l'article est placé entre guillemets; celui de l'ouvrage collectif se met en italique.
Si l'auteur de l'article est aussi le directeur de l'ouvrage collectif, on le mentionne deux fois.

Note   Si un autre article contenu dans l'ouvrage collectif a déjà été cité, il n'est pas nécessaire de répéter la référence complète (voir Références et notes infra-paginales : notions de base – références ultérieures).

E.   CHRONIQUES BIBLIOGRAPHIQUES

Exemples   H. Brun, **Compte rendu** (1982) 23 C. de D. 251.
N. L'Heareux, **Compte rendu : Abréviations juridiques par E. Casaubon et D. LeMay** (1984) 25 C. de D. 428.
M. Tancelin, **«Que sais-je?»** (1984) 25 C. de D. 493.

Règles   Auteur, Compte rendu (année) volume périodique première page du compte rendu.
Inclure les initiales complètes de l'auteur du compte rendu.
L'indication «Compte rendu» n'est jamais suivie d'une virgule, mais peut, au choix de l'auteur, être suivie du titre du livre en question et du nom de l'auteur. On peut aussi lui substituer le titre du compte rendu, s'il en a un, lequel se met entre guillemets.

F.   AVANT-PROPOS, PRÉFACES, ETC.

Exemples   M. le juge M. Proulx, **«Préface»** dans P. Béliveau, *Les garanties juridiques dans les chartes des droits*, Montréal, Thémis, 1991, ix.
J. de Larosière, **«Foreword»** dans R.H. Floyd, C.S. Gray et R.P. Short, *Public Enterprise in Mixed Economies*, Washington, D.C., International Monetary Fund, 1984, v à la p. v.

Règles   Auteur, «Avant-propos», etc. dans auteur, *titre*, renseignements sur l'édition, première page de l'avant-propos référence précise.
Inclure les initiales des deux auteurs au complet.
Les mots «avant-propos», «préface», «introduction», etc., se mettent entre guillemets.

G. CHRONIQUES DE LÉGISLATION ET DE JURISPRUDENCE

Exemples M.A. Tancelin, **Chronique de législation** (1974) 52 R. du B. can. 90.

C. D'Aoust, **«Réflexions sur l'arbitrage des diffé- rends»** (1984) 14 R.D.U.S. 625.

A.-M. Boisvert, **«Légitime défense et le «syndrome de la femme battue» : *R. c. Lavallée»*** (1991) 36 R.D. McGill 191.

Règles Inclure les initiales complètes de l'auteur.

Si la chronique a un titre, on le met entre guillemets : Auteur, «titre» (année) volume périodique première page de la chronique.

Si elle n'a pas de titre, y substituer la mention «Chroni- que de législation/jurisprudence», sans guillemets.

Le nom de l'arrêt peut être mentionné au choix de l'au- teur :

Auteur, Chronique de législation/jurisprudence (année) volume périodique première page de la chronique.

OU

Auteur, Chronique de jurisprudence : *X* c. *Y* (année) vo- lume périodique première page de la chronique.

H. COMMENTAIRES, REMARQUES, NOTES

Exemples E.L. Meyrowitz, **Commentaires** (1981) 75 Proc. Am. Soc. Int'l L. 214.

Note, '"Round and 'Round the Bramble Bush : From Legal Realism to Critical Legal Scholarship" (1982) 95 Harv. L. Rev. 1669.

Règles Auteur, Commentaires (année) volume périodique pre- mière page.

Inclure les initiales de l'auteur.

Pour les notes anonymes : Note, «titre» (année) volume périodique première page.

La mention «Commentaires», «Note», etc. ne se met pas entre guillemets.

I.   ALLOCUTIONS, DISCOURS, CONFÉRENCES

(a)   Portant un titre

Exemples   J.-Y. Morin, «Pour une nouvelle Constitution du Québec», Conférence de la Revue de droit de McGill, Université McGill, 29 octobre 1984 (1985) 30 R.D. McGill 171.

M.E. Agazzi, «Problèmes éthiques de la procréation artificielle» dans *Procréation artificielle, génétique et droit : Colloque de Lausanne des 29 et 30 novembre 1985*, Zurich, Publications de l'Institut suisse de droit comparé, 1986, 55.

Règles   Conférencier, «titre», Conférence, lieu, date.

Donner les initiales complètes du conférencier.

On peut omettre la mention de la fonction du conférencier; si ce renseignement est pertinent, il sera mentionné dans le texte.

On met le titre en évidence en le plaçant entre guillemets.

Si l'allocution n'est pas publiée, on ajoute la mention «non publié» entre crochets à la fin de la référence.

(b)   Sans titre

Exemple   P.E. Trudeau, Allocution, Conférence sur la réforme des institutions fédérales, Québec, 30 mars 1984.

Règles   Conférencier, Allocution, lieu, date.

On donne les initiales du conférencier au complet.

On peut omettre la fonction qu'occupe le conférencier.

On sépare le lieu et la date avec une virgule.

Si l'allocation n'est pas publiée, on ajoute la mention «non publié» entre crochets à la fin de la référence.

J.   THÈSES, LETTRES, ENTREVUES NON PUBLIÉES

Exemples   Lettre du Chef B. Diamond au Premier Ministre R. Lévesque, 30 novembre 1982.

J.-G. Cardinal, *Le droit de superficie*, thèse de doctorat en droit, Université de Montréal, 1957 [non publiée].

J.E.C. Brierley, *Bibliographical Guide to Canadian Legal Materials*, Faculté de droit, Université McGill, 1968 [non publié].

Règles

Manuscrits inédits :

Auteur, *titre*, diplôme pour lequel la thèse a été écrite, lieu, année [non publié].

Lettres et entrevues :

Lettre de X à Y [ou Entrevue avec X], date, localisation. On donne les initiales complètes de toutes les personnes mentionnées.

Par localisation, on entend par exemple : le lieu de l'entrevue ou «reproduit dans» auteur, *titre*, renseignements sur l'édition, numéro de page.

K. ARTICLES DE JOURNAUX

3

(a) Signés

Exemple

M. Adam, «Pour l'écrivain Jacques Renaud, la clause dérogatoire est une bombe à retardement» *La Presse [de Montréal]* **(12 septembre 1991) B3.**

Règles

Auteur(s), «titre» *journal* (jour mois année) page.

Inclure les initiales de l'auteur au complet. Le nom de l'auteur est suivi d'une virgule.

Le titre de l'article est placé entre guillements.

Le titre du journal se met en italique. Pour faciliter le repérage, on ajoute entre crochets toute indication géographique qui ne fait pas vraiment partie du titre du journal.

L'indication de la page doit aussi comprendre celle du cahier si les pages sont numérotées séparément dans chaque cahier.

Si l'article se trouve sur une seule page, il n'est pas nécessaire de répéter le numéro de la page pour une référence précise.

Indiquer le numéro de la colonne si cela peut être utile.

(b) Anonymes

Exemple

«Charter a Poor Safeguard to Citizens, Ex-Justice Says» *The [Toronto] Globe and Mail* **(13 février 1982) 11.**

Règles   «Titre» *journal* (jour mois année) page.
Les mêmes règles s'appliquent, sauf que l'auteur n'est pas mentionné.

(c)   Sans titre

Exemple   **B. Savoie, Lettre au Devoir, *Le Devoir [de Montréal]* (13 août 1985) 6.**

Règles   Auteur(s), description de l'extrait auquel on fait référence, *journal* (jour mois année) page.
On donne les initiales au complet.
On ne met pas la description de l'extrait entre guillemets.

L.   COMMUNIQUÉS DE PRESSE

Exemple   **Office national de l'énergie, Communiqué 91/30, «L'ONE délivre des permis d'exportation d'électricité à Ontario Hydro» (14 mai 1991).**

Règles   Organisme responsable, désignation du document et numéro, «titre» (date au complet).
La mention du titre est facultative.
Indiquer la désignation du document telle qu'elle apparaît sur le document («Communiqué», etc.).
Si possible, donner le numéro du document.

DOCUMENTS GOUVERNEMENTAUX CANADIENS

A. DÉBATS

Éléments

1. Indication géographique
2. Nom de l'assemblée législative
3. Titre
4. Numéro (s'il y a lieu)
5. Date au complet
6. Page

Exemples   **Québec, Assemblée nationale, *Journal des débats* (27 août 1991) à la p. 9751.**
Journals of the House of Assembly of the Province of New Brunswick (20 février 1875) à la p. 19.
***Débats de la Chambre des communes* (14 juin 1991) à la p. 1741.**
***Débats du Sénat* (20 juillet 1988) à la p. 4057.**
Nouvelle-Écosse, House of Assembly, *Debates and Proceedings*, n° 85-29 (18 avril 1985) à la p. 1343.

Règles   L'indication géographique est suivie d'une virgule. Cet élément de la référence est omis au niveau fédéral (débats de la Chambre des communes et du Sénat) et si le

nom de la province ou du territoire se trouve déjà dans le nom de l'assemblée législative ou dans le titre des débats.

Indiquer le nom de l'assemblée législative, à moins qu'il ne soit déjà mentionné dans le titre.

Donner le titre, en italique, tel qu'il apparaît sur la page titre du document. Cet élément est suivi d'une virgule uniquement lorsqu'on fait mention du numéro du document.

Inclure le numéro du document, s'il y a lieu.

Placer la date complète entre parenthèses.

Toute référence précise se met à la fin de la référence introduite par l'expression «à la p.».

B. RAPPORTS PARLEMENTAIRES

1. SI LE RAPPORT EST PUBLIÉ COMME PARTIE D'UN OUVRAGE PRINCIPAL

(a) Débats

Exemple **Québec, Assemblée nationale, Commission permanente des transports, «Auditions de personnes et d'organismes en regard du transport en commun dans la région de Montréal» dans *Journal des débats : Commissions parlementaires* à la p. B-8397 (14 octobre 1982).**

Règles Suivre les règles relatives aux débats (voir la partie A ci-dessus) en tenant compte des points suivants :

Il faut intercaler deux éléments supplémentaires entre le nom de l'assemblée législative et le titre des débats, soit le nom de l'organisme responsable et le titre du rapport.

Le nom de l'organisme responsable, que l'on peut abréger s'il est trop long, est suivi d'une virgule.

Mettre le titre du rapport entre guillemets.

Le mot «dans» sert de pont entre le titre du rapport et le titre des débats.

(b) «Sessional Papers»

Exemple **Ontario, Legislative Assembly, «Report on Workmen's Compensation for Injuries» par J. Mavor dans *Sessional Papers* (1900) aux pp. 6-7.**

Règles   Indication géographique, nom de l'assemblée législative, «titre du rapport» dans *Sessional Papers* (date) référence précise.

L'indication géographique et le nom de l'assemblée législative sont suivis de virgules.

On met le titre du rapport entre guillemets, suivi de «dans».

L'année se met entre parenthèses.

Au choix de l'auteur, on peut ajouter le numéro du document et le nom de l'auteur.

Remarque   Les *Sessional Papers* se faisaient rares dès 1940.

2.   SI LE RAPPORT EST PUBLIÉ SÉPARÉMENT

On suit les règles établies ci-dessous pour les documents n'émanant pas directement d'un parlement.

C.   DOCUMENTS N'ÉMANANT PAS D'UN PARLEMENT

4

1.   MODÈLE DE BASE

Exemples   **Québec, Office de révision du Code civil, *Rapport sur le Code civil du Québec : Commentaires*, Québec, Éditeur officiel, 1978.**

Conseil de la radiodiffusion et des télécommunications canadiennes, *Rapport annuel : 1978-79*, Hull, Approvisionnements et services Canada, 1979 à la p. 24.

Règles   Indication géographique, organisme responsable, *titre du document*, lieu d'édition, éditeur, date complète, référence précise.

L'indication géographique est omise si elle est déjà mentionnée dans le titre.

Indiquer l'organisme responsable, à moins qu'il ne soit déjà mentionné dans le titre.

Dans la mesure où cela peut être utile, on donne les détails de la structure de l'organisme.

Mentionner le titre du rapport tel qu'il apparaît sur la page titre, y compris le sous-titre s'il est utile.

On ajoute des renseignements complets sur la publication en prenant soin de donner une date aussi précise que possible.

La référence précise est introduite par «à la p.».
D'autres éléments peuvent venir s'ajouter à ceux-ci, y
compris ceux qui sont énoncés dans les règles suivantes.

2. DOCUMENTS DE TRAVAIL, DOCUMENTS D'ÉTUDE, ETC.

Exemple   Canada, *Les subventions fédérales-provinciales et le pouvoir de dé-
penser du Parlement canadien* **(Document de travail sur la
Constitution)** (juin 1969).

Règle   Si une indication de la nature du document («Document
de travail», «Document d'étude», etc.) apparaît sur la
page titre, on mentionne cette indication entre parenthèses après le titre.

3. AUTEUR(S) INDIVIDUEL(S)

Exemple   Commission d'enquête sur la santé et le bien-être social,
*L'organisation et la réglementation des professions de la santé et du
bien-être au Québec* **par C.-A. Sheppard**, annexe 12, t. 1,
Québec, Éditeur officiel, mai 1970 à la p. 1.3.13.

Règle   Si une personne a assumé une part de responsabilité
dans la préparation du document, on mentionne son
nom après le titre et on l'introduit par le mot «par».

4. RENSEIGNEMENTS SUPPLÉMENTAIRES

Exemple   Québec, *Rapport de la Commission d'enquête Brossard sur l'affaire
Coffin*, vol. 1, Québec, Office d'information et de publi-
cité, 27 novembre 1964 **(Commissaire : R. Brossard)**.

Règle   On ajoute le nom du ministre, du président ou du commissaire à la fin de la référence comme renseignement
supplémentaire.

5. PARTIES D'UN OUVRAGE PRINCIPAL

(a)   Parties portant le même titre

Exemple   Canada, **Rapport de la Commission royale d'enquête
sur le bilinguisme et le biculturalisme,** livres 1, 2, Ottawa, Imprimeur de la Reine, 8 octobre 1967, 23 mai
1968 (Présidents : A. Laurendeau et A.D. Dunton).

Règles   Si un document portant un seul titre est divisé en plusieurs parties publiées séparément et que chaque partie porte le même titre, on donne toujours la référence en se conformant aux modèles ci-dessus, en ajoutant les éléments qui permettent de distinguer les différentes parties tels que le numéro de volume et la date.

Si le mot «Livre», «Book» ou «Cahier» apparaît sur la page titre du document, on le mentionne immédiatement après le titre.

(b)   Parties portant des titres différents

Exemples   ***Rapport de la Commission d'enquête sur la situation de la langue française et sur les droits linguistiques au Québec : La langue de travail***, livre 1, Québec, Éditeur officiel, 31 décembre 1972 aux pp. 155, 305 (Président : J.-D. Gendron); ***Rapport de la Commission d'enquête sur la situation de la langue française et sur les droits linguistiques au Québec : Les droits linguistiques***, livre 2, Québec, Éditeur officiel, 31 décembre 1972 aux pp. 33, 78 (Président : J.-D. Gendron).

Règle   Lorsqu'on fait référence à des parties d'un ouvrage principal portant des titres différents, on donne l'identification de chaque partie et on les sépare par un point-virgule.

6.   DOCUMENTS DE CONFÉRENCES INTERGOUVERNEMENTALES

Exemple   **Conférence fédérale-provinciale des Premiers ministres sur la Constitution, *Commentaires du Premier ministre John A. Buchanan sur les pêcheries et la réforme constitutionnelle*, Document n° 800-10/031, Ottawa, 5-6 février 1979.**

Règles   Organisme responsable, *titre*, Document n°, localisation, date au complet.

Mettre une virgule après le nom de l'organisme et après le titre.

Indiquer le lieu et la date après le numéro de document, en plaçant une virgule entre ces éléments.

5

ROYAUME-UNI

A. LÉGISLATION

1. LOIS

Exemples   ***Companies Act*** **(R.-U.), 1980, c. 22, art. 4.**
Finance Act 1981 **(R.-U.), 1981, c. 35, art. 2(1)(2).**

Règle   On fait référence aux lois du Royaume-Uni de la même
manière qu'aux lois canadiennes sauf en ce qui concerne
les points suivants :

(a) Ponctuation lorsque l'année fait partie du titre

Exemples   ***Covent Garden Market Act, 1961*** (R.-U.), 1961, c. 49.
Criminal Justice (Amendment) Act 1981 (R.-U.), 1981,
c. 27, art. 2(1).

Règles   Si la date est incluse dans le titre d'une loi adoptée avant
le 1er janvier 1963, elle est précédée d'une virgule.
Si la date est incluse dans le titre d'une loi adoptée après
le 1er janvier 1963, il n'y a pas de virgule qui précède
l'année.

(b)   **Place de l'indication «R.-U.»**

Exemple   *Sale of Goods Act 1979* **(R.-U.)**, 1979, c. 54, art. 4.
ET NON
Sale of Goods Act 1979, 1979, c. 54, art. 4, (R.-U.).

Règles   On met l'indication «R.-U.» entre parenthèses immédiatement après le titre.
Ne pas mettre de virgule après le titre. En mettre une après les parenthèses.

(c)   **Année du règne ou année civile**

Exemples   *Law of Property Act, 1925* (R.-U.), **15 & 16 Geo. 5**, c. 20.
Policyholders Protection Act 1975 (R.-U.), **1975**, c. 75.

Règles   On renvoie à l'année du règne pour toutes les lois adoptées avant le 1ᵉʳ janvier 1963.
On renvoie à l'année civile pour toutes les lois adoptées après le 1ᵉʳ janvier 1963.

2.   RÈGLEMENTS

Exemples   **S.I. 1980/726.**
***Fabrics (Misdescription) Regulations 1980*, S.I. 1980/958.**
***Iso-propyl Alcohol Regulations 1927*, S.R. & O. 1927/783.**

Règles   *Titre*, S.I. [ou S.R. & O.] année/nᵒ.
La mention du titre est facultative.
1948 à ce jour – L'abréviation de «Statutory Instruments» est «S.I.».
Avant 1948 – L'abréviation de «Statutory Rules & Orders» est «S.R. & O.».

B.   JURISPRUDENCE

INTRODUCTION

Exemples   ***Constantine* c. *Imperial Hotels Ltd*, [1944] 1 K.B. 693, [1944] 2 All E.R. 171.**
***John Summers & Sons* c. *Frost*, [1955] A.C. 740, [1955] 1 All E.R. 870 (H.L.).**

Règle   On fait référence à la jurisprudence du Royaume-Uni de la même façon qu'à la jurisprudence canadienne, en prenant note des points suivants :

1. RECUEILS ANGLAIS MODERNES

(a) Modèle de base

Exemples   *R. c. Brittain* (1971), [1972] 1 **Q.B.** 357, [1972] 2 **W.L.R.** 450, [1972] 1 **All E.R.** 353 (C.A.).

R. c. Bullock (1954), [1955] 1 **W.L.R.** 1, [1955] 1 **All E.R.** 15, 119 **J.P.** 65 (C.C.A.).

Règles   On fait référence à un recueil semi-officiel avant un recueil non officiel.

On fait référence aux «Law Reports» avant les «Weekly Law Reports».

On fait référence à un recueil général avant un recueil spécialisé.

On donne deux autres références parallèles si cela est possible.

L'usage de ces règles est laissé au choix de l'auteur.

(b) «Law Reports»

(i) Les cinq collections actuelles

Exemples   *Co-op. Committee on Japanese Canadians* c. *Canada (P.G.)* (1946), [1947] **A.C.** 87 (P.C.).

Re Robson (1915), [1916] 1 **Ch.** 116.

Hongkong Fir Shipping Co. c. *Kawasaki Kisen Kaisha Ltd.* (1961), [1962] 2 **Q.B.** 26 (C.A.).

E. & S. Ruben Ltd. c. *Faire Bros.* (1948), [1949] 1 **K.B.** 254.

Countess De Gasquet James c. *Duke of Mecklenburg-Schewerin*, [1914] **P.** 53.

Ansah c. *Ansah* (1976), [1977] **Fam.** 138 (C.A.).

Re Associated Transformer Manufacturers' Agreement (1961), **L.R. 2 R.P.** 295.

H.T.C. Ltd. c. *Price Commission*, [1976] **I.C.R.** 170 (C.A.).

Règles   On ajoute «Court of Appeal», dont l'abréviation est «C.A.», à la fin de chaque référence à une cause entendue devant cette cour parce que les décisions de cette cour ne sont pas publiées dans des recueils séparés. Les cinq collections des «Law Reports» de 1891 jusqu'à présent s'abrègent de la façon suivante :

Appeal Cases (arrêts de la Chambre des Lords et du Comité judiciaire du Conseil privé) : «A.C.».

Chancery (décisions de la «Chancery Division» et appels de ces décisions devant la Cour d'appel) : «Ch.».

Queen's (King's) Bench (décisions de la «Queen's Bench Division» et appels de ces décisions devant la Cour d'appel) : «Q.B.» ou «K.B.».

Family et *Probate* (décisions de la «Family Division» ou de la «Probate, Divorce and Admiralty Division» et appels de ces décisions et des décisions des «Ecclesiastical Courts») : «Fam.» (de 1972 jusqu'à ce jour) et «P.» (de 1891 à 1971).

Industrial Cases Reports : «I.C.R.» (de 1975 jusqu'à ce jour); *Industrial Court Reports* : «I.C.R.» (de 1972 à 1974); *Law Reports Restrictive Practices* : «L.R. R.P.» (de 1957 à 1972). Les trois recueils ci-dessus contiennent des jugements de la «National Industrial Relations Court» et de la «Restrictive Practices Court» et appels de ces décisions et des décisions de la «High Court» en matière de relations industrielles.

Indiquer le numéro de volume avant l'abréviation «R.P.» pour la jurisprudence qui se trouve dans les *Law Reports Restrictive Practices*.

(*ii*) «Law Reports» de 1875 à 1890

Exemples   *Derry* c. *Peek* (1889), 14 **App. Cas.** 337 (H.L.).
Boston Deep Sea Fishing and Ice Co. c. *Ansell* (1888), 39 **Ch.D.** 339, [1886-90] All E.R. Rep. 65 (C.A.).
R. c. *Keyn* (1876), 2 **Ex.D.** 63 (C.C.R.).
Heaven c. *Pender* (1883), 11 **Q.B.D.** 503 (C.A.).
Foulkes c. *Metropolitan District Railway Co.* (1879), 4 **C.P.D.** 267 (Div. Ct.), conf. par (1880), 5 **C.P.D.** 157 (C.A.).
The Moorcock (1889), 14 **P.D.** 64, [1886-90] All E.R. Rep. 530 (C.A.).

Règles   On ajoute «Division», dont l'abréviation est «D.» afin de faire la distinction entre les collections de recueils publiées entre 1875 et 1890 et les collections plus récentes de recueils portant le même nom.

On ajoute le numéro de volume du recueil parce que cette collection est numérotée consécutivement.

On fait référence aux collections des «Law Reports» de 1875 à 1890 en abrégeant leur titre de la façon suivante :

Appeal Cases (arrêts de la Chambre des Lords et du Comité judiciaire du Conseil privé) : «App. Cas.».

Chancery (décisions de la «Chancery Division» et appels de ces décisions) : «Ch.D.».

Exchequer (décisions de la «Exchequer Division» et appels des décisions des «Inferior Courts» devant les «Divisional Courts of Appeal») : «Ex.D.».

Queen's Bench (décisions de la «Queen's Bench Division» et appels de ces décisions et des «Crown Cases Reserved») : «Q.B.D.».

Common Pleas (décisions de la cour de «Common Pleas» et appels de ces décisions) : «C.P.D.».

Probate (décisions de la cour «Probate, Divorce, Admiralty and Ecclesiastical» et appels de ces décisions devant la Cour d'appel et le Conseil privé) : «P.D.».

5

(iii) «Law Reports» de 1865 à 1875

Exemples   *Evans* c. *Smallcombe* (1868), **L.R. 3 H.L.** 249.

Rowley c. *Rowley* (1866), **L.R. 1 Sc. & Div.** 63 (H.L.).

Dow c. *Black* (1875), **L.R. 6 P.C.** 272.

Alexander c. *Mills* (1870), **L.R. 6 Ch.** 124.

Wilkinson c. *Joughin* (1866), **L.R. 2 Eq.** 319.

Powell Duffryn Steam Coal Co. c. *Taff Vale Railway Co.* (1874), **L.R. 9 Ch. App.** 331.

Baylis c. *Lintott* (1873), **L.R. 8 C.P.** 345.

George c. *Skivington* (1869), **L.R. 5 Ex.** 1.

R. c. *Allen* (1872), **L.R. 1 C.C.R.** 367.

Cattle c. *Stockton Waterworks Co.* (1875), **L.R. 10 Q.B.** 453.

The American and The Syria (1874), **L.R. 4 A. & E.** 226, en appel **L.R. 6 P.C.** 127.

Hyde c. *Hyde* (1866), **L.R. 1 P. & D.** 130 (Ct. Div. & Matr.).

Règles   On ajoute l'abréviation «L.R.» pour «Law Reports» pour faire la distinction avec d'autres collections du même nom.

On fait référence aux collections des «Law Reports» de 1865 à 1875 en abrégeant leur titre de la façon suivante :

House of Lords (recueils intitulés «English and Irish Appeal Cases»; causes devant la Chambre des Lords) : «L.R. H.L.».

Scotch and Divorce (causes en droit écossais et appels des décisions de droit matrimonial devant la Chambre des Lords) : «L.R. Sc. & Div.».

Privy Council (causes devant le Comité judiciaire du Conseil privé) : «L.R. P.C.».

Chancery (causes entendues par la «Chancery») : «L.R. Ch.».

Equity (causes d'«Equity» devant le «Master of the Rolls» et le «Vice-Chancellor») : «L.R. Eq.».

Chancery Appeal Cases (appels devant la «Chancery» et décisions de la «Court of Appeal in Chancery») : «L.R. Ch. App.».

Common Pleas (causes devant la «Court of Common Pleas») : «L.R. C.P.».

Exchequer (causes devant la «Court of Exchequer») : «L.R. Ex.».

Crown Cases Reserved (décisions de la «Court for Crown Cases Reserved») : «L.R. C.C.R.».

Queen's Bench (causes devant la «Court of Queen's Bench») : «L.R. Q.B.».

Admiralty and Ecclesiastical (causes devant la «High Court of Admiralty» et les «Ecclesiastical Courts») : «L.R. A. & E.».

Probate & Divorce (causes devant les cours de «Probate» et de «Divorce») : «L.R. P. & D.».

2. LES «NOMINATE REPORTERS» (1537-1865)

(a) Modèle de base

Exemples   *Baglehole* c. *Walters* (1811), 3 **Camp.** 154, 170 E.R. 1338, [1803-13] All E.R. Rep. 500, 13 R.R. 778 (K.B.).

Ayre c. *Craven* (1834), 2 **Ad. & E.** 2, 4 **N. & M.** 220, 111 E.R. 1, 41 R.R. 359 (K.B.).

Règles   On fait d'abord référence au «nominate reporter», même s'il n'a pas été consulté, puis aux autres recueils, en abrégeant leur titre, dans l'ordre suivant :
English Reports : «E.R.».
All England Reports Reprints : «All E.R. Rep.».
All England Reports Reprints Extension : «All E.R. Rep. Ext.».
Revised Reports : «R.R.».

(b) Lorsqu'une décision se trouve dans plusieurs «nominate reporters»

Exemples   *Barnett* c. *Allen* (1858), 3 **H. & N.** 376, 1 **F. & F.** 125, 157 E.R. 516, 175 E.R. 655, 117 R.R. 736 (Ex. Dic.)
Christ's Hospital c. *Grainger* (1849), 1 **Mac. & G.** 460, 1 **H. & Tw.** 533, 41 E.R. 1343, 47 E.R. 1521, [1843-60] All E.R. Rep. 204, 84 R.R. 128 (Ch.).

Règle   On fait référence aux réimpressions parallèlement aux «nominate reporters».

3. LES «YEARBOOKS»

(a) Modèle de base

5

Exemples   **Waldon c. Marshall (1370), Y.B. Mich. 43 Edw. 3, pl. 38, fol. 33.**
Doige's Case (1422), Y.B. Trin. 20 Hen. 6, pl. 4, fol. 34.

Règles   Intitulé de la décision [si possible] (année de la décision d'après le calendrier grégorien), «Y.B.» trimestre année du règne, numéro du plaidoyer («plea»), numéro du feuillet («folio»).
L'abréviation de «Yearbook» est «Y.B.».
Indiquer le trimestre en l'abrégeant : «Michaelmas» (trimestre d'automne) : «Mich.»; «Hilary» (trimestre d'hiver) : «Hil.»; «Easter» (trimestre du printemps) «Pach.»;
«Trinity» (trimestre d'été) : «Trin.».
L'abréviation de «plea» est «pl.».
L'abréviation de «folio» est «fol.».

(b) **Réimpressions des «Yearbooks»**

Exemples   *Beauver* c. *Abbot of St Albans* (1312), Y.B. Mich. 6 Edw. 2,
reproduit dans (1921) **38** *Selden Society* **32.**
Jordan's Case (1528), Y.B. Mich. 19 Hen. 8, pl. 3, fol. 24,
trad. dans C.H.S. Fifoot, *History and Sources of the
Common Law : Tort and Contract*, Londres, Stevens,
1949 à la p. 353.

Règle   On fait référence à l'original tel qu'indiqué ci-dessus en
mentionnant autant d'éléments que possible, avant de
faire référence à la réimpression.

4.   JURISPRUDENCE ÉCOSSAISE

(a) **Modèle de base**

Exemples   **M'Lean c. Bell, [1932] Sess. Cas. 21, [1932] S.L.T. 286
(H.L.).**
**Urquhart c. Baxter & Sons (Contractors), [1961] Sess.
Cas. 149, [1961] S.L.T. 331 (Ct. Sess.).**
**Gray c. Caledonian Railway Co. (1911), [1912] Sess.
Cas. 339, [1912] S.L.T. 1 Reports 76 (Ct. Sess.).**

Règles   On fait référence au recueil semi-officiel (*Session Cases*)
avant le recueil général (*Scottish Law Times*) et ensuite à
tout recueil spécialisé.
La mention «Scot.» et/ou le nom du tribunal se mettent
entre parenthèses après la référence à la page si l'un ou
l'autre de ces renseignements ne se déduit pas du titre
du recueil.

(b) **Décisions dans les «Session Cases»**

Exemples   *A.E. Abrahams Ltd.* c. *Campbell* (1910), [1911] **Sess. Cas.
353 (Ct. Sess., Scot.).**
Thompson c. *Great North of Scotland Railway* (1899), 2 **F.** 22
(Ct. Just., Scot.).
Brownlie c. *Miller* (1880), 7 **R.** 66 **(H.L., Scot.).**
Fernie c. *Robertson* (1871), 9 **M.** 531 **(Ct. Sess., Scot.).**
Thompson c. *Fowler* (1859), 21 **D.** 265 **(Ct. Sess., Scot.).**
Ferrier c. *Graham's Trustees* (1828), 6 **S.** 818 **(Ct. Sess.,
Scot.).**

Règles On fait référence aux six séries de recueils des «Session Cases» en abrégeant le nom du rédacteur de la façon suivante :
1906 à ce jour – «Sess. Cas.».
1898 à 1906 – «Fraser» : «F.».
1873 à 1898 – «Rettie» : «R.».
1862 à 1873 – «MacPherson» : «M.».
1838 à 1862 – «Dunlop» : «D.».
1821 à 1838 – «Shaw» : «S.».

Indiquer le nom du tribunal parce que chaque volume est divisé en parties selon les tribunaux et que chaque partie est paginée séparément.

5. JURISPRUDENCE IRLANDAISE JUSQU'À 1924 ET D'IRLANDE DU NORD

Exemples ***Walker*** c. ***Glass***, [1979] N.I. 129 (Ch.D.).
Johnson c. ***Egan***, [1894] 2 I.R. 480 (Q.B.D.).
Hardman c. ***Maffett*** (1884), 13 L.R.Ir. 499 (Ch.D.).
Leclerc c. ***Greene*** (1870), I.R. 4 C.L. 388 (Ex.).

Règles On fait référence aux différents recueils en abrégeant leurs titres de la façon suivante :
Northern Ireland Law Reports (1924 jusqu'à ce jour) : «N.I.».
Irish Law Reports (1894 à 1924) : «I.R.».
Law Reports (Ireland) (1878 à 1893) : «L.R.Ir.».
Irish Reports Common Law Series (1867 à 1878) : «I.R. C.L.».
Irish Reports Equity Series (1867 à 1878) : «I.R. Eq.».
Irish Law Times Reports : «Ir. L.T.R.».
On fait référence à la jurisprudence irlandaise de la même façon qu'à la jurisprudence canadienne.
On fait référence à un recueil semi-officiel avant un recueil général et à un recueil général avant un recueil spécialisé.
La mention «Ir.» et/ou le nom du tribunal se mettent entre parenthèses après la référence à la page si l'un ou l'autre de ces renseignements ne se déduit pas du titre du recueil.

C. DOCUMENTATION GOUVERNEMENTALE

INTRODUCTION

Exemples R.-U., Standing Committee D, «Minutes of Procee-dings on the Contracts of Employment Bill» no 189 dans *Sessional Papers* (1962-63) vol. 4 à la p. 787.
R.-U., Law Revision Committee, «Fifth Interim Report (Statutes of Limitation)» Cmd 5334 dans *Sessional Papers* (1936-37) vol. 13 à la p. 37.

Règle On suit le modèle de base énoncé au chapitre 4 pour la documentation gouvernementale canadienne.

1. DÉBATS

(a) De 1803 jusqu'à ce jour

Exemples R.-U., H.C., *Parliamentary Debates*, 5e sér., vol. 362, col. 1177 (10 juillet 1940).
R.-U., H.L., *Parliamentary Debates*, 3e sér., vol. 185, col. 1011 à la col. 1018 (26 février 1867, Earl of Carnarvon).

Règles R.-U., organisme responsable, *Parliamentary Debates*, no sér., vol. no, col. no (date des débats, autre information pertinente).
L'abréviation de «Royaume-Uni» est «R.-U.».
L'abréviation de «House of Commons» est «H.C.».
L'abréviation de «House of Lords» est «H.L.».
On donne le titre comme étant *Parliamentary Debates* pour les six séries.
Mettre le numéro de la série immédiatement après le titre et les séparer par une virgule.
«Série» s'abrège «sér.» au singulier comme au pluriel.
Mettre le numéro de volume après le numéro de série avec une virgule entre les deux.
Indiquer le numéro de la colonne initiale.
«Col.» est l'abréviation de «colonne».
On donne la date complète des débats entre parenthèses.
La mention «à la col.» sert à indiquer une référence précise et on met le nom de l'orateur entre parenthèses après la date.

(b)   Débats d'avant 1803

Exemple   R.-U., H.C., *Parliamentary History of England*, vol. 12, col. 1357 (27 mai 1774).

Règles   On donne le titre comme étant *Parliamentary History of England*.

R.-U., organisme responsable, *Parliamentary History of England*, vol. n°, col. n° (date des débats).

2.   JOURNAUX

Exemples   R.-U., *Journals of the House of Commons*, vol. 185 à la p. 424 (3 juillet 1930).

R.-U., *Journals of the House of Lords*, vol. 118 à la p. 313 (24 juin 1886).

Règles   R.-U., *titre*, vol. n° à la p. (date complète).

On ne mentionne pas l'organisme responsable car il apparaît dans le titre.

Le titre – «*Journals of the House of Commons*» ou «*Journals of the House of Lords*» – est suivi d'une virgule.

3.   DOCUMENTS PARLEMENTAIRES

5

(a)   Les «Sessional Papers»

Exemples   R.-U., H.C., «Copy of the Reply of Mr Doyle to Miss Rye's Report on the Emigration of Pauper Children to Canada» n° 263 dans *Sessional Papers* (1877) vol. 71, 1.

R.-U., H.C., «Reports of the Commissioners Appointed to Inquire into the Grievances Complained of in Lower Canada» n° 50 dans *Sessional Papers* (1837) vol. 24, 1.

Règles   R.-U., organisme responsable (s'il n'est pas déjà mentionné dans le titre) «titre» n° dans *Sessional Papers* (date) vol. n°, première page du rapport (référence à une page précise à l'intérieur du document).

Mentionner le titre tel qu'il apparaît sur la page titre.

Mettre le numéro de session du document après le titre.

Une virgule sépare le numéro du volume de l'indication de la première page.

Toute référence précise renvoie à la pagination interne du document.

On fait référence aux *Sessional Papers* de la Chambre des communes à moins que le document n'apparaisse seulement dans les *Sessional Papers* de la Chambre des Lords.

(b)   Les «Command Papers»

Exemples   R.-U., H.L., «**Reports from Her Majesty's Representatives Abroad Showing the Earliest Age at Which Marriages Can Be Legally Solemnized in Each of the States of the Continent of Europe**» C. 1096 dans *Sessional Papers* (1874) vol. 28, 201.

R.-U., Law Revision Committee, «**Fifth Interim Report (Statutes of Limitation)**» Cmd 5334 dans *Sessional Papers* (1936-37) vol. 13, 37.

R.-U., H.C., «**Report of the Committee on the Law Relating to Rights of Light**» Cmnd 473 dans *Sessional Papers* (1957-58) vol. 17, 955 (Président : C.E. Harman).

Règles   Suivre le mode de référence établi pour les «Sessional Papers».

Le mot «Command» s'abrège de différentes façons selon l'époque :

1833 à 1869	1re série (1 – 4222)	– «c.»
1870 à 1899	2e série (1 – 9550)	– «C.»
1900 à 1918	3e série (1 – 9239)	– «Cd»
1919 à 1956	4e serie (1 – 9889)	– «Cmd»
1957 à ce jour	5e série (1 –)	– «Cmnd»

On peut ajouter le nom du président du comité entre parenthèses à la fin de la référence.

L'abréviation appropriée apparaît à la première page de chaque «command paper».

4.   DOCUMENTS N'ÉMANANT PAS DU PARLEMENT

Exemples   R.-U., Royal Commission on the Press, *Studies on the Press* (Working Paper No. 3) par O. Boyd-Barrett, C. Seymour-Ure & J. Turnstall, Londres, H.M.S.O.,

1978.

R.-U., Commission on the Constitution, *Research Papers 2 : Federalism in the United States, Canada and Australia* **par M.J.C. Vile, Londres, H.M.S.O., 1973.**

Règles R.-U., organisme responsable, *titre du document* par nom des personnes responsables, renseignements sur l'édition.

On donne le titre intégral tel qu'il apparaît à la page titre du document.

Si une personne a assumé une part de responsabilité dans la préparation du document, on mentionne son nom après le titre du document en l'introduisant par le mot «par».

On ajoute le lieu d'édition et le nom de l'éditeur commercial suivis d'une date aussi précise que possible.

5

6

FRANCE

A. LÉGISLATION

Modèle de base

Loi n° 91-593 du 25 juin 1991,	J.O., 27 juin 1991, 8271,	D.1991.Lég.276.
Titre	Journal officiel	Référence parallèle

6

Éléments

1. Titre
2. Référence au «Journal officiel de la République Française»
3. Références parallèles

1. TITRE

Exemples   **Loi n° 81-4 du 7 janvier 1981**, J.O., 8 janvier 1981, 192, Gaz. Pal. 1981. 1er sem. Lég.83.
Arrêté du 6 avril 1984 fixant le taux de la taxe intérieure de consommation sur les produits pétroliers dt assimilés, J.O., 10 avril 1984, 1107, D.1984.Lég.293.
Ordonnance n° 45-174 du 2 février 1945 relative à l'enfance délinquante, J.O., 9 février 1945, 652, D.1945.Lég.41.

Règles   Législation n° du jour mois année titre descriptif.

Le titre est écrit en italique.

Lorsque la législation a un numéro, l'indication du titre descriptif est facultative.

Lorsque la législation n'a pas de numéro, on indique le titre descriptif de la législation au complet après la date.

On n'abrège pas le nom de la législation.

Ne pas mettre de virgule entre le nom de la législation et le numéro.

Ne pas mettre de virgule entre la date et le numéro de la législation.

Mettre en majuscules seulement la première lettre du premier mot du titre et la première lettre de tout nom propre.

2.   JOURNAL OFFICIEL DE LA RÉPUBLIQUE FRANÇAISE

(a)   La publication régulière

Exemple   *Décret n° 84-854 du 21 septembre 1984*, **J.O., 23 septembre 1984, 2977**, D.1984.Lég.538.

Règles   La première référence renvoie toujours au «Journal officiel de la République Française», abrégé «J.O.».

Indiquer la date de publication au complet et la page.

Mettre une virgule après chaque partie de la référence.

(b)   Le numéro complémentaire

Exemple   *Décret du 5 décembre 1978 portant classement d'un site pittoresque*, **J.O., 6 décembre 1978 (N.C.), 9250**.

Règles   La mention «N.C.» (pour «numéro complémentaire») se met entre parenthèses après la date de publication.

Cette référence est suivie d'une virgule.

3.   RÉFÉRENCES PARALLÈLES

Exemples   *Décret n° 78-160 du 10 février 1978*, J.O., 14 février 1978, 719, **Gaz. Pal. 1978. 1er sem. Lég.185**.

Loi n° 68-978 du 12 novembre 1968, J.O., 13 novembre 1968, 10679, **D.1968.317**.

Règles   On fait référence aux recueils «Dalloz», «Sirey», «Gazette du Palais» et la «Semaine Juridique» de la même façon que lorsqu'on fait référence à la partie jurisprudence de ces recueils (voir la partie C ci-dessous).
Le «Recueil de législation Sirey» s'abrège «S.».

B. CODES

Exemples   **Art. 1713 C. civ.**
Art. 1382-1384 C.N.
Art. 49 C. proc. pén.

Règles   Le numéro de l'article précède l'abréviation du code.
Employer les abréviations suivantes :
Code civil . . . .**C. civ.**
Code civil des Français (1804) . . . . **C.N.**
Code pénal . . . . **C. pén.**
Nouveau Code de procédure civile . . . **N.C. proc. civ.**
Code de procédure pénale . . . . **C. proc. pén.**

C. JURISPRUDENCE

Modèle de base

Cass. com.,	30 juin 1953,	J.C.P.	1953	.	II	.	7811	(note R. Savatier).
Juridiction	Date	Recueil	Année		Partie		Page	Note

6

Éléments

1. Juridiction
2. Date de la décision
3. Intitulé de la décision (s'il y a lieu)
4. Abréviation du titre du recueil
5. Année de publication du recueil
6. Partie du recueil
7. Page et/ou numéro
8. Référence parallèle
9. Note, rapport ou conclusion (s'il y a lieu)

1. JURIDICTION

(a) Modèle de base

Exemples   **Cass. com.**, 27 février 1973, Bull. civ. 1973.IV.89, n°
105, J.C.P. 1973.II.17445 (note R. Savatier).
Lyon, 18 décembre 1952, D.1953.Jur.241.
Cass. civ. 2e, 5 juin 1971, Bull. civ. 1971.II.145, n° 203.
Trib. com. Seine, 16 avril 1953, Gaz. Pal. 1953. 2e sem.
Jur.121.

Règle   On indique le nom de la cour ou du tribunal qui a rendu
la décision et la date de la décision; une virgule sépare
les deux.

(b) Tribunaux de première instance

Exemples   **Trib. civ. Cholet**, 17 février 1954, D.1954.Jur.308.
Trib. gr. inst. Aix-en-Provence, 21 octobre 1982, Gaz.
Pal. 1983. 2e sem. Jur.623 (note H. Vray).
Trib. com. Paris, 27 avril 1983, Gaz. Pal. 1983. 2e sem.
Jur.375.
Trib. admin. Nantes, 27 novembre 1981, *Mme Robin*,
Rec. 1981.544.

Règles   Les noms des tribunaux s'abrègent comme suit :
«Tribunal civil» ou «Tribunal de première instance» (tri-
bunal civil de droit commun avant 1958) : «Trib. civ.».
«Tribunal de grande instance» (tribunal civil de droit
commun depuis 1958) : «Trib. gr. inst.».
«Justice de Paix» (tribunal civil de droit commun pour
les petites créances avant 1958) : «J.P.».
«Tribunal d'instance» (tribunal civil de droit commun
pour les petites créances depuis 1958) : «Trib. inst.».
«Tribunal commercial» : «Trib. com.».
«Tribunal administratif» : «Trib. admin.».
Indiquer le nom de la ville où siège le tribunal.

(c) Cour d'appel

Exemples   **Paris**, 3 mars 1976, D.1978.Jur.233 (note J. Massip).
Toulouse, 11 février 1977, D.1978.Jur.206 (note J. Mestre), J.C.P. 1978.II.18898 (note J.-P. Verschaeve).

Règles   Indiquer seulement le nom de la ville où siège la cour.
On omet le nom de la cour.

(d) Cour de cassation

Exemples   **Cass. civ.**, 3 janvier 1951, S.1952.I.58.
Cass. civ. 1re, 26 janvier 1983, Bull. civ. 1983.I.33, n° 38,
D.1983.Jur.436 (note J. Massip).
Cass. civ. 2e, 4 juin 1984, Bull. civ. 1984.II.73, n° 103.
Cass. civ. 3e, 11 mai 1976, Bull. civ. 1976.III.155, n° 199,
D.1978.Jur.269 (note J.-J. Taisne).
Cass. com., 27 février 1973, Bull. civ. 1973.IV.89, n°
105, J.C.P. 1973.II.17445 (note R. Savatier).
Cass. soc., 29 octobre 1980, Bull. civ. 1980.V.586, n°
796.
Cass. Req., 21 octobre 1925, D.P. 1926.I.9.
Cass. Ch. réun., 17 mars 1954, Bull. civ. 1954. Ch. réun.,
n° 2, D.1954.Jur.328.
Cass. Ass. plén., 15 avril 1983, Bull. civ. 1983. Ass.
plén., n° 4, D.1983.Jur.461 (note F. Derreda).
Cass. Ch. mixte, 23 mars 1973, Bull. civ. 1973. Ch.
mixte, n° 1.

Règles   Indiquer le nom abrégé de la cour et le nom abrégé de la
chambre qui a rendu la décision de la façon suivante :

«Chambre civile» : «civ. 1re», «civ. 2e » ou «civ. 3e » selon
qu'il s'agit d'une décision provenant de la première,
deuxième ou troisième chambre civile, depuis 1952.
«Chambre commerciale» : «com.».
«Chambre sociale» : «soc.».
«Chambre criminelle» : «crim.».
«Chambre des requêtes» : «Req.».
«Chambres réunies» (avant 1967) : «Ch. réun.».
«Assemblée plénière» (depuis 1967) : «Ass. plén.».
«Chambre mixte» : «Ch. mixte».

(e) Conseil d'État

Exemple   **Cons. d'État**, 15 octobre 1982, *Ministère de l'éducation nationale*, Rec. 1982.341.
Règle   On abrège «Conseil d'État» par «Cons. d'État».

2. DATE DE LA DÉCISION

Exemples   Bordeaux, **27 juin 1983**, Gaz. Pal. 1983. 2ᵉ sem. Jur.467
(note J.-P. Marchi).
Cass. civ., **2 décembre 1891**, D.1892.I.161 (note L. Sarrut), S.1892.I.92.

Règles   On indique au complet la date à laquelle la décision a été rendue.
Mettre une virgule après la date.

3. INTITULÉ DE LA DÉCISION

Exemples   Cass. civ. 3ᵉ, 28 novembre 1978, Bull. civ. 1978.III.275, nº 358.
Cons. d'État, 27 mai 1977, **Pagoaga Gallastegui**, Rec. 1977.244.
Cass. Ass. plén., 3 juin 1983, **C.P.A.M. de la Corrèze c. Garoux**, Bull. civ. 1983. Ass. plén., nº 6, Gaz. Pal. 1983. 2ᵉ sem. Jur.462.

Règles   En général, ne pas indiquer les noms des parties.
Cependant, lorsqu'on fait référence à une décision rendue par un tribunal administratif ou par le Conseil d'État, on indique le nom du demandeur.
Lorsqu'on fait référence à une décision inédite ou seulement résumée dans la partie «Sommaire» d'un recueil, on indique les noms des parties.
Il est laissé au choix de l'auteur d'indiquer les noms des parties si la décision est mieux connue sous cette dénomination, ou s'il risque d'y avoir confusion entre deux décisions rendues le même jour par le même tribunal. Le nom d'une ou des partie(s) est alors indiqué en italique, entre virgules, après la date de la décision.

4. RECUEIL

(a) Modèle de base

Exemples   Trib. gr. inst. Caen, 30 octobre 1962, **S.1963.Jur.152**.
Trib. admin. Dijon, *Commune de Saint-Denis-les-Sens*, 12 mai 1981, **Rec. 1981.527**.
Cass. com., 16 octobre 1973, **Bull. civ. 1973.IV.256, nº 285, J.C.P. 1974.II.17846**.

Règles	Indiquer le titre abrégé du recueil, l'année de publication, le numéro ou le titre abrégé de la partie et le numéro de page ou de décision.

On sépare ces éléments par des points.

On fait référence à un recueil officiel avant un recueil non officiel.

L'utilisation de références parallèles est facultative.

(b) Titre

Exemples

Cass. civ., 12 novembre 1884, **D.P.** 1885.I.357.

Anger, 9 juillet 1935, **D.H.** 1935.513.

Paris, 4 février 1941, **D.A.** 1941.Jur.216.

Cass. civ., 10 novembre 1942, **D.C.** 1943.Jur.21.

Trib. gr. inst. Basse-Terre, 26 octobre 1982, **D.**1983.Jur.92 (note J.-C. Groslière).

Trib. civ. Riom, 9 novembre 1950, **S.**1952.II.28.

Cons. d'État, 28 février 1964, *Ministère des Armées,* **A.J.D.A.** 1964.580.

Aix-en-Provence, 10 mai 1983, **Gaz. Pal.** 1983. 2e sem. Jur.620 (note C. Dureuil).

Cass. civ. 1re, 9 mars 1964, **Bull. civ.** 1964.I.105, no 139.

Cass. com., 30 juin 1953, **J.C.P.** 1953.II.7811 (note R. Savatier).

Trib. admin. Dijon, 12 mai 1981, *Commune de Saint-Denis-les-Sens,* **Rec.** 1981.527.

Cass. Req., 11 mars 1931, **Sem. Jur.** 1931.605.

Règles

On fait référence aux différents recueils de la façon suivante :

Recueil périodique et critique Dalloz (1845 à 1940) : «D.P.».

Recueil hebdomadaire Dalloz (1924 à 1940) : «D.H.».

Recueil analytique Dalloz (1941 à 1944) : «D.A.».

Recueil critique Dalloz (1941 à 1944) : «D.C.».

Recueil Dalloz et *Recueil Dalloz et Sirey* (1945 à aujourd'hui) : «D.».

Recueil Sirey (jusqu'en 1964) : «S.».

Gazette du Palais : «Gaz. Pal.».

Bulletin de la Cour de cassation, section civile : «Bull. civ.».

Semaine Juridique (1927 à 1936) : «Sem. Jur.».

Semaine Juridique (1937 à aujourd'hui) : «J.C.P.».

Recueil des décisions du Conseil d'État ou *Recueil Lebon* : «Rec.».

Actualité juridique de droit administratif : «A.J.D.A.».

5. ANNÉE DE PUBLICATION DU RECUEIL

Exemples Cass. civ. 1re, 19 janvier 1965, D.1965.Jur.389.
Cass. com., 31 mai 1949, Bull. civ. **1949**.II.502, n° 221.
Trib. admin. Dijon, *Commune de Saint-Denis-les-Sens*, 12 mai
1981, Rec. **1981**.527.
Rouen, 20 mars 1959, Gaz. Pal. **1959. 2e sem.** Jur. 117.

Règles On renvoie au volume en question en indiquant l'année
de sa publication après l'abréviation du titre du recueil.
Omettre le numéro de volume dans les cas exception-
nels où il y a plus d'un volume par année, soit pour le
«Recueil Dalloz» depuis 1972, le «Bulletin civil» et la
«Semaine Juridique» depuis 1968.
On indique le numéro de semestre après l'année de pu-
blication lorsqu'on réfère à la «Gazette du Palais».

6. PARTIE DU RECUEIL

Exemples Rouen, 28 novembre 1925, D.P. 1927.**II**.172 (note G. Le-
pargneur).
Cass. Req., 7 octobre 1940, D.H. 1940.**Jur**.180.
Poitiers, 9 février 1942, D.A. 1942.**Jur**.114.
Trib. civ. Seine, 13 juillet 1944, D.C. 1944.**Jur**.173 (note
H. Lalou).
Cass. Ass. plén., 15 avril 1983, D.1983.**Jur**.461 (note F.
Derrida).
Cass. civ., 12 novembre 1884, S.1886.I.149.
Trib. gr. inst. Caen, 30 octobre 1962, S.1963.**Jur**.152.
Cass. Req., 5 juin 1929, Gaz. Pal. 1929. 2e sem. **Jur**.433.
Cass. com., 2 mai 1984, Bull. civ. 1984.**IV**.123, n° 145.
Trib. Seine, 22 janvier 1930, Sem. Jur. 1930.**Jur**.578.
Trib. gr. inst. Nancy, 15 octobre 1976, J.C.P.
1977.**II**.18526 (note R. Lindon).
Cass. Ass. plén., 15 avril 1983, Bull. civ. 1973. **Ass.
plén.**, n° 4.

Règles On indique le numéro de la partie en chiffres romains
après l'année de publication chaque fois que les parties
sont numérotées dans le volume.
On indique l'abréviation du titre de la partie pour les
sections qui ne sont pas numérotées dans le volume.
Abréger les titres des sections de la façon suivante :
«Jur.» pour «Jurisprudence».

«Lég.» pour «Législation», «Lois et décrets», «Textes de lois», etc.
«Chron.» pour «Chroniques».
«Doctr.» pour «Doctrine».
«Somm.» pour «Sommaire».
«Inf.» pour «Informations rapides».
«Pan.» pour «Panorama de jurisprudence».
«Req.» pour «Chambre des requêtes».
«Ch. réun.» pour «Chambres réunies».
«Ass. plén.» pour «Assemblée plénière».
«Ch. mixte» pour «Chambre mixte».
La référence à la partie est précédée et suivie d'un point.

Exception   Lorsqu'on fait référence au «Recueil Lebon» ou à l'«Actualité juridique de droit administratif», on n'indique pas la partie.

7.   PAGE ET/OU NUMÉRO

Exemples   Cass. civ. 1re, 26 janvier 1983, Bull. civ. 1983.I.**33, n° 38**, D.1983.Jur.**436** (note J. Massip).
Cass. soc., 27 janvier 1939, J.C.P. 1940.**1393**.
Cass. Ch. mixte, 23 mars 1973, Bull. civ. 1973.
Ch. mixte, **n° 1**.
Cass. crim., 31 mars 1981, D.1983.Jur.**39 à la p. 40**.

Règles   On indique le numéro de page (ou le numéro de la décision lorsqu'on renvoie à la «Semaine Juridique») après l'indication de la partie (ou de l'année de publication). Lorsqu'on fait référence au «Bulletin de la Cour de cassation», on mentionne le numéro de page et le numéro de décision, séparés par une virgule.

Note   Vu le caractère concis de la plupart des jugements, les références précises ne sont guère employées. S'il faut en mettre une, elle se place toujours directement après le numéro de la première page, introduite par «à la p.».

8.   RÉFÉRENCE PARALLÈLE

Exemple   Cass. com., 16 octobre 1973, Bull. civ. 1973.IV.256, n° 285, **J.C.P. 1974.II.17846**.

6

Règles   On fait référence à un recueil officiel avant un recueil non officiel.

L'indication d'une ou de plusieurs références parallèles est laissée au choix de l'auteur.

9. NOTES, RAPPORTS ET CONCLUSIONS

Exemples   Cass. civ. 1re, 13 février 1985, J.C.P. 1985.II.20388 **(Concl. Gulphe)**, D.1985.Inf.403 **(note J. Penneau)**. Cass. com., 27 octobre 1970, Bull. civ. 1970.IV.249, no 285, J.C.P. 1971.II.16655 **(note P.L.)**.

Règles   À la fin de la référence, il importe de mentionner si la décision est suivie d'une note, d'un rapport ou d'une conclusion.

On écrit «note», «rapport» ou «concl.», suivi du nom de l'auteur, le tout entre parenthèses.

Note   Si on veut citer ou faire allusion à une annotation de ce genre, voir la règle D 2, ci-dessous.

D. DOCTRINE

INTRODUCTION

Exemples   **J. Mestres, «La pluralité d'obligés accessoires» (1981) 79 R.T.D.C. 1.**

P. Dubois, «La responsabilité civile des dirigeants de sociétés anonymes du secteur public» (1986) 8 Rev. soc. 47.

Règle   On fait référence à la doctrine française selon les règles énoncées au chapitre 3, Doctrine, en tenant compte des exceptions suivantes.

1. CHRONIQUES PUBLIÉES DANS LES RECUEILS GÉNÉRAUX

Exemples   **R. Savatier, «Les contrats de conseil professionnel en droit privé» D.1972.Chron.137, no 10.**

R. Meurisse, «Les interférences du rapport à fin d'égalité et du rapport à fin de réduction» S.1962.Chron.61.

M.P. Malinvaud, «La responsabilité civile du fabricant en droit français» Gaz. Pal. 2e sem. 1973. Chron.463, no 15 et s.

J. Robert, «L'avant-projet du Code pénal» J.C.P.
1976.I.281 à la p. 283.

Règles   On fait référence à l'auteur et au titre de la chronique
selon les règles énoncées au chapitre 3, Doctrine.

On fait référence aux recueils «Dalloz», «Sirey», «Gazette du Palais» et la «Semaine Juridique» de la même façon que lorsqu'on fait référence à la partie «jurisprudence» de ces recueils (voir la partie C ci-dessus).

Lorsqu'un volume contient deux parties appelées «Chroniques», l'une contenant des chroniques de jurisprudence et l'autre des chroniques de législation, on utilise les abréviations «Chron. jur.» et «Chron. lég.»

Les références précises renvoient soit au paragraphe (n°), soit à la page en question.

2. NOTES ACCOMPAGNANT LE TEXTE D'UNE DÉCISION

Exemples   **P. Jestaz, note sous Cass. civ. 3e, 23 mars 1968, D.1970.Jur.663 à la p. 665.**

M. Boitard et J.-C. Dubarry, note sous Paris, 15 mai 1975, J.C.P. 1976.II.18265.

Règles   Auteur, «note sous» nom du tribunal, date de la décision, titre abrégé du recueil.année.partie.page.

On fait référence à la décision sous laquelle se retrouve la note et au recueil de la même façon que lorsque l'on fait référence à la jurisprudence (voir, ci-dessus, la partie C, «Jurisprudence»).

Toute référence précise se met après le numéro de la première page de la note, introduite par l'expression «à la p.».

6

E. ENCYCLOPÉDIES

INTRODUCTION

Exemples   *Encyclopédie juridique Dalloz : Répertoire de droit civil*, 2e éd., «Astreintes», par J. Bauré.

Juris-classeur civil, art. 3, fasc. N, par P. Malaurie, n° 38.

Règles   *Titre du répertoire,* rang de l'édition [s'il y a lieu], identification de la rubrique, par Auteur de la rubrique, référence précise.

Ne pas donner de référence parallèle lorsqu'une même rubrique est publiée dans plus d'un répertoire du «Juris-classeur».

On fait référence au «Juris-classeur civil» de préférence à tout autre répertoire du «Juris-classeur».

1.   TITRE DU RÉPERTOIRE

Exemples   ***Juris-classeur commercial : Banque et crédit,*** vol. 2, fasc. 32, par J. Stoufflet, n° 1-5.
Juris-classeur civil, art. 1315 à 1316, par G. Wiederkehr.
Encyclopédie juridique Dalloz : Répertoire de droit civil, 2ᵉ éd., «Publicité foncière», par M. Donnier, n° 528.

Règles   *Titre du répertoire,* rang de l'édition [s'il y a lieu], identification de la rubrique, par Auteur de la rubrique, référence précise.

Indiquer le titre du répertoire au long.

Mettre le titre du répertoire en italique.

2.   EMPLOI DE L'EXPRESSION «CI-APRÈS»

Exemple   *Juris-classeur civil,* art. 1315 à 1316, par G. Wiederkehr [ci-après *J.-cl. civ.*].

Règles   Lorsqu'on veut réutiliser le nom d'une encyclopédie ultérieurement dans le texte, on utilise l'expression «ci-après» pour indiquer le nom abrégé de l'encyclopédie en question.

Les abréviations des principaux répertoires sont :
«J.-cl. civ.» pour «Juris-classeur civil».
«J.-cl. com.» pour «Juris-classeur commercial».
«J.-cl. com. : Banque et crédit» pour «Juris-classeur commercial : Banque et crédit».
«J.-cl. resp. civ.» pour «Juris-classeur responsabilité civile».
«J.-cl. civ. annexe» pour «Juris-classeur civil annexe».
«J.-cl. rép. not.» pour «Juris-classeur répertoire notarial».
«J.-cl. admin.» pour «Juris-classeur administratif».

«Rép. civ. Dalloz» pour «Encyclopédie juridique Dalloz : Répertoire de droit civil».

«Rép. com. Dalloz» pour le «Répertoire de droit commercial» de la même encyclopédie

«Rép. admin. Dalloz» pour le «Répertoire de droit administratif».

On met en italique le titre abrégé du répertoire.

3. RANG DE L'ÉDITION

Exemples   *Encyclopédie juridique Dalloz : Répertoire de droit civil*, **2ᵉ éd.**, «Publicité foncière», par M. Donnier.

Encyclopédie juridique Dalloz : Répertoire de droit commercial, **2ᵉ éd.**, «Ventes commerciales», par L. Bihl, nº 256 et s.

Règles   Lorsqu'il y a plus d'une édition, indiquer le rang de l'édition dans la formule abrégée indiquée au chapitre 3 du *Manuel*.

Indiquer le rang de l'édition après le titre du répertoire.

Lorsque le répertoire est publié sous forme de fascicules, on ne fait pas référence à la date de refonte du fascicule.

4. IDENTIFICATION DE LA RUBRIQUE

(a) Lorsque les rubriques sont classées par ordre alphabétique

Exemples   *Encyclopédie juridique Dalloz : Répertoire de droit international*, **«Propriété littéraire et artistique»**, par H. Desbois.

Juris-classeur civil annexes, **«Associations» fasc. 1-A**, par R. Brichet.

Règles   Indiquer le nom de la rubrique (mot-clé sous lequel se trouve la rubrique) entre guillemets.

Mettre en majuscule seulement la première lettre du premier mot.

On ajoute «fasc. nº» après le nom de la rubrique s'il y a un numéro de fascicule qui correspond à la rubrique.

(b) Lorsque les rubriques sont classées par les articles d'un code

Exemples   *Juris-classeur civil*, **app. art. 3, fasc. 4**, par Y. Luchaine.

Juris-classeur civil, **art. 1354 à 1356, fasc. A**, par R. Perrot.

Règles   On fait référence à la rubrique en indiquant l'article (ou les articles) sous lequel elle est classée, de la manière indiquée dans le répertoire, soit «art. nº», «app. art. nº» ou «art. nº à nº», etc.

On ajoute «fasc. nº» après le numéro de l'article s'il y a lieu.

(c) Lorsque les rubriques sont classées selon un plan méthodique

Exemples   *Juris-classeur commercial : Concurrence consommation,* **vol. 1, fasc. 360,** par V. Sélinsky.

Juris-classeur administratif, **vol. 6, fasc. 530,** par J. Dufau, nº 29-30.

Règles   On indique le numéro du volume où se trouve la rubrique.

Indiquer le numéro du fascicule après le numéro du volume.

Mettre une virgule entre le titre du répertoire et le volume.

Mettre une virgule entre le numéro du volume et le fascicule.

7

ÉTATS-UNIS

A. CONSTITUTIONS

Exemples   **U.S. Const. préambule.**
U.S. Const. art. IV, § 2, cl. 3.
U.S. Const. amend. XX, § 2.
La. Const. art. V, § 14.

Règles   Pour la constitution américaine, il faut employer l'abréviation «U.S. Const.».

Se servir aussi des abréviations suivantes : «art.» pour «article», «amend.» pour «amendement», «§» ou «sec.» pour «section» et «cl.» pour «clause».

Indiquer les numéros d'articles et d'amendements en chiffres romains majuscules, ceux des sections et des clauses en chiffres arabes.

Suivre les mêmes règles pour les constitutions des États, en abrégeant le nom de l'État.

B. LOIS

INTRODUCTION

Règle   Par ordre de préférence, on renvoie le lecteur aux sources suivantes :

1. Un code officiel. Pour les lois fédérales, il s'agit du *United States Code* (U.S.C.).

2. Un code non officiel. Au niveau fédéral, il y en a deux : le *United States Code Annotated* (U.S.C.A.) et le *United States Code Service* (U.S.C.S.).
3. Les recueils sessionnels («session laws»). Pour les lois fédérales, le recueil officiel est les *Statutes at Large*.
4. Une source secondaire. En matière de législation fédérale, il y a le *United States Code Congressional and Administrative News*.
5. Une édition à feuilles mobiles.

1.   LES CODES

Modèle de base

17 U.S.C. § 201(b) (1988).
Conn. Gen. Stat. Ann. § 38-376 (West 1987).

Éléments

(a)   Titre de la loi (exceptionnellement)
(b)   Partie du code
(c)   Titre abrégé du code
(d)   Article
(e)   Éditeur (codes non officiels seulement)
(f)   Année de publication

(a)   Titre de la loi (exceptionnellement)

Exemple   ***Deepwater Ports Act***, 33 U.S.C. § 1517(m)(4) (1988).
Règles   On omet d'ordinaire le titre original d'une loi qui a été intégrée dans un code. On le donne lorsque les circonstances l'exigent (si elle est bien connue sous ce titre, par exemple).
Le titre se met en italique.

(b)   Partie du code

Exemples   **15** U.S.C. § 4 (1988).
Pa. Stat. Ann. **tit. 63**, § 425.3 (Supp. 1986).

Règles   Un code peut se diviser en «titles», chapitres ou volumes. Il faut alors identifier la partie en question. Cette indication se place avant ou après le titre du code selon le mode de référence du code en question.

(c) Titre abrégé du code

Exemples   17 **U.S.C.** § 104 (1988).
            W. Va. Code § 30-3C-2 (1986).
Règles   Le titre du code s'abrège.
            On ne le met pas en italique.

(d) Article

Exemples   Utah Code Ann. § **58-12.43(8)** (1986).
            29 U.S.C. §§ **701-796** (1988).
Règles   Le symbole «§» («§§» au pluriel) désigne l'article. On peut aussi utiliser l'abréviation «art.» au singulier comme au pluriel.

(e) Éditeur

Exemples   Cal. Penal Code § 4500 (**West** 1982).
            S.C. Code Ann. § 40-71-10 (**Law. Co-op.** 1986).
Règles   Si le code n'est pas officiel, on mentionne le nom de l'éditeur entre parenthèses. Cela ne se fait pas pour un code officiel, par exemple le U.S.C.

(f) Année de publication

Exemples   21 U.S.C. § 34 (**1988**).
            Fla. Stat. Ann. § 448.075 (West **1981**).
            Wash. Rev. Code Ann. § 4.24.240 (**Supp. 1987**).
            28 U.S.C.A. § 991 (West **Supp. 1987**).
Règles   L'année se met entre parenthèses après le nom de l'éditeur. S'il s'agit de l'édition reliée, l'année en question est celle qui figure sur le dos du volume. S'il s'agit plutôt d'un supplément inséré dans une pochette, on indique l'année figurant sur la page titre du

supplément en la faisant précéder de la mention «Supp.».

2.   RECUEILS SESSIONNELS («SESSION LAWS»)

Modèle de base

Economic Recovery Tax Act of 1981, Pub. L. No. 97-34, 95 Stat. 172.
The Indian Child Welfare Act of 1978, Pub. L. No. 95-608, 92 Stat. 3069 (codifié tel qu'amendé au 25 U.S.C. §§ 1901-1963 (1988)).

Éléments

(a)   Titre de la loi
(b)   Numéro («public law number») ou chapitre de la loi
(c)   Volume
(d)   Titre abrégé du recueil
(e)   Page
(f)   Année
(g)   Article
(h)   Référence au code (facultatif)

(a)   Titre de la loi

> *Exemples*   ***Water Quality Act of 1987***, Pub. L. No. 100-4, 100 Stat. 7.
> **Act of Aug. 21, 1974**, ch. 85, 1974 N.J. Laws 385.
> *Règles*   Le titre de la loi se met en italique.
> Si elle n'en a pas, elle s'identifie par la date de promulgation («Act of ...»).
> Le titre est suivi d'une virgule.

(b)   Numéro («public law number») ou chapitre de la loi

> *Exemples*   *Employee Retirement Income Security Act*, **Pub. L. No. 93-406**, 88 Stat. 829 (1974) (codifié tel qu'amendé au 29 U.S.C. §§ 1001-1461 (1988)).
> *Federal Trademark Act*, **ch. 79-540**, 60 Stat. 427 (1946).
> *Règle*   L'indication du numéro suit le titre de la loi. Cette numérotation se fait tantôt au moyen d'un «public law number», tantôt sous forme de chapitre.

(c) Volume

Exemple   *Omnibus Budget Reconciliation Act of 1986*, Pub. L. No. 99-509, **100** Stat. 1874.

Règle   Mentionner le volume du recueil.

(d) Titre abrégé du recueil

Exemple   *The Deficit Reduction Act of 1984*, Pub. L. No. 98-369, 98 **Stat.** 494 (1984) (codifié tel qu'amendé au 26 U.S.C. §§ 1-9504 (1988)).

Règle   Le titre du recueil s'abrège. On écrit «Stat.» pour les *Statutes at Large* au niveau fédéral.

(e) Page

Exemple   *The Balanced Budget and Emergency Deficit Control Act of 1985*, Pub. L. No. 99-177, 99 Stat. **1037**.

Règle   Indiquer la première page de la loi.

(f) Année de publication

Exemples   *National Labor Relations Act*, ch. 372, 49 Stat. 449 **(1935)** (codifié tel qu'amendé au 29 U.S.C. §§ 151-169 (1988)). *National Environmental Policy Act of 1969*, Pub. L. No. 91-190, 83 Stat. 852 **(1970)**.

Règle   L'année se met entre parenthèses, si elle ne figure pas déjà dans le titre de la loi.

Note   L'année qui figure dans le titre d'une loi n'est pas nécessairement celle durant laquelle elle a été publiée; dans un tel cas, la mention de l'année de publication s'impose.

(g) Article

Exemple   *National Environmental Policy Act of 1969*, Pub. L. No. 91-190, § 102, 83 Stat. 852 à la p. 853 (1970).

Règle   Pour renvoyer à un article de la loi, on indique le numéro de celui-ci entre le numéro de la loi et la référence au recueil, ainsi que la page où se trouve l'article en question après le numéro de la première page.

(h) Référence au code (facultatif)

Exemple   *Health Insurance for the Aged and Disabled,* Pub. L. No. 89-97, 79 Stat. 290 (1965) **(codifé tel qu'amendé au 42 U.S.C. §§ 1395-1396(d) (1988), et dans diverses sections du 26 U.S.C. et du 45 U.S.C.).**

Règle   Si ces informations sont connues, on peut en faire mention entre parenthèses. Il arrive que les lois soient éparpillées dans plusieurs parties d'un code.

3. **LE *UNITED STATES CODE CONGRESSIONAL AND ADMINISTRATIVE NEWS***

Exemples   ***Persian Gulf Conflict Supplemental Authorization and Personnel Benefits Act of 1991,* Pub. L. No. 102-25, 1991 U.S.C.C.A.N. (105 Stat.) 75.**

    Act of March 22, 1991, Pub. L. No. 102-16, 1991 U.S.C.C.A.N. (105 Stat.) 48.

Règles   On mentionne le titre de la loi ou, s'il n'y en a pas, la date de promulgation.

    Sont également nécessaires le numéro, l'année et le titre abrégé du *United States Code Congressional and Administrative News* : «U.S.C.C.A.N.».

    Il convient d'indiquer aussi le volume et la page où la loi se trouvera plus tard dans les «*Statutes at Large*».

C. SOURCES QUASI-LÉGISLATIVES

Exemples   **U.C.C. § 6-109 (1991).**
    ***Uniform Partnership Act* § 23 (1969).**
    ***Restatement (Second) of Agency* § 78 (1957).**
    ***Restatement (Second) of Torts* § 599 (1976).**
    ***Restatement of Contracts* § 104 (1932).**

Règles   Dans le cas des codes et lois uniformes, ainsi que pour les *Restatements*, on donne le titre de la source suivi de l'article et, entre parenthèses, l'année d'adoption ou de promulgation, laquelle est souvent indiquée à la page titre.

    Le titre se met en italique, sauf s'il s'agit d'un code.

    Si plus d'un *Restatement* a été fait sur le sujet, il importe de préciser de quelle version il s'agit; cette indication se place entre parenthèses après le mot «*Restatement*».

D. JURISPRUDENCE

Modèle de base

Lojuk c. Quandt,	706	F.2d	1456	(7th Cir.	1983).
Intitulé	Volume	Recueil et série	Page	Tribunal	Année

Éléments

1. Intitulé de la décision
2. Volume
3. Recueil et série
4. Page
5. Référence précise
6. Tribunal
7. Année

1. INTITULÉ DE LA DÉCISION

Exemple **United States c. Nixon**, 418 U.S. 683 (1974).

Règles On met les noms des parties en italique.
Ne pas mettre le «c.» en italique.
L'intitulé est suivi d'une virgule.

2. VOLUME

Exemples *Jackson c. People's Republic of China*, **794** F.2d 1490 (11th Cir. 1986).
Marbury c. Madison, **5** U.S. **(1 Cranch)** 137 (1803).

Règles On mentionne le volume en question.
Avant 1875, les différents volumes des *U.S. Reports* portaient aussi une deuxième numérotation qui recommençait chaque fois que la direction du recueil changeait. Ce numéro ainsi que le nom du directeur se mettent entre parenthèses après «U.S.».

7

3.   RECUEIL ET SÉRIE

Exemples   *Henningsen* c. *Bloomfield Motors, Inc.*, 32 **N.J.** 358, 161 **A.2d** 69 (1960).
       Shaffer c. *Heitner*, 433 **U.S.** 186 (1977).
Règles   Le titre du recueil s'abrège.
       Il est suivi, le cas échéant, du numéro de la série.
       Les principaux recueils et leurs abréviations sont :

       United States Reports . . . . **U.S.**
       Supreme Court Reporter . . . . **S. Ct.**
       Lawyers' Edition . . . . **L. Ed.**
       Federal Reporter . . . . **F.**
       Federal Supplement . . . . **F. Supp.**
       Atlantic Reporter . . . . **A.**
       Pacific Reporter . . . . **P.**
       North Eastern Reporter . . . . **N.E.**
       North Western Reporter . . . . **N.W.**
       South Eastern Reporter . . . . **S.E.**
       South Western Reporter . . . . **S.W.**
       Southern Reporter . . . . **So.**
       New York Supplement . . . . **N.Y.S.**
       California Reporter . . . . **Cal. Rptr.**

4.   PAGE

Exemple   *Miranda* c. *Arizona*, 384 **U.S.** **436** (1966).
Règle   Indiquer la première page de l'arrêt.

5.   RÉFÉRENCE PRÉCISE

Exemples   *Morrissey* c. *Curran*, 567 F.2d 546 **à la p. 549** (2d Cir. 1977).
       South Carolina c. *Gathers*, 490 U.S. 805 **à la p. 824** (1989).
Règle   La référence précise se place après l'indication de la première page, introduite par «à la p.» ou «aux pp.».

6.   TRIBUNAL

Règle   On met le nom du tribunal entre parenthèses avant l'année en tenant compte des règles suivantes :

(a) Tribunaux fédéraux

(i) Cour suprême des États-Unis

Exemples *Burger King* c. *Rudzewicz*, 471 U.S. 462 (1985).
North Dakota c. *United States*, 58 U.S.L.W. 4574 (U.S. 21 mai 1990).

Règle La Cour suprême se passe de mention, la seule exception étant une référence au *United States Law Week* (U.S.L.W.), auquel cas la mention «U.S.» suffit pour indiquer la Cour suprême.

(ii) Les cours d'appel

Exemples *United States* c. *Dorsey*, 852 F.2d 1068 (**8th Cir.** 1988).
Naartex Consulting Corp. c. *Watt*, 722 F.2d 779 (**D.C. Cir.** 1983).

Règles La cour d'appel de chaque circuit s'identifie par le numéro du circuit («1st Cir.», «2d Cir.», «3d Cir.», «4th Cir.», etc.)
«D.C. Cir.» désigne la cour d'appel du circuit du District of Columbia, et «Fed. Cir.» celle du circuit fédéral.

(iii) Cours de district

Exemples *Jackson* c. *People's Republic of China*, 596 F. Supp. 386 (**N.D. Ala.** 1984).
Callahan c. *Scott Paper Co.*, 541 F. Supp. 550 (**E.D. Pa.** 1982).

Règle On mentionne le nom du district en abrégé.

(b) Tribunaux des États

Exemples *Sucher* c. *Sucher*, 416 N.W.2d 182 (**Minn. Ct. App.** 1987).
Kelly c. *Mississippi Valley Gas Co.*, 397 So. 2d 874 (**Miss.** 1981).
Nunes Turfgrass, Inc. c. *Vaughan-Jacklin Seed Co.*, 200 Cal. App. 3d 1518, 246 Cal. Rptr. 823 (**Ct. App.** 1988).
Chrysler Corp. c. *Wilson Plumbing Co.*, 132 Ga. App. 435, 208 S.E.2d 321 (1974).

7

Règles On doit indiquer l'État et la cour entre parenthèses.
Ne pas mettre le nom de l'État si celui-ci figure dans le
titre du recueil.
Ne pas mettre le nom de la cour s'il s'agit du plus haut
tribunal de l'État.
Omettre les deux si les deux règles ci-dessus s'appliquent.

7. ANNÉE

Exemples *Johnson* c. *Mobil Oil Corp.*, 415 F. Supp. 264 (E.D. Mich.
1976).
Upjohn Co. c. *United States*, 449 U.S. 383 (**1981**).

Règle L'année se met entre parenthèses après le nom de la
cour.

Pour plus de détails sur la référence juridique américaine, voir *The Bluebook : A Uniform System of Citation*, 15ᵉ éd., Cambridge, Harvard Law Review Association, 1991.

8

DOCUMENTATION INTERNATIONALE

A. TRAITÉS

Modèle de base

Charte des Nations Unies, 26 juin 1945, R.T. Can. 1945 n⁰ 7, 59 Stat. 1031, 145 U.K.F.S. 805, art. 2(7).

Convention européenne de sauvegarde des droits de l'homme et des libertés fondamentales, 4 novembre 1950, S.T.E. 5, 213 R.T.N.U. 221 [ci-après *Convention européenne des droits de l'homme*].

Charte de l'Organisation des États Américains (telle qu'amendée), 30 avril 1948, R.T. Can. 1990 n⁰ 23, 21 U.S.T. 607, T.I.A.S. n⁰ 6847 [ci-après *Charte de l'OÉA*] (en vigueur le 13 décembre 1951, signée par le Canada le 13 novembre 1989, en vigueur pour le Canada le 8 janvier 1990).

Échange de notes entre le Canada et la France concernant la construction, l'entretien et le fonctionnement d'une station de quarantaine pour bovins sur le territoire des Îles Saint-Pierre-et-Miquelon, 3 avril 1969, R.T. Can. 1969 n⁰ 10 [ci-après *Accord de l'Île Saint-Pierre*].

Éléments

1. Titre
2. Date
3. Noms des parties [s'il y a lieu]
4. Référence aux recueils de traités
5. Référence précise
6. Renseignements supplémentaires

1.   TITRE

Exemples   ***Accord entre le Canada et la Pologne sur l'encouragement et la protection réciproques des investis-
sements,*** 6 avril 1990, R.T. Can. 1990 n° 43 [ci-après *Accord sur la protection des investissements*].

***Traité entre le Canada et les États-Unis relatif à la
mise en valeur des ressources hydrauliques du bassin
du fleuve Columbia,*** 17 janvier 1961, R.T. Can. 1964 n°
2, 15 U.S.T. 1555, T.I.A.S. n° 5638, 542 R.T.N.U. 244 [ci-
après *Accord du fleuve Columbia*].

Règles   Indiquer le titre abrégé du traité, suivi d'une virgule.

Abréger les noms des signataires s'ils sont mentionnés
dans le titre de l'acccord afin de se conformer à l'usage
courant.

Retenir dans le titre les éléments essentiels qui permet-
tront d'identifier facilement le traité.

Mettre en majuscules la première lettre du premier mot
ainsi que la première lettre des noms propres.

À la fin de la référence, l'expression «ci-après» introduit
soit le titre abrégé officiel ou, s'il n'y en a pas, la forme
abrégée choisie par l'auteur, le tout entre crochets.

2.   DATE

Exemples   *Convention relative aux infractions et à certains autres actes surve-
nant à bord des aéronefs,* **14 septembre 1963,** R.T. Can. 1970
n° 5, 704 R.T.N.U. 219.

*Convention sur l'élimination de toutes les formes de discrimination à
l'égard des femmes,* **1er mars 1980,** R.T. Can. 1982 n° 31.

Règles   Indiquer la date complète à laquelle le traité fut signé ou
présenté pour signatures; dans le cas des traités bilaté-
raux, ne mentionner que la première date de signature.

3.   NOMS DES PARTIES (S'IL Y A LIEU)

Exemples   *Protocole d'accord en vue de promouvoir certains échanges de pro-
grammes de télévision à caractère culturel, scientifique, technique et
éducatif*, 15 janvier 1967, **France-Québec**, R.E.I.Q. nº 1.
Accord sur les dettes extérieures allemandes, 27 février 1953, **Canada et al.-Allemagne Fédérale**, R.T. Can. 1953 nº 2, 4
U.S.T. 443, T.I.A.S. nº 2792, 33 R.T.N.U. 4.

Règles   S'ils ne sont pas mentionnés dans le titre, les noms des
États signataires d'un traité bilatéral se placent après la
date, séparés par un trait d'union.

Les noms d'États ne s'abrègent pas, à l'exception de
l'«URSS». On peut cependant utiliser les formes brèves
reconnues par l'usage.

Les signataires d'un traité multilatéral peuvent être
mentionnés à la fin de la référence entre parenthèses
(voir la règle 6 ci-dessous).

4.   RÉFÉRENCE AUX RECUEILS DE TRAITÉS

Exemples   *Accord entre le Canada et les États-Unis relatif à la qualité de l'eau
dans les Grands Lacs*, 15 avril 1972, **R.T. Can. 1972 nº 12,
23 U.S.T. 301, 837 R.T.N.U. 213, T.I.A.S. nº 7312, 11
I.L.M. 694** [ci-après *Accord sur les Grands Lacs*].

*Acte général pour le règlement pacifique des différends
internationaux*, 26 septembre 1928, **R.T. Can. 1931 nº 4,
93 R.T.S.N. 343.**

*Convention de Vienne sur le droit des traités entre États et organisa-
tions internationales ou entre organisations internationales*, 20
mars 1986, **Doc. NU A/CONF.129/15 (1986), 5 DJI 314.**

*Convention des Nations Unies sur les contrats de vente internatio-
nale de marchandises*, 11 avril 1980, **Doc. NU A/
CONF.97/18 (1980), 7 DJI 133.**

Règle   Par ordre de préférence, on renvoie aux recueils officiels
suivants, s'il y a lieu : *Recueil des traités du Canada*, recueil
officiel de l'autre État (ou recueil des États pertinents),
série principale de traités internationaux (par exemple
«R.T.N.U.» ou «R.T.S.N.»), autre série de traités internationaux (par exemple «Con. T.S.» ou «Rec. G.T.F.») et
référence parallèle (par exemple «DJI»).

Une liste d'abréviations des séries de traités se trouve à
l'appendice 8.

8

Dans le cas d'une convention des Nations Unies qui n'est pas encore en vigueur, on renvoie au document de l'ONU dans lequel elle se trouve en fournissant, si possible, une référence parallèle.

5. RÉFÉRENCE PRÉCISE

Exemples   *Accord entre le Canada et le Pakistan relatif à la construction de la centrale nucléaire à Karachi*, 24 décembre 1965, R.T. Can. 1965 nº 26, 869 R.T.N.U. 203, **art. 3**.

Accord général sur les tarifs douaniers et le commerce, 30 octobre 1947, R.T. Can. 1947 nº 27, 55 R.T.N.U. 187, T.I.A.S. nº 1700, **art. 23**.

Convention internationale sur l'élimination de toutes les formes de discrimination raciale, 7 mars 1966, R.T. Can. 1970 nº 28, 660 R.T.N.U. 195, **art. 3**.

Règle   La référence précise à un article ou à un appendice se place après la mention du recueil.

6. RENSEIGNEMENTS SUPPLÉMENTAIRES

Exemples   *Pacte international relatif aux droits civils et politiques*, 19 décembre 1966, R.T. Can. 1976 nº 47, 999 R.T.N.U. 171, 6 I.L.M. 368 **(au 31 décembre 1989, ratifié par 89 États mais non par les États-Unis; en vigueur le 23 mars 1976)**.

Convention relative au statut des réfugiés, 28 juillet 1951, R.T. Can. 1969 nº 6, 189 R.T.N.U. 150 **(en vigueur pour le Canada le 2 septembre 1969)**.

Accord de libre-échange entre le Canada et les États-Unis d'Amérique, 22 décembre 1987, R.T. Can. 1989 nº 3, 7 DJI 209, art. 1806 [ci-après *Accord de libre-échange*] **(Partie A, Annexe à la *Loi de mise en oeuvre de l'Accord de libre-échange entre le Canada et les États-Unis d'Amérique*, S.C. 1988, c. 65)**.

Règles   On peut inclure des renseignements supplémentaires (la date d'entrée en vigueur, les noms des États ayant ou n'ayant pas signé le traité, les références aux sources autres que le traité, etc.) entre parenthèses à la fin de la référence.

B. JURISPRUDENCE

1. COUR INTERNATIONALE DE JUSTICE

(a) Jugements

Exemples   **Activités militaires et paramilitaires au Nicaragua et contre celui-ci (Nicaragua c. États-Unis), [1984] C.I.J. Rec. 392** [ci-après *Activités militaires et paramilitaires au Nicaragua*].
Compétences en matière de pêcheries (Royaume-Uni c. Islande), [1974] C.I.J. Rec. 3 à la p. 6.

Règles   *Intitulé de la décision (parties)*, [volume] abréviation du titre du recueil numéro de page référence précise, référence parallèle [s'il y a lieu] [ci-après...].
Indiquer l'intitulé tel qu'il est énoncé par la Cour; inclure les noms des États entre parenthèses après l'intitulé, suivis d'une virgule; les noms des parties sont séparés par un «c.», même si la Cour utilise une barre oblique («/»).
L'abréviation de *Cour internationale de justice : Recueil des arrêts, avis consultatifs et ordonnances* est «C.I.J. Rec.».

(b) Ordonnances et avis consultatifs

Exemples   **Demande de réformation du jugement n⁰ 333 du Tribunal administratif des Nations Unies, Ordonnance du 30 novembre 1984, [1984] C.I.J. Rec. 639 (Requête pour avis consultatif).**
Différend frontier, terrestre, insulaire et maritime (El Salvador c. Honduras), Ordonnance du 13 décembre 1989, [1989] C.I.J. Rec. 129.
Certaines terres à phosphates à Nauru, (Nauru c. Australie), Ordonnance du 18 juillet 1989, [1989] C.I.J. Rec. 12.

Règles   *Intitulé de la décision ou avis consultatif (parties [s'il y a lieu])*, Ordonnance du [date]/Avis consultatif, [volume] abréviation du titre du recueil numéro de page référence précise.
Suivre les règles de base relatives à la Cour, en tenant compte des exceptions suivantes :

8

Après le titre, indiquer s'il s'agit d'une ordonnance ou d'un avis consultatif; cette indication est précédée et suivie d'une virgule.

Lorsqu'il s'agit d'une ordonnance, on donne la date au complet.

On peut ajouter des renseignements supplémentaires entre parenthèses à la fin de la référence.

(c)   Plaidoiries

Exemples   ***Droit de passage sur territoire indien (Portugal c. Inde)*** vol. I, «Mémoire du Gouvernement de la République Portugaise», [1960] C.I.J. Mémoires 11.
Personnel diplomatique et consulaire des États-Unis à Téhéran, (États-Unis c. Iran), «Mémoire du gouvernement des États-Unis d'Amérique», [1981] C.I.J. Mémoires 123.

Règles   *Intitulé de la décision (parties* [s'il y a lieu]), «Titre» (date [s'il y a lieu]), [volume] abréviation du titre du recueil numéro de page.

Suivre les règles de base relatives à la Cour, en tenant compte des exceptions suivantes :

Mentionner le titre du document en question selon l'indication dans le recueil, suivi de la date entre parenthèses.

Lorsque les plaidoiries d'un jugement sont publiées en plusieurs volumes, le numéro du volume se place après le titre.

Renvoyer au recueil intitulé *Cour internationale de justice : Mémoires, plaidoiries et documents*, abrégé «C.I.J. Mémoires».

2.   COUR PERMANENTE DE JUSTICE INTERNATIONALE

(a)   Jugements

Exemples   ***Statut juridique du Groenland Oriental (Danemark c. Norvège)*** (1933), C.P.J.I. Sér. A/B, n⁰ 53.
Juridiction territoriale de la Commission internationale de l'Oder (Royaume-Uni c. Pologne) (1929), C.P.J.I. Sér. A, n⁰ 23 à la p. 3.

Règles   *Intitulé de la décision (parties)* (année de la décision), abréviation du titre du recueil indication de la série, numéro de la décision référence précise.

Suivre les règles de base relatives à la Cour internationale de justice, en tenant compte des exceptions suivantes :

L'année de la décision se met entre parenthèses, suivie d'une virgule.

Indiquer la série après l'abréviation du recueil.

Inclure le numéro de la décision après l'indication de la série, précédé d'une virgule.

La référence précise, s'il y a lieu, se place après le numéro de la décision.

Renvoyer aux sources suivantes : *Publications de la Cour permanente de justice internationale : Série A : Recueil des arrêts,* dont l'abréviation est «C.P.J.I. Sér. A»; *Série A/B : Arrêts, ordonnances et avis consultatifs,* qui s'abrège «C.P.J.I. Sér. A/B».

(b)   Ordonnances et avis consultatifs

Exemples   **Compagnie d'électricité de Sofia et de Bulgarie, Ordonnance du 5 décembre 1939, C.P.J.I. Sér. A/B, n⁰ 79 (Mesures conservatoires).**

Compétence des tribunaux de Dantzig, Avis consultatif (1928), C.P.J.I. Sér. B, n⁰ 15.

Règles   *Intitulé de la décision ou avis consultatif (parties* [s'il y a lieu]), Ordonnance du [date]/Avis consultatif, (année [s'il y a lieu]), abréviation du titre du recueil, indication de la série, numéro de la décision référence précise.

Suivre les règles de base relatives à la Cour, en tenant compte des exceptions suivantes :

Indiquer s'il s'agit d'une ordonnance ou d'un avis consultatif; cette indication est précédée d'une virgule.

On met la date au complet lorsqu'il s'agit d'une ordonnance.

Renvoyer aux sources suivantes : *Publications de la Cour permanente de justice internationale : Série A/B : Arrêts, ordonnances et avis consultatifs,* dont l'abréviation est «C.P.J.I. Sér. A/B», *Série B : Recueil des avis consultatifs,* dont l'abréviation est «C.P.J.I. Sér. B».

On peut inclure des renseignements supplémentaires entre parenthèses à la fin de la référence.

8

(c)   Plaidoiries

Exemple   ***Chemin de Fer Panevezys-Saldutiskis*, «Mémoire du gouvernement estonien» (1939), C.P.J.I. Sér. C, n⁰ 86, 11.**

Règles   *Intitulé de la décision*, «Titre du document» (année), abréviation du titre du recueil indication de la série, numéro de la collection, numéro de page.

Suivre les règles de base relatives à la Cour, en tenant compte des exceptions suivantes :

Mentionner le titre du document en question tel qu'il apparaît dans le recueil, suivi de la date complète entre parenthèses.

L'abréviation de *Série C : Plaidoiries, exposés oraux et documents* est «C.P.J.I. Sér. C».

L'indication du numéro de la collection, précédée et suivie d'une virgule, se place après la mention de la série.

3.   COUR EUROPÉENNE DES DROITS DE L'HOMME

(a)   Jugements

Exemples   ***Affaire Le Compte, van Leuven et de Meyere* (1981), Cour Eur. D.H. Sér. A, n⁰ 43 à la p. 8, 25 Ann. Conv. Eur. D.H. 26, (*sub nom. Le Compte and de Meyere* c. *Belgium*) 4 E.H.R.R. 1.**

***Affaire Dudgeon* (1981), Cour Eur. D.H. Sér. A, n⁰ 45, 24 Ann. Conv. Eur. D.H. 444, (*sub nom. Dudgeon* c. *Royaume-Uni*) 4 E.H.R.R. 149.**

Règles   *Intitulé de la décision* (année de la décision), Cour Eur. D.H. Sér. A, numéro de la décision référence précise, référence(s) parallèle(s).

Indiquer l'intitulé selon le premier recueil mentionné.

Utiliser l'abréviation «Cour Eur. D.H.» pour la Cour européenne des Droits de l'Homme.

La première référence doit renvoyer à la source officielle : *Publications de la Cour européenne des Droits de l'Homme : Série A : Arrêts et décisions* dont l'abréviation est «Cour Eur. D.H. Sér. A».

Si possible, inclure au moins une référence parallèle.

On renvoie à *l'Annuaire de la Convention européenne des Droits de l'Homme,* dont l'abréviation est «Ann. Conv. Eur. D.H.».

Une deuxième référence parallèle peut renvoyer aux *European Human Rights Reports,* dont l'abréviation est «E.H.R.R.».

(b)   Mémoires, plaidoiries et documents

Exemples   **Affaire Kjeldsen, Busk Madsen et Pedersen, «Mémoire du gouvernement danois sur le fond» (11 mars 1976), Cour Eur. D.H. Sér. B, n⁰ 21, 123 à la p. 124.**
Affaire Golder, «Compte rendu intégral des audiences publiques des 11 et 12 octobre 1974», Cour Eur. D.H. Sér. B, n⁰ 16, 161.

Règles   *Intitulé de la décision,* «Titre de document» (date [s'il y a lieu]), Cour Eur. D.H. Sér. B, numéro de la décision, numéro de page référence précise [s'il y a lieu].
On renvoie au document officiel : *Publications de la Cour européenne des Droits de l'Homme : Série B : Mémoires, plaidoiries et documents,* qui s'abrège «Cour Eur. D.H. Sér. B».
Indiquer la date complète entre parenthèses après le titre de la source si elle ne fait pas partie du titre du document.

4.   COMMISSION EUROPÉENNE DES DROITS DE L'HOMME

Exemples   **Br c. République fédérale d'Allemagne (n⁰ 6959/75) (1977), 10 Comm. Eur. D.H. D.R. 100 aux pp. 140-42, 21 Ann. Conv. Eur. D.H. 638, 3 E.H.R.R. 244.**
De Wilde, Ooms et Versyp c. Belgique (n⁰ˢ 2832/66, 2835/66 et 2899/66) (1967), 25 Comm. Eur. D.H. Rec. 47, 10 Ann. Conv. Eur. D.H. 421.

Règles   *Intitulé de la décision* (numéro de la décision) (année de la décision), volume abréviation du titre du recueil numéro de page référence précise, référence(s) parallèle(s).
On renvoie au document officiel de la Commission : *Décisions et rapports* (1975 jusqu'à ce jour), dont l'abréviation est «Comm. Eur. D.H. D.R.»; *Recueil de décisions de la Commission européenne des Droits de l'Homme* (1960-74), dont l'abréviation est «Comm. Eur. D.H. Rec.».

8

Si possible, fournir des références parallèles à l'*Annuaire de la Convention européenne des Droits de l'Homme* et aux *European Human Rights Reports*.

5.   COUR DE JUSTICE DES COMMUNAUTÉS EUROPÉENNES

Exemples   **Moser c. Land Baden-Wurttemberg (n⁰ 180/83),** [1984] C.J.C.E. Rec. 2539 à la p. 2541, [1984] 3 C.M.L.R. 720, [1983-85] C.M.R. 14,931.
Auer c. Ministère public (n⁰ 271/82), [1983] C.J.C.E. Rec. 2727, [1985] 1 C.M.L.R. 123, (sub nom. Auer c. Public Prosecutor) [1983-85] C.M.R. 14760.

Règles   *Intitulé de la décision* (numéro de la décision), [volume] abréviation du titre du recueil numéro de page référence précise, référence(s) parallèle(s).
On renvoie au recueil officiel de la Cour : *Recueil de la Jurisprudence de la Cour*, dont l'abréviation est «C.J.C.E. Rec.».
Si possible, fournir des références parallèles aux *Common Market Law Reports*, dont l'abréviation est «C.M.L.R.», ou au *Common Market Reporter*, qui s'abrège «C.M.R.».

6.   COUR INTERAMÉRICAINE DES DROITS DE L'HOMME

(a)   Jugements

Exemples   **Velásquez Rodríguez Case (Honduras) (1988), Cour Interam. D.H. Sér. C n⁰ 4, para. 149, Annual Report of the Inter-American Court of Human Rights : 1988, OEA/Ser.L/V/ III.19/doc.13 (1988) 35 à la p. 66, 28 I.L.M. 321.**
Godínez Cruz Case (Honduras) (1989), Cour Interam. D.H. Sér. C n⁰ 5, para. 197, Annual Report of the Inter-American Court of Human Rights : 1989, OEA/ Ser.L/V/ III.21/doc.14 (1989) 15 à la p. 58.

Règles   *Intitulé de la décision (État)* (année), Cour Interam. D.H. Sér. C numéro de la décision, référence précise au paragraphe, référence(s) parallèle(s).
S'il n'y a pas de version française, on fait référence à la version anglaise.
Mettre l'intitulé tel qu'il est énoncé dans la Série C.

«Cour interaméricaine des Droits de l'Homme» s'abrège «Cour Interam. D.H.».

L'abréviation de *Series C : Decisions and Judgments* est «Cour Interam. D.H. Sér. C».

Indiquer, s'il y a lieu, l'État qui est impliqué.

Fournir au moins une référence parallèle; si on renvoie au rapport annuel de la Cour comme référence parallèle, il faut suivre les règles relatives au rapport annuel de la Commission (voir la règle 7 ci-dessous).

(b) Avis consultatifs

Exemples **In the Matter of Viviana Callardo et al (*Costa Rica*) (1981), Cour Interam. D.H. Avis consultatif nº G. 101/81, Sér. A, *Annual Report of the Inter-American Court of Human Rights : 1981*, OEA/Ser.L/III.5/ doc.13 (1981) 13, 20 I.L.M. 1424.**

Compulsory Membership in an Association Prescribed by Law for the Practice of Journalism (*Arts. 13 and 29 American Convention on Human Rights) (sub nom. Costa Rican Law for the Practice of Journalism*) (*Costa Rica*) (1985), Cour Interam. D.H. Avis consultatif OC-5/85, Sér. A nº 5, para. 73, *Annual Report of the Inter-American Court of Human Rights : 1985*, OEA/Ser.L/V/ III.12/doc.13 (1985) 19 à la p. 42, 25 I.L.M. 142.

Habeas Corpus in Emergency Situations (1987), Cour Interam. D.H. Avis consultatif OC-8/87, Sér. A nº 8, para. 24, *Annual Report of the Inter-American Court of Human Rights : 1987*, OEA/Ser.L/V/III.17/ doc.13 (1987) 17 à la p. 24, 27 I.L.M. 519.

Règles *Intitulé de la décision (sub nom. [s'il y a lieu]) (État) (année),* Cour Interam. D.H. Avis consultatif numéro, Sér. A nº [s'il y a lieu], référence précise, référence(s) parallèle(s).

Indiquer l'intitulé selon *Series A : Judgments and Opinions*, dont l'abréviation est «Sér. A».

Suivre les règles relatives aux références parallèles énoncées plus haut (voir la règle 6 (a) sur les jugements, ci-dessus).

Mentionner l'État impliqué dans l'affaire, s'il y a lieu.

(c)   Mémoires, plaidoiries et documents

Exemples   *Restrictions to the Death Penalty [Arts. 4(2) and 4(4) American Convention on Human Rights]* (1983), «Verbatim Record of Public Hearing» (26 juillet 1983), Cour Interam. D.H. Avis consultatif OC-3/83, Sér. B n° 3 192 à la p. 203.

Proposed Amendments to the Naturalization Provisions of the Constitution of Costa Rica (1984), «Observations Received from the Supreme Electoral Tribunal of Costa Rica» (6 septembre 1983), Cour Interam. D.H. Avis consultatif OC-4/84, Sér. B n° 4 à la p. 21.

Règles   *Intitulé de la décision* (année), «Titre du document» (date [s'il y a lieu]), Cour Interam. D.H. Avis consultatif numéro, Sér. B numéro de la décision numéro de page référence précise.

Indiquer le titre tel qu'il apparaît dans la table des matières; on peut le modifier si cela est nécessaire.

La mention de la date complète s'impose, entre parenthèses, si elle ne figure pas dans le titre.

On doit également mentionner l'État s'il n'apparaît pas dans l'intitulé.

L'abréviation du document *Series B : Pleadings, Oral Arguments and Documents* est «Sér. B».

7.   COMMISSION INTERAMÉRICAINE DES DROITS DE L'HOMME

Exemples   *In the Matter of Viviana Gallardo and Others* (*Costa Rica*) (1983), Comm. Interam. D.H. Rés. n° 13/83, *Annual Report of the Inter-American Commission on Human Rights : 1982-1983*, OÉA/Ser.L/V/II.61/Doc.22 rev.1 (1983).

Case 9647 (*États-Unis*) (1987), Comm. Interam. D.H. Rés. n° 3/87, para. 46, *Annual Report of the Inter-American Commission on Human Rights : 1986-1987*, OÉA/ Ser.L/V/II.71/ Doc.9 rev.1 (1987) 147 à la p. 165.

Case 10.252 (*El Salvador*) (1989), Comm. Interam. D.H. Res. no 28/89, *Annual Report of the Inter-*

Règles

American Commission on Human Rights : 1989-1990,
OÉA/Ser.L/V/ II.77/Doc.7 rev.1 (1990).
Intitulé de la décision (État) (année), Comm. Interam. D.H.
numéro de la résolution, référence précise au paragra-
phe, *Annual Report of the Inter-American Commission on Human*
Rights, numéro du document (année du document) nu-
méro de page référence précise.
On fait référence au rapport annuel de la Commission :
inclure l'année ou les années mentionnées dans le titre,
introduites par un deux-points.
Indiquer l'intitulé tel qu'il apparaît au début de la résolution.
L'abréviation de «Commission interaméricaine des
Droits de l'Homme» est «Comm. Interam. D.H.».
«Résolution» s'abrège «Rés.».
Remarquer les différences entre les règles relatives aux
rapports annuels et celles qui s'appliquent aux documents de l'OÉA (voir la partie D, règle 4).

8.   **ACCORD GÉNÉRAL SUR LES TARIFS DOUANIERS ET LE**
COMMERCE (GATT) (GROUPES SPÉCIAUX)

Exemples

Subventions australiennes aux importations de sul-
fate d'ammonium (Chili c. Australie) (1950), GATT
Doc. CP.4/39, para. 12, 2 I.B.D.D. (1952) 204 à la p.
209.
Pratiques suivies par les Pays-Bas en matière d'impôt
sur le revenu (États-Unis c. Pays-Bas) (1976), GATT
Doc. L/4425, Supp. nº 23 I.B.D.D. (1977) 150.
CEE–Restrictions quantitatives à l'importation de
certains produits en provenance de Hong-Kong
(Royaume-Uni c. Communauté européenne) (1983),
GATT Doc. L/5511, para. 31, Supp. nº 23 I.B.D.D.
(1984) 135 à la p. 146.
États-Unis–Taxes sur le pétrole et certains produits
d'importation (Canada et al. c. États-Unis) (1987),
GATT Doc. L/6175, para. 3.1.4, Supp. nº 34 I.B.D.D.
(1988) 154 à la p. 159.
République de Corée–Restrictions à l'importation de
la viande de boeuf, plainte de la Nouvelle-Zélande
(Nouvelle-Zélande c. République de Corée) (1989)
GATT Doc. L/6505, Supp. nº 36 I.B.D.D. (1990) 260.

8

Règles   *Intitulé de la décision* (*parties*) (année), GATT numéro du document, référence précise au paragraphe [s'il y a lieu], numéro de volume I.B.D.D. (année) numéro de page référence précise, référence parallèle.

Les noms des parties se mettent entre parenthèses.

Inclure, s'il y a lieu, la référence précise au paragraphe directement après la référence au document.

On fait référence aux *Instruments de base et documents divers*, dont l'abréviation est «I.B.D.D.».

9.   ACCORD DE LIBRE-ÉCHANGE ENTRE LE CANADA ET LES ÉTATS-UNIS (GROUPES SPÉCIAUX)

Exemples   **Dans l'affaire de l'obligation du Canada en matière de débarquement du saumon et du hareng de la côte du Pacifique (1989), 2 T.C.T 7162 (Ch. 18 Groupe spéc.), 1 T.T.R. 237.**

Dans l'affaire des homards du Canada (1990), 3 T.C.T. 8182 (Ch. 18 Groupe spéc.), 2 T.T.R. 72.

Dans l'affaire des framboises rouges du Canada (1990), 3 T.C.T. 8175 (Ch. 19 Groupe spéc.), 2 T.T.R. 214.

Si la décision n'est pas publiée,

Dans l'affaire des homards du Canada (25 mai 1990), USA-89-1807-01 (Ch. 18 Groupe spéc.).

Dans l'affaire des nouveaux rails d'acier du Canada, à l'exception des rails légers (30 août 1990), USA-89-1904-08 (Ch. 19 Groupe spéc.).

Dans l'affaire du porc frais, frigorifié et congelé du Canada (14 juin 1991), ECC-91-1904-01 USA (Comité con. extr.).

Règles   *Intitulé de la décision* (année de la décision) volume T.C.T. numéro de page (Tribunal d'arbitrage), référence parallèle.

Si la décision n'a pas encore été publiée dans un recueil, *Intitulé de la décision* (date de la décision) numéro du dossier du Secrétariat (Tribunal d'arbitrage).

On fait référence au premier recueil.

Employer la mention «Ch. 18 Groupe spéc.» pour indiquer le «Groupe spécial» créé en vertu du chapitre 18, «Ch. 19 Groupe spéc.» pour désigner le «Groupe spécial» établi par le chapitre 19, et «Comité con. extr.» pour le

«Comité pour contestation extraordinaire» du chapitre 19.

C.   DOCUMENTS DES NATIONS UNIES

Dans les références aux documents des Nations Unies, se servir des abréviations suivantes :

Décision . . . . Déc.
Document . . . . .doc.
Document officiel . . . . Doc. off.
Extraordinaire . . . . .extra.
Miméographié . . . . miméo.
Numéro . . . . nº
Paragraphe . . . . para.
Plénière . . . . plén.
Recommandation . . . . Rec.
Régulier . . . . rég.
Résolution . . . . .Rés.
Session . . . . sess.
Spécial . . . . spéc.
Supplément . . . . .supp.
Urgence . . . . urg.

1.   DOCUMENTS OFFICIELS

(a)   Procès-verbaux/Comptes rendus des séances

Modèle de base

Doc. off. CCED CNUCED, 23ᵉ sess., 565ᵉ séance, nº 24, Doc. NU TD/ B/SR.565 (1981) [ci-après Doc. NU TD/B/SR.565].

Éléments

8

(*i*) Document officiel de l'organe de l'ONU
(*ii*) Session ou année
(*iii*) Séance
(*iv*) Numéro du document NU, (nº de vente) [facultatif]
(*v*) Année du document
(*vi*) Référence précise [facultative]
(*vii*) Documents provisoires

(*i*)   Document officiel de l'organe de l'ONU

Exemples   **Doc. off. AG NU C.1, 1ʳᵉ sess., 9ᵉ séance, Doc. NU A/ C.1/16 (1946).**

Doc. off. AG NU, 36ᵉ sess., 78ᵉ séance plén., Doc. NU A/36/PV.78 (1981).

Règles   On identifie le document officiel de l'organe de l'ONU, suivi d'une virgule.

Les abréviations des organes principaux sont les suivantes :

Assemblée générale . . . . **AG**
Bureau . . . . **Bur.**
Conférence des Nations Unies sur le commerce
    et le développement . . . . **CNUCED**
Conseil de sécurité . . . . **CS**
Conseil de tutelle . . . . **CT**
Conseil du commerce et du
    développement . . . . **CCED**
Conseil économique et social . . . . **CES**
Première Commission, Deuxième
    Commission, etc. . . . . **C.1, C.2, etc.**
Pour les abréviations des autres organes de l'ONU, voir le *Lexique général anglais-français*, Doc. NU ST/DCS/1/Rev.2 (1982) et le *Terminology Bulletin nᵒ 311/Rev.1*, Doc. NU ST/CS/SER.F/311/Rev.1 (1981).

Pour les organes de l'ONU qui n'ont ni acronyme ni abréviation officiels, on donne le nom au complet, suivi de «OR».

(*ii*) Session ou année

Exemples   Doc. off. CS NU, **4ᵉ année**, 426ᵉ séance (1949).

Doc. off. AG NU C.1, **1ʳᵉ sess.**, 9ᵉ séance, Doc. NU A/ C.1/16 (1946).

Doc. off. CT NU, **15ᵉ sess. extra.**, 1542ᵉ séance, Doc. NU T/PV.1542 (1982).

Règle   Indiquer le numéro de la session, l'année de l'organe de l'ONU ou l'année civile immédiatement après l'indication du document officiel, suivie d'une virgule.

(*iii*) Séance

Exemples Doc. off. CS NU, 4ᵉ année, **426ᵉ séance** (1949).
Doc. off. AG NU C.1, 1ʳᵉ sess., **9ᵉ séance**, Doc. NU A/
C.1/16 (1946).

Règles Le numéro de la séance se place après l'indication de la
session ou de l'année, suivi d'une virgule.
Si le document n'a ni session ni année, le numéro de la
séance se place après la mention du document officiel.

(*iv*) Numéro de document NU (nº de vente (facultatif))

Exemples Doc. off. CS NU, 4ᵉ année, 426ᵉ séance (1949).
Doc. off. AG NU C.1, 1ʳᵉ sess., 9ᵉ séance, **Doc. NU A/
C.1/16** (1946).

Règles Le numéro du document se met après le numéro de la
séance.
Lorsqu'un document porte deux numéros, on inclut les
deux, séparés par un trait d'union.
Le numéro de vente du document peut être inclus au
choix de l'auteur au moyen de la mention «nº de vente».
Le numéro de vente se met entre parenthèses après le
numéro du document.

(*v*) Année du document

Exemples Doc. off. CS NU, 4ᵉ année, 426ᵉ séance **(1949)**.
Doc. off. AG NU C.1, 1ʳᵉ sess., 9ᵉ séance, Doc. NU A/
C.1/16 **(1946)**.
Doc. off. CES NU, **1984**, 23ᵉ séance plén., Doc. NU
e/1984/SR.23.

Règles L'indication de l'année du document se place entre parenthèses après le numéro du document; elle est suivie
d'un point s'il n'y a pas de référence précise.
Si le volume du document est indiqué par l'année civile
plutôt que par la session ou par l'année de l'organe, on
omet la référence à l'année civile à la fin de la référence.
L'année en question est celle du document (souvent indiqué au-dessous du numéro) ou bien celle de l'événe-
ment, mais non celle de la publication du document.

8

(*vi*) Référence précise

Exemples	Doc. off. CCED CNUCED, 23e sess., 565e séance, Doc. NU TD/B/SR.565 (1981), **nº 24.**
	Doc. off. AG NU C.1, 1re sess., 9e séance, Doc. NU A/C.1/16 (1946) **à la p. 23.**
Règles	Mettre la référence précise après l'année du document ou, le cas échéant, après le numéro du document, suivie d'un point.
	On peut renvoyer soit aux pages soit aux paragraphes.

(*vii*) Documents provisoires

Exemple	Doc. off. CS NU, 2917e séance, Doc. NU S/PV.2917 (1990) **[provisoire]**
Règles	On fait référence à un document officiel avant un document provisoire.
	Lorsque le document officiel n'est pas disponible, on indique le caractère provisoire en incluant la mention «provisoire», entre crochets, après l'année.

(b) Suppléments

(*i*) Rapports

Exemple	***Rapport du Comité spécial des réfugiés et personnes déplacées*, Doc. off. CES NU, 2e sess., Supp. spéc. nº 1, à la p. 59, Doc. NU E/REF/75 (1946).**
Règles	Organe-auteur [s'il y a lieu], *titre*, document officiel de l'organe de l'ONU, session ou année, numéro de supplément, numéro de l'ONU (nº de vente [facultatif]) (année du document) référence précise [facultative].
	S'il y a lieu, on mentionne l'organe-auteur du document, suivi d'une virgule, s'il n'apparaît pas dans le titre.
	On peut abréger le titre, mais seulement d'une façon qui ne prête à aucune équivoque.
	La forme abrégée (introduite par l'expression «ci-après»), pour les fins des références ultérieures, peut être soit le numéro du document soit une forme abrégée du titre.

(*ii*) Résolutions et décisions

Exemples **Principes de base concernant le statut juridique des combattants qui luttent contre la domination coloniale et étrangère et les régimes racistes,** Rés. AG 3103 (XXVIII), Doc. off. AG NU, 28e sess., Supp. no 30, p. 152 (1973).

Pétition de M. Paul Wamba Kudililwa relative au Territoire sous tutelle du Tanganyika , Rés. CT 41(III), Doc. off. CT NU, 3e Sess., p. 5, Doc. NU T/215 (1948).

Transfert de ressources réelles aux pays en développement, Rés. CCED CNUCED 150 (XVI), Doc. off. CCED CNUCED, 16e sess., Supp. no 1, p. 1, Doc. NU TD/B/638 (1976).

Règles *Titre*, numéro de résolution/décision, document officiel et session ou année, numéro de supplément [s'il y a lieu], numéro de document NU (année du document) première page du document, référence précise.

Lorsque le document fait partie d'une collection qui est paginée de façon consécutive, indiquer la première page du document après l'année.

La forme abrégée (introduite par l'expression «ci-après»), pour les fins des références ultérieures, peut être soit le numéro du document soit une forme abrégée du titre.

(c) Annexes

Exemple **Projet de résolution,** Doc. off. AG NU, 39e sess., Annexes, Point 34, Doc. NU A/39/L.35 et Add.1 (1984).

Règles *Titre*, document officiel, session ou année, Annexe(s), Point no, numéro de document NU (ou no de vente [facultatif]) (année du document) référence précise.

L'identification de la série s'effectue au moyen de la mention «Annexe(s)», telle qu'elle apparaît sur la page titre du document, suivie d'une virgule et du numéro du point de l'ordre du jour, identifié par l'indication «Point».

8

2.   DOCUMENTS MIMÉOGRAPHIÉS

Exemples   NU CES, Commission des Droits de l'Homme, 24ᵉ
sess. *République-Unie de Tanzanie : Projet de résolu-*
tion revisé, Doc. NU E/CN.4/L.991/Rev.1 (février
1968) (miméo., Limité).

NU PNUD, Conseil d'administration, 28ᵉ sess., *Assis-*
tance complémentaire pour un projet mondial : pro-
gramme de recherche, de formation et de production
en vue de l'obtention de ma qualité nutritive, assorti
d'enquêtes au niveau des exploitations agricoles, Doc.
NU DP/PROJECTS/R.14/Add. 6 (mars 1981) (miméo., Restreint).

Règles   NU organe-auteur, session ou année [s'il y a lieu], *titre du*
document, numéro du document de l'ONU (date com-
plète) (miméo., renseignements sur la distribution [s'il y
a lieu]).

Si la version miméographiée est la seule disponible, on y
fait référence selon les règles relatives au document officiel correspondant.

On peut également inclure d'autres informations sur la
nature du document, *i.e.*, «Limité», «Restreint» ou «Pro-
visoire», en plus de «miméo.»

3.   PÉRIODIQUES ET ANNUAIRES

(a)   Périodiques

Exemple   «Emplois rémunérés dans les activités non agricoles»
(1989) 63 :9 *Bulletin mensuel de statistiques* 12 (Nations Unies, Département des affaires économiques et
sociales internationales) (Doc. NU ST/ESA/STAT/
SER.Q/201)

Règles   Les références aux périodiques de l'ONU se font de la
même manière qu'aux périodiques ordinaires selon les
règles énoncées au chapitre 3, avec les modifications
suivantes :

Le titre du périodique se met en italique.

Si possible, donner le nom de l'auteur, qu'il s'agisse d'un
organe ou d'un individu.

S'il n'est pas évident d'après le titre qu'il s'agit d'un périodique provenant de l'ONU, on met, à la fin de la réfé-

rence entre parenthèses, «Nations Unies» et le nom du département en question, séparés par une virgule.

Inclure le numéro du document entre parenthèses s'il est disponible.

Lorsqu'on cite une table de statistiques, on peut mentionner le titre de celle-ci.

(b) Annuaires

Exemple **Annuaire statistique du commerce international 1987, vol. II, New York : Nations Unies, Département des affaires économiques et sociales internationales, Bureau de statistique, 1989 à la p. 683 (Doc. NU ST/ ESA/STAT/ SER.G/36/Add.1, n° de vente E/ F.89.XVII.2, Vol.II)**

Règles Les références aux articles d'annuaires se font selon les règles relatives aux ouvrages collectifs énoncées au chapitre 3, en omettant le nom de l'auteur et/ou celui de l'éditeur intellectuel si ces informations ne sont pas connues.

S'il y a lieu, inclure le numéro du document et le numéro de vente entre parenthèses.

4. PUBLICATIONS DE VENTE

Exemple **CNUCED, *Manuel de statistiques du commerce international et du développement, Supplément 1973*, New York, 1974 à la p. 18 (Doc. NU TD/Stat.5, n° de vente E/F.74.II.D.7)**

Règles Pour ce qui est des publications de vente, suivre les règles relatives aux monographies énoncées au chapitre 3, le nom de l'organe de l'ONU étant à la place de l'auteur. Là où les circonstances s'y prêtent, on inclut le numéro du document et le numéro de vente entre parenthèses.

8

D. DOCUMENTS D'AUTRES ORGANISATIONS INTERNATIONALES

Les abréviations suivantes sont employées dans les références aux documents d'autres organisations internationales :

Décision . . . . Déc.
Document . . . . .doc.
Document officiel . . . . Doc. off.
Extraordinaire . . . . .extra.
Miméographié . . . . miméo.
Numéro . . . . .nº
Paragraphe . . . . para.
Plénière . . . . plén.
Recommandation . . . . Rec.
Régulier . . . . rég.
Résolution . . . . .Rés.
Session . . . . sess.
Spécial . . . . spéc.
Supplément . . . . .supp.
Urgence . . . . urg.

1. COMMUNAUTÉ EUROPÉENNE

(a) Journal Officiel

Exemples   CE, *Niveaux maximaux admissibles de radioactivité,* J.O. Débats (1987) nº 2-356 à la p. 6.
CE, *Règlement (CEE) nº 1799/91 de la Commission du 25 juin 1991,* J.O. Législation (1991) nº L161 à la p. 5.
CE, *Règlement (CEE) nº 1396/82 du Conseil du 4 juin 1982,* J.O. Législation (1982) nº L155 à la p. 38.
CE, *Communication des décisions prises dans le cadre de diverses procédures d'adjudication dans le secteur agricole (produits laitiers),* J.O. Communications (1991) nº C165 à la p. 11.
CE, *Affaire T26/91 : Recours introduit le 14 mai 1991 contre la Commission des Communautés européennes par Imperial Chemical Industries plc (ICI),* J.O. Communications (1991) nº C165 à la p. 16.

Règles   CE, *Titre,* titre de la série (année) numéro du document référence précise.
Un titre long peut être abrégé.
Utiliser les abréviations suivantes : «J.O. Législation» pour *Journal Officiel des Communautés européennes : Législation;* «J.O. Communications» pour *Journal Officiel des Communautés européennes : Communications et Information,* et «J.O. Dé-

bats» pour *Journal Officiel des Communautés européennes : Débats du Parlement européen.*

(b) **Séries**

Exemples **CE, Centre européen pour le développement de la formation professionnelle,** *Situation de la formation professionnelle des jeunes étrangers en France,* **Série de document du CEDEFOP, Luxembourg : CE, 1986. CE, Commission,** *Qui prend soin des enfants de l'Europe?* **Série Objectif 92, Luxembourg : CE, 1989.**

Règle CE, organe-auteur, *titre du document,* titre de la série, information de publication.

(c) **Périodiques**

Exemples **CE,** *Commerce extérieur : Statistiques mensuelles (4-6, 1988),* **1988. CE,** *Conjoncture industrielle : Statistiques mensuelles (2-3, 1990)* **1990.**

Règles CE, *titre,* année.

S'il y a lieu, inclure entre parenthèses dans le titre la période de temps en question, telle qu'elle apparaît sur la page titre du document.

(d) **Publications générales**

Exemples **CE, Commission,** *La Communauté européenne, les organisations internationales et les accords multilatéraux,* **3ᵉ éd., Luxembourg : CE, 1983. CE, Commission,** *Les Droits du citoyen européen,* **Luxembourg : CE, 1990.**

Règle CE, organe-auteur, *titre,* renseignements sur la publication.

8

2. ACCORD GÉNÉRAL SUR LES TARIFS DOUANIERS ET LE COMMERCE (GATT)

(a) Décisions, recommandations, etc.

Exemples   *Liberté de contrat en matière d'assurance-transport,* GATT P.C. Rec. (27 mai 1959), 15e sess., Supp. no 8 I.B.D.D. (1960) 27.

Déclaration ministérielle (29 novembre 1982), 38e sess. à l'échelon ministériel, GATT Doc. L/5424, para. 6, Supp. no 29 I.B.D.D. (1983) 9 à la p. 11.

Accord relatif aux arrangements commerciaux préférentiels entre États membres de l'ANASE, GATT P.C. Déc., 35e sess., GATT Doc. L/4768, Supp. no 26 I.B.D.D. (1980) 246.

Uruguay–Surtaxes à l'importation : Prorogation du délai, GATT P.C. Déc. L/6207, 43e sess., Supp. no 34 I.B.D.D. (1988) 39.

Amélioration des règles et procédures de règlement des différends du GATT, GATT P.C. Déc. L/6489, 45e sess., Supp. no 36 I.B.D.D. (1990) 64.

Règles   *Titre de la décision/recommandation,* GATT P.C. décision/ recommandation, session ou séance, numéro du document du GATT, volume I.B.D.D. (année) première page du document.

Lorsque la décision ou la recommandation ne porte pas de numéro du GATT, indiquer la date complète entre parenthèses après la mention de l'organe du GATT en question.

Si possible, on renvoie aux suppléments des I.B.D.D. Employer les abréviations suivantes : «P.C.» pour «Parties contractantes à l'Accord général sur les tarifs douaniers et le commerce»; «I.B.D.D.» pour *Instruments de Base et documents divers.*

(b) Rapports

Exemples   GATT, Comité des concessions tarifaires, *Rapport présenté au Conseil le 7 novembre 1989,* GATT Doc. TAR/177, Supp. no 36 I.B.D.D. (1990) 48.

GATT, *Libéralisation des échanges commerciaux, protectionisme et interdépendance,* GATT Études sur

le commerce international, nº 5, Genève : GATT, 1977.

GATT, *Les relations commerciales en régime de changes flottants*, GATT Études sur le commerce international, nº 8, Genève : GATT, 1980.

GATT, *Les marchés internationaux de la viande : 1990/91* Genève : GATT, 1991.

Règles   GATT, organe-auteur [s'il y a lieu], *titre*, numéro du document du GATT, volume I.B.D.D. (année) première page du document.

Si possible, revoyer aux I.B.D.D. ou à leurs suppléments. Si le rapport n'a pas de numéro ou s'il est publié comme monographie, la référence se fait selon les règles relatives à la doctrine :

Organe-auteur, *titre*, renseignements sur l'édition.

3. ORGANISATION DE COOPÉRATION ET DE DÉVELOPPEMENT ÉCONOMIQUES

(a) Séries

Exemples   OCDE, *Politiques nationales de la science et de la technologie : Suède*, OCDE Série des examens des politiques scientifiques et technologiques nationales, Paris : OCDE, 1987.

OCDE, *Les Services reposant sur les réseaux de télécommunications : Conséquences pour la politique*, OCDE Série des politiques d'information, d'informatique et de communication nº 18, Paris : OCDE, 1989.

OCDE, Centre de développement, *Changements sociaux et productivité agricole en Afrique centrale*, OCDE Études du Centre de développement, Paris : OCDE, 1986.

Documents de travail :

OCDE, *Mécanismes de transmission et effets macro-économiques de la politique monétaire en France : Les principaux enseignements économiques*, Document de travail nº 33, mars 1986.

Règles   OCDE, organe-auteur [s'il y a lieu], *titre*, titre de la série numéro [s'il y a lieu], renseignements sur l'édition.

Ne pas mettre le titre de la série en italique.

Documents de travail :

8

OCDE, organe-auteur [s'il y a lieu], *titre du document*, Document de travail, numéro du document [s'il y a lieu], mois année.

(b)   Périodiques et publications annuelles

Exemples   OCDE, *Statistiques mensuelles du commerce extérieur, Série A*, mars 1985.
OCDE, *Commerce extérieur par produits : Série C, 1985, Vol. 2 : Importations*, 1987.
OCDE, *Comptes financiers des pays de l'OCDE*, 1988.
OCDE, *Statistiques financières mensuelles*, mai 1991.

Règles   OCDE, *titre*, année.
Donner le titre complet du périodique, y compris le numéro de série.
S'il y a lieu, indiquer les mois de la publication.

4.   ORGANISATION DES ÉTATS AMÉRICAINS

Modèle de base

OÉA, Assemblée générale, 14e sess. extra., *Protocole d'amendements de la Charte de l'Organisation des États américains*, Doc. off. OÉA/Ser.P/AG/doc.16 (XIV-E/85) rev. 1 (1986) à la p. 3.

Éléments

(a)   OÉA, Organe-auteur
(b)   Session ou séance [s'il y a lieu]
(c)   Titre
(d)   Désignation de Documents officiels avec numéro du document
(e)   Année du document
(f)   Référence précise

(a)   OÉA, Organe-auteur

Exemples   **OÉA, Assemblée générale, Commission préparatoire**, *Proposition d'ajustements du budget du fonds ordinaire présentée par le secrétariat général 1985*, Doc. off. OÉA/Ser.P/AG/CP/

doc.364/84 (1984).

OÉA, Conseil permanent, *Compte rendu analytique de la séance ordinaire du Conseil permanent tenue le 10 janvier 1990*, Doc. off. OÉA/Ser.G/CP/SA.803/90 (1990).

Règle   La mention «OÉA» identifie l'Organisation des États américains; elle est suivie d'une virgule ainsi que du nom de l'organe-auteur, s'il y a lieu, tel qu'il apparaît sur la page titre, lui aussi suivi d'une virgule.

(b)   Session ou séance

Exemple   OÉA, Réunion de consultation des ministres des Relations extérieures, **20ᵉ réunion**, *Note de la mission permanente d'Argentine transmettant le communiqué de presse émis par son gouvernement le 3 janvier 1987 en relation avec les Îles Malouines*, Doc. off. OÉA/Ser.F /II.20 /Doc.124/87 (1987).

Règle   S'il y a lieu, indiquer la session ou le numéro de la séance après l'organe-auteur, cette indication étant suivie d'une virgule.

(c)   Titre

Exemple   OÉA, Commission interaméricaine des Droits de l'Homme, ***Rapport sur l'oeuvre accomplie par la Commission interaméricaine des Droits de l'Homme au cours de la vingt-septième session***, Doc. off. OÉA/Ser.L/V/II.27/ doc. 42 rev. 1 (1972) à la p. 59.

Règle   Donner le titre tel qu'il apparaît sur la page titre du document, suivi d'une virgule.

(d)   Désignation de Documents officiels avec numéro du document

Exemple   OÉA, Conseil permanent, *Compte rendu analytique de la séance ordinaire du Conseil permanent tenue le 10 janvier 1990*, **Doc. off. OÉA/Ser.G/CP/SA.803/90** (1990).

Règles   Indiquer le numéro complet du document tel qu'il apparaît sur la page titre, précédé de «OR»; si le numéro est composé de plusieurs parties, on les sépare au moyen d'une barre oblique («/»).

8

(e)   Année du document

Exemple   OÉA, Réunion de Consultation des ministres des Relations extérieures, 12ᵉ réunion, *Projet de résolution présenté par la Délégation du Vénézuela,* Doc. Off. OÉA/Ser.F/II.12/Doc. 56 **(1967).**

Règle   On mentionne entre parenthèses l'année du document telle qu'elle apparaît sur la page titre, suivie d'un point s'il n'y a pas de référence précise.

(f)   Référence précise

Exemple   OÉA, Assemblée générale, 20ᵉ sess., *Exécution de la Résolution AG/Res.941 (XVIII-0/88) relative à la coopération entre l'Organisation des États américains et les Nations Unies,* Doc. off. OÉA/Ser/P/AG/ doc.2553/90 (1990) **à la p. 3.**

Règle   La référence précise se met après l'année, suivie d'un point.

5.   CONSEIL DE L'EUROPE

(a)   Comptes rendus sténographiques des débats

Exemple   **Conseil de l'Europe, A.P., 29ᵉ sess., Débats, vol. I (1977) à la p. 94**

Règles   Conseil de l'Europe A.P./A.C., numéro de session, Débats, volume (année) référence précise.

Utiliser les abréviations suivantes : «A.P.» pour «Assemblée parlementaire»; «A.C.» pour «Assemblée consultative»; «Débats» pour «Comptes rendus sténographiques des débats»; et «C.A.» pour «Consultative Assembly», dans le cas de documents publiés avant 1974.

(b)   Textes adoptés

Exemple   **Conseil de l'Europe, A.C., 21ᵉ sess., IIIᵉ partie, Textes adoptés, Rec. 585 (1970) à la p. 1.**

Règles   Conseil de l'Europe, A.P./A.C., numéro de session, partie de session, Textes adoptés, numéro de la recommandation, la résolution, l'avis ou la directive (année) titre descriptif [facultatif] référence précise.
La mention «Textes adoptés» renvoie aux *Textes adoptés par l'Assemblée.*

(c)   Documents de séance

Exemples   **Conseil de l'Europe, A.C., 21e sess., Documents, vol. I, Doc. 2573 (1969) à la p. 3.**
Conseil de l'Europe, A.P., 38e sess., *Déclaration écrite nº 150 relative à la protection du site archéologique de Pompéi* (1987), Documents, vol. VII, Doc. 5700, à la p. 1.

Règles   Conseil de l'Europe, P.A./C.A., numéro de session, *Titre* [facultatif] (année), Documents, volume, numéro de document, référence précise.
La mention «Documents» renvoie aux *Documents de séance.*

(d)   Ordres du jour et procès-verbaux

Exemple   **Conseil de l'Europe, A.C., 21e sess., IIe partie, Ordres, 10e séance (1969) à la p. 20.**

Règles   Conseil de l'Europe, A.P./A.C., numéro de session, partie de session, Ordres, numéro de séance (année) référence précise.
La mention «Ordres» renvoie aux *Ordres du jour et procès-verbaux.*

(e)   Documents en série

Exemples   **Conseil de l'Europe, *Réglementation législative et autoréglementation de la presse*, Dossiers sur les mass media nº 2, (Strasbourg, 1982) à la p. 26.**
Pour *Bulletin d'information sur les activités juridiques* :
Conseil de l'Europe, Comité des Ministres, Rec. nº R(81)1 (1980) 10 Bull. inf. 49.

Règles   Conseil de l'Europe, *titre du document*, titre de la série numéro du document dans la série (informations sur la publication) référence précise.
Pour *Bulletin d'information sur les activités juridiques* :

Conseil de l'Europe, Comité des Ministres, numéro de recommandation titre descriptif [s'il y a lieu] (année) numéro Bull. inf. première page du document référence précise.

La mention «Bull. inf.» renvoie au *Bulletin d'information sur les activités juridiques.*

APPENDICE 1

STATUT DES RECUEILS

A. CANADA

D'après la règle 8(a) du chapitre 2, les références aux recueils officiels et semi-officiels doivent précéder celles qui renvoient aux recueils non officiels. Les recueils officiels sont ceux qui sont publiés par l'Imprimeur de la Reine; les recueils semi-officiels sont publiés sous l'égide du barreau de la province ou du territoire en question. Tous les recueils qui ne sont pas mentionnés dans cet appendice sont non officiels.

Officiel   Recueils des arrêts de la Cour suprême du Canada [1970-à ce jour] . . . . R.C.S.

Officiel   Rapports judiciaires du Canada, Cour suprême du Canada [1963-69] . . . . R.C.S.

Officiel   Canada Law Reports, Supreme Court of Canada [1923-62] . . . . S.C.R.

Officiel   Canada Supreme Court Reports (1876-1922), vol. 1-64 . . . . S.C.R.

Officiel   Recueils des arrêts de la Cour fédérale [1971-à ce jour] . . . . .C.F.

Officiel   Rapports judiciaires du Canada, Cour de l'Échiquier du Canada [1963-70] . . . . R.C. de l'É.

Officiel   Canada Law Reports, Exchequer Court of Canada
[1923-62] . . . . .Ex. C.R.

Officiel   Reports of the Exchequer Court of Canada (1881-1922),
vol. 1-21 . . . . .Ex. C.R.

B. ALBERTA

Semi-officiel Alberta Reports (1976-à ce jour),
vol. 1-à ce jour . . . . A.R.

Non officiel Alberta Law Reports (2e) (1976-à ce jour), vol. 1-à ce
jour . . . . Alta. L.R. (2e)

Semi-officiel Alberta Law Reports (1907-32),
vol. 1-26 . . . . .Alta. L.R.

C. COLOMBIE-BRITANNIQUE

Non officiel British Columbia Law Reports (1976-à ce jour), vol. 1-à
ce jour . . . . .B.C.L.R.

Semi-officiel British Columbia Reports (1867-1947),
vol. 1-63 . . . . B.C.R.

D. MANITOBA

Non officiel Manitoba Reports (2e) (1979-à ce jour),
vol. 1-à ce jour . . . . .Man. R. (2e)

Semi-officiel Manitoba Reports (1883-1961), vol. 1-67 . . . .Man. R.

Non officiel Manitoba Law Reports [1875-83] . . . . Man. L.R.

E. NOUVEAU-BRUNSWICK

Semi-officiel Recueil du Nouveau-Brunswick (2e) (1984-à ce jour),
vol. 44-à ce jour . . . . .N.B.R. (2e)

Semi-officiel New Brunswick Reports (2e) (1968-83), vol. 1-43 . . .
. . . . .N.B.R. (2e)

Non officiel New Brunswick Reports (1825-1929),
vol. 1-54 . . . . .N.B.R.

F. NOUVELLE-ÉCOSSE

Semi-officiel Nova Scotia Reports (2e) (1969-à ce jour), vol. 1-à ce jour . . . . N.S.R. (2e)

Semi-officiel Nova Scotia Reports (1965-69), vol. 1-5 . . . . . N.S.R.

Non officiel Nova Scotia Reports (1834-1929), vol. 1-60 . . . . N.S.R.

G. ONTARIO

Non officiel Ontario Appeal Cases (1983-à ce jour), vol. 1-à ce jour . . . . O.A.C.

Semi-officiel Ontario Reports (2e) (1973-à ce jour), vol. 1-à ce jour . . . . O.R. (2e)

Semi-officiel Ontario Reports [1931-73] . . . . O.R.

Semi-officiel Ontario Law Reports (1900-31), vol. 1-66 . . . O.L.R.

Non officiel Ontario Reports (1882-1900), vol. 1-32 . . . . . . O.R.

Non officiel Ontario Appeal Reports (1876-1900), vol. 1-27 . . . . O.A.R.

Semi-officiel Ontario Weekly Notes . . . . O.W.N.

H. QUÉBEC

Semi-officiel Recueils de jurisprudence du Québec [1986-à ce jour] . . . . R.J.Q.

Semi-officiel Recueils de jurisprudence du Québec, Cour d'appel [1970-85] . . . . C.A.

Semi-officiel Recueils de jurisprudence du Québec, Cour du Banc de la Reine/du Roi [1942-69] . . . . B.R.

Semi-officiel Rapports judiciaires officiels de Québec, Cour du Banc de la Reine/du Roi (1892-1941), vol. 1-71 . . . . B.R.

Semi-officiel Recueils de jurisprudence du Québec, Cour supérieure [1967-85] . . . . C.S.

Semi-officiel Rapports judiciaires officiels de Québec, Cour supérieure [1942-66] ........................C.S.

Semi-officiel Rapports judiciaires officiels de Québec, Cour supérieure (1892-1941), vol. 1-79 ..............C.S.

Semi-officiel Recueils de jurisprudence du Québec, Cour provinciale, Cour des Sessions de la paix, Cour du bien-être social [1975-85] .... C.P./C.S.P./C.B.E.S.

I. SASKATCHEWAN

Non officiel Saskatchewan Reports (1979-à ce jour), vol. 1-à ce jour ....Sask. R.

Semi-officiel Saskatchewan Law Reports (1907-31), vol. 1-25 .... Sask. L.R.

J. TERRE-NEUVE ET ÎLE-DU-PRINCE-ÉDOUARD

Semi-officiel Newfoundland & Prince Edward Island Reports (1970-à ce jour), vol. 1-à ce jour .... Nfld. & P.E.I.R.

Non officiel Newfoundland Law Reports (1817-1946), vol. 1-15 .... Nfld. L.R.

K. TERRITOIRES DU NORD-OUEST

Semi-officiel Northwest Territories Reports [1983-à ce jour] ...................N.W.T.R.

Semi-officiel Territories Law Reports (1885-1907), vol. 1-7 ....Terr. L.R.

L. TERRITOIRE DU YUKON

Semi-officiel Yukon Reports .... Y.R.

APPENDICE 2

RECUEILS DE JURISPRUDENCE

APPEN-
DICES

Canadian Human Rights Reporter . . . . C.H.R.R.
Canadian Insurance Law Reporter . . . . .I.L.R.
Canadian Intellectual Property Reports . . . . C.I.P.R.
Canadian Labour Law Cases . . . . .C.L.L.C.
Canadian Labour Law Reporter .C.L.L.R.
Canadian Labour Relations Boards Reports . . . . .Can. L.R.B.R.
Canadian Native Law Cases . . . . C.N.L.C.
Canadian Native Law Reporter . . . . C.N.L.R.
Canadian Patent Reporter . . . . C.P.R.
Canadian Radio-television and Telecommunications
    Decision and Policy Statements . . . . C.R.T.
Canadian Railway Cases . . . . .C.R.C.
Canadian Railway and Transport Cases . . . . C.R.T.C.
Canadian Rights Reporter . . . . .C.R.R.
Canadian Transport Cases . . . . .C. Trans. C.
Carswell's Practice Cases . . . . C.P.C.
Causes en appel au Québec . . . . Q.A.C.
Charter of Rights Decisions . . . . .C.R.D.
Construction Law Reports . . . . C.L.R.
Criminal Reports . . . . C.R.
Décisions de la Commission des Affaires sociales . . . . C.A.S.
Décisions des Tribunaux du Bas-Canada (1851-1867) . . . Déc. B.-C.
Décisions et énoncés de pratique sur la
    radiodiffusion et les télécommunications canadiennes . . . R.T.C.
Dominion Law Reports . . . . D.L.R.
Dominion Tax Cases . . . . .D.T.C.
Eastern Law Reporter (1906-1914) . . . . E.L.R.
Estates and Trusts Reports . . . . E.T.R.
Exchequer Court of Canada Reports . . . . .Ex. C.R.
Family Law Reform Act Cases . . . . F.L.R.A.C.
Federal Court Reports (voir Canada Federal Court Reports)
Fox's Patent, Trademark, Design and
    Copyright Cases . . . . Fox Pat. C.
Immigration Appeal Cases . . . . I.A.C.
Jurisprudence Express . . . . J.E.
Labour Arbitration Cases . . . . L.A.C.
Land Compensation Reports . . . . L.C.R.
Lower Canada Reports (1851-1867) . . . . L.C. Rep.
Manitoba Reports . . . . .Man. R.
Maritime Provinces Reports . . . . .M.P.R.
Motor Vehicle Reports . . . . M.V.R.
Municipal and Planning Law Reports . . . . M.P.L.R.
National Reporter . . . . N.R.

New Brunswick Reports ..........................N.B.R.
Newfoundland & Prince Edward Island Reports ... Nfld. & P.E.I.R.
Newfoundland Reports ....Nfld. R.
Northwest Territories Reports ...................N.W.T.R.
Nova Scotia Reports ............................N.S.R.
Ontario Appeal Cases ..........................O.A.C.
Ontario Labour Relations Board Reports ..........O.L.R.B. Rep.
Ontario Law Reports ...........................O.L.R.
Ontario Municipal Board Reports .................O.M.B.R.
Ontario Reports ...............................O.R.
Ontario Weekly Notes ..........................O.W.N.
Ontario Weekly Reporter .......................O.W.R.
Personal Property Security Act Cases .............P.P.S.A.C.
Quebec Appeal Cases ..........................Q.A.C.
Quebec Practice Reports ....Que. P.R.
Rapports de pratique de Québec .................R.P. Qué.
Rapports judiciaires officiels de Québec :
    Cour du banc du roi (de la reine) ...............B.R.
Rapports judiciaires officiels de Québec :
    Cour supérieure ...........................C.S.
Real Property Reports .........................R.P.R.
Recueil de droit de la famille ...................R.D.F.
Recueil de droit fiscal québécois ................R.D.F.Q.
Recueils de jurisprudence de la Cour de l'Échiquier ....R.C. de l'É.
Recueils de jurisprudence du Québec (1986-à ce jour) ......R.J.Q.
Recueils de jurisprudence du Québec :
    Cour d'appel (1970-1985) .....................C.A.
Recueils de jurisprudence du Québec :
    Cour de Bien-être social (1975-1985) ..............C.B.E.S.
Recueils de jurisprudence du Québec :
    Cour provinciale (1975-1985) ...................C.P.
Recueils de jurisprudence du Québec :
    Cour des Sessions de la paix (1975-1985) ...........C.S.P.
Recueils de jurisprudence du Québec :
    Cour supérieure (1970-1985) ..................C.S.
Recueils de jurisprudence du Québec :
    Tribunal de la jeunesse (1975-1985) ..............T.J.
Recueils des arrêts de la Cour fédérale du Canada .........C.F.
Recueils des arrêts de la Cour suprême du Canada ........R.C.S.
Reports of Family Law .........................R.F.L.
Reports of Patent Cases .......................R.P.C.
Revue de droit du travail .......................R.D.T.
Revue de droit judiciaire ......................R.D.J.

APPEN-
DICES

Revue légale ....R.L.
Saskatchewan Reports ....Sask. R.
Sentences arbitrales de griefs ........................S.A.G.
Supreme Court Reports (voir Canada Supreme Court Reports)
Tariff Board Reports .... T.B.R.
Tax Appeal Board Cases Tax ........................A.B.C.
Tribunal du travail (Jurisprudence en droit du travail) ........T.T.
Upper Canada Common Pleas Reports (1850-1882) ...... U.C.C.P.
Upper Canada King's Bench Reports (1831-1844) .... U.C.K.B.
Upper Canada Queen's Bench Reports (1844-1882) ...... U.C.Q.B.
Weekly Digest of Civil Procedure .................W.D.C.P.
Western Labour Arbitration Cases .................W.L.A.C.
Western Law Reporter (1905-1916) .... W.L.R.
Western Weekly Reports ..........................W.W.R.
Yukon Reports .... Y.R.

A.C.W.S. ....All Canada Weekly Summaries
Admin. L.R. .... Administrative Law Reports
A.I.A. ....Affaires d'immigration en appel
Alta. L.R. ....Alberta Law Reports
A.R. .... Alberta Reports
A.P.R. .... Atlantic Provinces Reports
B.C.L.R. ....British Columbia Law Reports
B.C.L.R.B. Dec. ....British Columbia Labour
Relations Board Decisions
B.C.R. .... British Columbia Reports
B.L.R. .... Business Law Reports
B.R. .... Rapports judiciaires officiels de Québec :
Cour du banc du roi (de la reine)
Can. L.R.B.R. .... Canadian Labour Relations Board Reports
C.A. ....Recueils de jurisprudence du Québec :
Cour d'appel (1970-1985)
C.A.S. .... Décisions de la Commission des Affaires sociales
C.B.E.S. .. Recueils de jurisprudence du Québec : Cour de Bien-être
social (1975-1985)
C.B.R. ....Canadian Bankruptcy Reports
C.E.R. ....Canadian Customs and Excise Reports
C.C.C. .... Canadian Criminal Cases
C.C.E.L. ....Canadian Cases on Employment Law
C.C.L. .... Canadian Current Law
C.C.L.I. ....Canadian Cases on the Law of Insurance
C.C.L.R. ....Canadian Computer Law Reporter
C.C.L.T. ....Canadian Cases on the Law of Torts

C.E.B. & P.G.R. . . . . Canadian Employment Benefits
and Pension Guide Reports
C.E.L.R. . . . . Canadian Environmental Law Reports
C.F. . . . . Recueils des arrêts de la Cour fédérale du Canada
C.H.R.R. . . . . Canadian Human Rights Reporter
C.I.L.R. . . . . Canadian Insurance Law Reports
C.I.P.R. . . . . Canadian Intellectual Property Reports
C.L.L.C. . . . . Canadian Labour Law Cases
C.L.L.R. . . . . Canadian Labour Law Reports
C.L.R. . . . . Construction Law Reports
C.N.L.C. . . . . Canadian Native Law Cases
C.N.L.R. . . . . Canadian Native Law Reporter
C.P. . . . . Recueils de jurisprudence du Québec :
Cour provinciale (1975-1985)
C.P.C. . . . . Carswell's Practice Cases
C.P.R. . . . . Canadian Patent Reporter
C.R. . . . . Criminal Reports
C.R.C. . . . . Canadian Railway Cases
C.R.D. . . . . Charter of Rights Decisions
C.R.R. . . . . Canadian Rights Reporter
C.R.T. . . . . Canadian Radio-television and Telecommunications
Decisions and Policy Statements
C.R.T.C. . . . . Canadian Railway and Transport Cases
C.S. . . . . Recueils de jurisprudence du Québec : Cour supérieure
(1970-1985)
C.S. . . . . Rapports judiciaires officiels de Québec :
Cour supérieure
C.S.P. . . . . Recueils de jurisprudence du Québec :
Cour des Sessions de la paix (1975-1985)
C.T.C. . . . . Canada Tax Cases
C. Trans. C. . . . . Canadian Transport Cases
Déc. B.-C. . . . Décisions des Tribunaux du Bas-Canada (1851-1867)
D.L.R. . . . . Dominion Law Reports
D.T.C. . . . . Dominion Tax Cases
E.T.R. . . . . Estates and Trusts Reports
E.L.R. Eastern Law Reporter (1906-1914)
Ex. C.R. . . . . Exchequer Court of Canada Reports
F.C. . . . . Canada Federal Court Reports
F.L.R.A.C. . . . . Family Law Reform Act Cases
Fox Pat. C. . . . . Fox's Patent, Trademark, Design
and Copyright Cases
I.A.C. . . . . Immigration Appeal Cases
I.L.R. . . . . Canadian Insurance Law Reports

APPEN-
DICES

J.E. . . . . .Jurisprudence Express
L.A.C. . . . . Labour Arbitration Cases
L.C.R. . . . . Land Compensation Reports
L.C. Rep. . . . . Lower Canada Reports
Man. R. . . . . .Manitoba Reports
M.P.L.R. . . . . Municipal and Planning Law Reports
M.P.R. . . . . Maritime Provinces Reports
M.V.R. . . . . .Motor Vehicle Reports
N.B.R. . . . . New Brunswick Reports
Nfld. & P.E.I.R. . . . . Newfoundland & Prince Edward Island Reports
Nfld. R. . . . . .Newfoundland Reports
N.R. . . . . .National Reporter
N.S.R. . . . . .Nova Scotia Reports
N.W.T.R. Northwest Territories Reports
O.A.C. . . . . .Ontario Appeal Cases
O.L.R. . . . . Ontario Law Reports
O.L.R.B. Rep. . . . . Ontario Labour Relations Board Reports
O.M.B.R. . . . . Ontario Municipal Board Reports
O.R. . . . . .Ontario Reports
O.W.N. . . . . Ontario Weekly Notes
O.W.R. . . . . Ontario Weekly Reporter
P.P.S.A.C. . . . . .Personal Property Security Act Cases
Q.A.C. . . . . Quebec Appeal Cases/Causes en appel au Québec
Que. P.R. . . . . .Quebec Practice Reports
Que. Q.B. . . . . . . .Quebec Court of Queen's (King's) Bench Reports
R.C. de l'É. . . . . Recueils de jurisprudence de la Cour de l'Échiquier
R.C.S. . . . . Recueils des arrêts de la Cour suprême du Canada
R.D.F. . . . . Recueil de droit de la famille
R.D.F.Q. . . . . Recueil de droit fiscal québécois
R.D.J. . . . . .Revue de droit judiciaire
R.D.T. . . . . Revue de droit du travail
R.F.L. . . . . Reports of Family Law
R.J.Q. . . . . . . .Recueils de jurisprudence du Québec (1986-à ce jour)
R.L. . . . . Revue légale
R.P.C. . . . . Reports of Patent Cases
R.P. Qué. . . . . Rapports de Pratique de Québec
R.P.R. . . . . .Real Property Reports
R.T.C. . . . . Décisions et énoncés de pratique sur la
                  radiodiffusion et les télécommunications canadiennes
S.A.G. . . . . .Sentences arbitrales de griefs
Sask. R. . . . . Saskatchewan Reports
S.C.R. .Canada Supreme Court Reports
Tax A.B.C. . . . . .Tax Appeal Board Cases

T.B.R. . . . . .Tariff Board Reports

T.J. . . . . .Recueils de jurisprudence du Québec :
Tribunal de la jeunesse (1975-1985)

T.T. . . . . Tribunal du Travail (Jurisprudence en droit du travail)

U.C.C.P. . . . . . . .Upper Canada Common Pleas Reports (1850-1882)

U.C.K.B. . . . . Upper Canada King's Bench Reports (1831-1844)

U.C.Q.B. . . . . . .Upper Canada Queen's Bench Reports (1844-1882)

W.D.C.P. . . . . Weekly Digest of Civil Procedure

W.L.A.C. . . . . .Western Labour Arbitration Cases

W.L.R. . . . . Western Law Reporter (1905-1916)

W.W.R. . . . . Western Weekly Reports

Y.R. . . . . .Yukon Reports

APPENDICE 3

ABRÉVIATIONS GÉOGRAPHIQUES

Alberta . . . . Alta.
Bas-Canada . . . . .B.-C.
Colombie-Britannique . . . . B.C.
Canada . . . . C.
Haut-Canada . . . . U.C.
Île-du-Prince-Édouard . . . . .P.E.I.
Manitoba . . . . .Man.
Nouveau-Brunswick . . . . .N.-B
Nouvelle-Écosse . . . . N.S.
Ontario . . . . Ont.
Province du Canada . . . . Prov. Can.
Québec . . . . Qué.
Saskatchewan . . . . Sask.
Terre-Neuve . . . . Nfld.
Territoires du Nord-Ouest . . . . .T.N.-O.
Territoire du Yukon . . . . Y.

APPENDICE 4

JURIDICTIONS

Admiralty Court	Adm. Ct.
County Court	Co. Ct.
Circuit Court	Circ. Ct.
Cour canadienne de l'impôt	C.C.I.
Cour d'appel	C.A.
Cour de circuit	C. circ.
Cour de district	C. dist.
Cour de magistrat	C. mag.
Cour de révision	C. rév.
Cour de l'Échiquier	C. de l'É.
Cour des Sessions de la paix	C.S.P.
Cour divisionnaire	C. div.
Cour du Banc de la Reine (du Roi)	B.R.
Cour du Québec	C.Q.
Cour fédérale d'appel	C.F.A.
Cour fédérale, première instance	C.F. (1re inst.)
Cour municipale	C. mun.
Cour provinciale	C.P.
Division civile	Div. civ.
Division criminelle	Div. crim.
Division de la famille	Div. fam.
Cour supérieure	C.S.
Cour suprême (provinciale)	C.S.
Cour suprême du Canada	C.S.C.
Court of Appeal	C.A.

Court of Criminal Appeals .... Ct. Crim. App.
Court of King's Bench .... K.B.
Court of Queen's Bench .... Q.B.
Court of Review .... Ct. Rev.
Court of Sessions of the Peace .... Ct. Sess. P.
District Court .... Dist. Ct.
Divisional Court .... Div. Ct.
Divorce and Matrimonial Causes Court ... Div. & Matr. Causes Ct.
Exchequer Court .... Ex. Ct.
Family Court .... Fam. Ct.
Federal Court Appeal Division .... F.C.A.
Federal Court Trial Division .... F.C.T.D.
General Division .... Gen. Div.
Haute Cour .... H.C.
High Court of Justice .... H.C.J.
Justice of the Peace Court .... Just. of Peace Ct.
Juvenile Court .... Juv. Ct.
Magistrate's Court .... Mag. Ct.
Municipal Court .... Mun. Ct.
Petites créances .... Pet. cré.
Probate court .... Prob. Ct.
Provincial Court .... Prov. Ct.
    Civil Division .... Civ. Div.
    Family Division .... Fam. Div.
    Criminal Division .... Crim. Div.
    Youth Division .... Youth Div.
    Small Claims Division .... Sm. Cl. Div.
Provincial Division .... Prov. Div.
Small Claims .... Sm. Claims
Superior Court .... Sup. Ct.
Supreme Court (provincial) .... S.C.
    Appellate Division .... A.D.
    Trial Division .... T.D.
Supreme Court of Canada .... S.C.C.
Surrogate Court .... Surr. Ct.
Tax Court of Canada .... T.C.C.
Territorial Court .... Terr. Ct.
Tribunal de la jeunesse .... Trib. jeun.
Unified Family Court .... Unif. Fam. Ct.
Youth Court .... Youth Ct.

APPENDICE 5

TRIBUNAUX ADMINISTRATIFS

Commission canadienne des droits de la personne . . . . C.C.D.P.
Commission canadienne des pensions . . . . C.C.P.
Commission canadienne des transports . . . . C.T.C.
Commission d'appel des pensions . . . . C.A.P.
Commission de contrôle de l'énergie atomique . . . . C.C.E.A.
Commission de l'immigration et du statut du réfugié . . . . . . C.I.S.R.
Commission des relations de travail
       dans la Fonction publique . . . . C.R.T.F.P.
Commission nationale des libérations conditionnelles . . . . . C.N.L.C.
Conseil canadien des relations de travail . . . . C.C.R.T.
Conseil de la radio-diffusion et des
       télécommunications canadiennes . . . . C.R.T.C.
Office national de l'énergie . . . . .O.N.E.
Tribunal canadien du commerce extérieur . . . . .T.C.C.E.
Tribunal d'appel des anciens combattants . . . . T.A.A.C.
Tribunal de la concurrence . . . . Trib. conc.
Tribunal de l'aviation civile . . . . T.A.C.
Tribunal des droits de la personne . . . . T.D.P.

APPENDICE 6

REVUES

Canadian Bar Association, British Columbia
Branch Lectures . . . . .B.C. Br. Lect.
Canadian Bar Journal . . . . .Can. Bar J.
Canadian Bar Review . . . . Can. Bar Rev.
Canadian Business Law Journal . . . . .Can. Bus. L.J.
Canadian Communications Law Review . . . .Can. Communic. L. Rev.
Canadian Community Law Journal . . . . Can. Community L.J.
Canadian Competition Policy Record . . . . Can. Comp. Pol. Rec.
Canadian Criminology Forum . . . . Can. Crim. Forum
Canadian Current Tax . . . . .Can. Curr. Tax
Canadian Council on International
Law, Proceedings . . . . .Can. Council Int'l L. Proc.
Canadian Environmental Law News . . . . Can. Env. L.N.
Canadian Human Rights Advocate . . . . .Can. H.R. Advoc.
Canadian Human Rights Yearbook . . . . .Can. Hum. Rts. Y.B.
Canadian Intellectual Property Review . . . . . Can. Intell. Prop. Rev.
Canadian Journal of Criminology . . . . Can. J. Crim.
Canadian Journal of Criminology
and Corrections . . . . Can. J. Crim. & Corr.
Canadian Journal of Family Law . . . . .Can. J. Fam. L.
Canadian Journal of Insurance Law . . . . .Can. J. Ins. L.
Canadian Journal of Law and Jurisprudence . . . . Can. J. Law & Jur.
Canadian Journal of Women and the Law . . . . .C.J.W.L.
Canadian Law Review (1901-1907) . . . . .Can. L. Rev.
Canadian Law Times (1881-1922) . . . . .Can. L.T.
Canadian Lawyer . . . . Can. Law.
Canadian Legal Studies .Can. Legal Stud.
Canadian Municipal Journal . . . . Can. Mun. J.
Canadian Public Policy . . . . Can. Pub. Pol.
Canadian Taxation : A Journal of
Tax Policy . . . . .Can. Tax'n : J. Tax Pol'y
Canadian Tax Foundation (Conference Report) . . . Can. Tax Found.
Canadian Tax Journal . . . . Can. Tax J.
Canadian Tax News . . . . .Can. Tax N.
Canadian Year Book of International Law . . . . . . Can. Y.B. Int'l L.
Chitty's Law Journal . . . . .Chitty's L.J.
Computer Law . . . . Computer L.
Corporate Management Tax Conference . . . . .Corp. Mgt. Tax Conf.
Correspondances judiciaires (1906) . . . . .Corr. jud.
Cours de perfectionnement du notariat . . . . .C.P. du N.
Criminal Law Quarterly . . . . .Crim. L.Q.
Criminologie . . . . Criminologie
Crown Counsel's Review . . . . Crown Coun. Rev.

Current Legal Problems . . . . Curr. Legal Probs.
Dalhousie Law Journal . . . . Dalhousie L.J.
Estates and Trusts Quarterly . . . . Est. & Tr. Q.
Examiner (L'observateur) (1861) . . . . Examiner (L'obervateur)
Family Law Review . . . . Fam. L. Rev.
Health Law In Canada . . . . Health L. Can.
Industrial Law Journal . . . . Indust. L.J.
Intellectual Property Journal . . . . I.P.J.
Journal of Business Law . . . . J. Bus. L.
Journal of Law and Social Policy . . . . J.L. & Social Pol'y
Journal of Planning and Environmental Law . . . . . J. Plan. & Env. L.
Journal of Social Welfare Law . . . . J. Social Welfare L.
Justice Report . . . . Justice Rep.
Law Librarian . . . . L. Lib.
Law Quarterly Review . . . . L.Q. Rev.
Law Society Gazette (Law Society of Upper Canada) . . . L. Soc. Gaz.
Legal News (1887-1897) . . . . Legal N.
Local Courts' and Municipal
        Gazette (1865-1872) . . . . Local Cts. & Mun. Gaz.
Lower Canada Jurist (1848-1891) . . . . L.C. Jurist
Lower Canada Law Journal (1865-1868) . . . . L.C.L.J.
Manitoba Bar News . . . . Man. Bar N.
Manitoba Law Journal . . . . Man. L.J.
McGill Law Journal . . . . McGill L.J.
National Banking Law Review . . . . Nat'l Banking L. Rev.
National Insolvency Review . . . . Nat'l Insolv. Rev.
National Journal of Constitutional Law . . . . N.J.C.L.
Osgoode Hall Law Journal . . . . Osgoode Hall L.J.
Ottawa Law Review . . . . Ottawa L. Rev.
Provincial Judges Journal . . . . Prov. Judges J.
Queen's Law Journal . . . . Queen's L.J.
Revue canadienne de propriété intellectuelle . . . . R.C.P.I.
Revue canadienne du droit d'auteur . . . . Rev. Can. D.A.
Revue critique (1870-1875) . . . . Rev. crit.
Revue critique de législation et
        de jurisprudence du Canada . . . . R.C.L.J.
Revue de droit, Université de Sherbrooke . . . . R.D.U.S.
Revue de droit de McGill . . . . R.D. McGill
Revue de droit d'Ottawa . . . . R.D. Ottawa
Revue de jurisprudence . . . . R. de J.
Revue de législation (1845-1848) . . . . R. de L.
Revue de planification fiscale et successorale . . . . R.P.F.S.

Revue juridique des étudiants et
   étudiantes de l'Université Laval .... R.J.E.L.
Revue du Barreau .... R. du B.
Revue du Barreau canadien .... R. du B. can.
Revue du droit (1922-1939) .... R. du D.
Revue du Notariat .... R. du N.
Revue générale de droit ...........................R.G.D.
Revue juridique «La femme et le droit» .... R.J.F.D.
Revue juridique Thémis ..........................R.J.T.
Revue nationale de droit constitutionnel .... N.J.C.L.
Revue québécoise de droit international .............R.Q.D.I.
Saskatchewan Bar Review .... Sask. Bar Rev.
Saskatchewan Law Review .... Sask. L. Rev.
Special Lectures of the Law Society of
   Upper Canada .... Spec. Lect. L.S.U.C.
Studia Canonica .... Stud. Canon.
Supreme Court Law Review .... Supreme Court L.R.
Trade Law Topics .... Trade L. Topics
Uniform Law Conference of
   Canada, Proceedings .... Unif. L. Conf. Proc.
University of British Columbia Law Review .... U.B.C. L. Rev.
University of New Brunswick Law Journal .... U.N.B.L.J.
University of Toronto Faculty of Law Review .... U.T. Fac. L. Rev.
University of Toronto Law Journal .... U.T.L.J.
University of Western Ontario Law Review ...... U.W.O. L. Rev.
Upper Canada Jurist (1844-1848) .... U.C. Jurist
Upper Canada Law Journal (1855-1864) .... U.C.L.J.
Western Law Review (1961-1966) ....West. L. Rev.
Western Ontario Law Review (1967-1976) .....West. Ont. L. Rev.
Windsor Yearbook of Access to Justice ...Windsor Y.B. Access Just.

A.C.D.I. .... Annuaire canadien de droit international
A.C.D.P. .... Annuaire canadien des droits de la personne
Acta Crim. ....Acta Criminologica
Actualités .... Actualités
Actualités-Justice .... Actualités-Justice
Admin. L.J. ....Administrative Law Journal
Advocate ....Advocate
Advocates' Q. .... Advocates' Quarterly
Advocates' Soc. J. .... Advocates' Society Journal
Alta. L. Rev. ....Alberta Law Review
Anal. de Pol. ....Analyse de Politiques
Ann. Air & Sp. L. .... Annals of Air and Space Law

Assurances . . . . .Assurances
Barrister . . . . Barrister (1894-1897)
B.C.L.N. . . . . .British Columbia Law Notes
Bus. & L. . . . . .Business and the Law
Bus. Q. . . . . .Business Quarterly
B.C. Br. Lect. .Canadian Bar Association,
British Columbia Branch Lectures
Can. Bar J. . . . . Canadian Bar Journal
Can. Bar Rev. . . . . Canadian Bar Review
Can. Bus. L.J. . . . . .Canadian Business Law Journal
Can. Communic. L. Rev. . . .Canadian Communications Law Review
Can. Community L.J. . . . . Canadian Community Law Journal
Can. Comp. Pol. Rec. . . . . . . .Canadian Competition Policy Record
Can. Council Int'l L. Proc. . . . . . .Canadian Council on International
Law, Proceedings
Can. Crim. Forum . . . . Canadian Criminology Forum
Can. Curr. Tax . . . . Canadian Current Tax
Can. Env. L.N. . . . . Canadian Environmental Law News
Can. H.R. Advoc. . . . . Canadian Human Rights Advocate
Can. Hum. Rts. . . . . .Y.B. Canadian Human Rights Yearbook
Can. Intell. Prop. Rev. . . . . . .Canadian Intellectual Property Review
Can. J. Crim. . . . . Canadian Journal of Criminology
Can. J. Crim. & Corr. . . . . Canadian Journal of Criminology
and Corrections
Can. J. Fam. L. . . . . .Canadian Journal of Family Law
Can. J. Ins. L. . . . . Canadian Journal of Insurance Law
Can. J. Law & Jur. . . . . . Canadian Journal of Law and Jurisprudence
Can. L.J. . . . . .Canada Law Journal
Can. L.T. . . . . Canadian Law Times (1881-1922)
Can. Law. . . . . .Canadian Lawyer
Can. Legal Stud. .Canadian Legal Studies
Can. L. Rev. . . . . Canadian Law Review (1901-1907)
Can. Mun. J. Canadian Municipal Journal
Can. Pub. Pol. . . . . .Canadian Public Policy
Can. Tax Found. . . . .Canadian Tax Foundation (Conference Report)
Can. Tax J. . . . . .Canadian Tax Journal
Can. Tax N. . . . . Canadian Tax News
Can. Tax'n : J. Tax Pol'y . . . . Canadian Taxation :
A Journal of Tax Policy
Can.-U.S. L.J. . . . . .Canada-United States Law Journal
Can. Y.B. Int'l L. . . . . Canadian Year Book of International Law
C.B.A. Papers . . . . .Canadian Bar Association Papers
C.B.A. Y.B. . . . . .Canadian Bar Association Year Book

C. de D. . . . . Cahiers de droit
C. de l'I.Q.A.J. . . . . .Cahiers de l'Institut québécois
d'administration judiciaire
Chitty's L.J. . . . . .Chitty's Law Journal
C.J.W.L. . . . . Canadian Journal of Women and the Law
Computer L. . . . . .Computer Law
Corp. Mgt. Tax Conf. . . . . .Corporate Management Tax Conference
Corr. jud. . . . . .Correspondances judiciaires (1906)
C.P. du N. . . . . Cour de perfectionnement du notariat
Crim. L.Q. . . . . Criminal Law Quarterly
Criminologie . . . . Criminologie
Crown Coun. Rev. . . . . Crown Counsel's Review
Curr. Legal Probs. . . . . Current Legal Problems
Dalhousie L.J. . . . . Dalhousie Law Journal
Est. & Tr. Q. . . . . .Estates and Trusts Quarterly
Examiner (L'observateur) . . . . Examiner (L'observateur) (1861)
Fam. L. Rev. . . . . Family Law Review
Health L. Can. . . . . Health Law in Canada
Indust. L. J. . . . . Industrial Law Journal
I.P.J. . . . . Intellectual Property Journal
J. Bus. L. . . . . Journal of Business Law
J.L. & Social Pol'y . . . . .Journal of Law and Social Policy
J. Plan. & Env. L. . . . . .Journal of Planning and Environmental Law
J. Social Welfare L. . . . . .Journal of Social Welfare Law
Justice Rep. . . . . Justice Report
L.C. Jurist . . . . .Lower Canada Jurist (1848-1891)
Legal N. . . . . Legal News (1878-1897)
L.C.L.J. . . . . .Lower Canada Law Journal (1865-1868)
L. Lib. . . . . Law Librarian
Local Cts. & Mun. Gaz. . . . . Local Courts' and Municipal
Gazette (1865-1872)
L.Q. Rev. . . . . Law Quarterly Review
L. Soc. Gaz. . . Law Society Gazette (Law Society of Upper Canada)
Man. Bar N. . . . . Manitoba Bar News
Man. L.J. . . . . Manitoba Law Journal
McGill L.J. . . . . McGill Law Journal
Nat'l Banking L. Rev. . . . . National Banking Law Review
Nat'l Insolv. Rev. . . . . National Insolvency Review
N.J.C.L. . . . . Revue nationale de droit constitutionnel
N.J.C.L. . . . . National Journal of Constitutional Law
Osgoode Hall L.J. . . . . Osgoode Hall Law Journal
Ottawa L. Rev. . . . . .Ottawa Law Review
Prov. Judges J. . . . . Provincial Judges Journal

Queen's L.J. . . . . Queen's Law Journal
R.C.L.J. . . . . .Revue critique de législation et de
jurisprudence du Canada
R.C.P.I. . . . . .Revue canadienne de propriété intellectuelle
R. de J. . . . . .Revue de jurisprudence
R. de L. . . . . Revue de Législation (1845-1848)
R.D. McGill . . . . Revue de droit de McGill
R.D. Ottawa . . . . Revue de droit d'Ottawa
R. du B. . . . . .Revue du Barreau
R. du B. can. . . . . .Revue du Barreau canadien
R. du D. . . . . .Revue du droit (1922-1939)
R. du N. . . . . Revue du Notariat
R.D.U.S. . . . . Revue de droit, Université de Sherbrooke
R.G.D. . . . . Revue générale de droit
R.J.F.D. . . . . Revue juridique «La femme et le droit»
R.J.T. . . . . Revue juridique Thémis
R.P.F.S. . . . . Revue de planification fiscale et successorale
R.Q.D.I. . . . . .Revue québécoise de droit international
Rev. Can. D.A. . . . . .Revue canadienne du droit d'auteur
Rev. crit. . . . . Revue critique (1870-1875)
Sask. Bar Rev. . . . . .Saskatchewan Bar Review
Sask. L. Rev. . . . . Saskatchewan Law Review
Spec. Lect. L.S.U.C. . . . . .Special Lectures of the Law
Society of Upper Canada
Stud. Canon. . . . . .Studia Canonica
Sup. Ct. L. Rev. . . . . Supreme Court Law Review
Trade L. Topics . . . . .Trade Law Topics
U.B.C. L. Rev. . . . . . . .University of British Columbia Law Review
U.C. Jurist . . . . .Upper Canada Jurist (1844-1848)
U.C.L.J. . . . . .Upper Canada Law Journal (1855-1864)
U.N.B.L.J. . . . . .University of New Brunswick Law Journal
Unif. L. Conf. Proc. . . . . Uniform Law Conference
of Canada, Proceedings
U.T. Fac. L. Rev. . . . . University of Toronto Faculty of Law Review
U.T.L.J. . . . . University of Toronto Law Journal
U.W.O. L. Rev. . . . . . . .University of Western Ontario Law Review
West. L. Rev. . . . . Western Law Review (1961-1966)
West. Ont. L. Rev. . . . . .Western Ontario Law Review (1967-1976)
Windsor Y.B. Access Just. . . Windsor Yearbook of Access to Justice

APPENDICE 7

REVUES DE DROIT INTERNATIONAL

APPEN-
DICES

Human Rights Law Journal ....HRLJ
Human Rights Quarterly ....Hum. Rts. Q.
ICSID Review .... ICSID Rev.
International and Comparative Law Quarterly ...........I.C.L.Q.
International Business Law Journal .... IBLJ
International Business Lawyer .... IBL
International Commission of Jurists Review . . Int'l Comm. Jur. Rev.
International Journal of Law and Psychiatry ......Int'l J. L. & Psy.
International Journal of Legal Information .... Int'l J. L. Inf.
International Lawyer ....Int'l Lawyer
International Legal Materials .... I.L.M.
International Legal Practitioner .... Int'l L. Pract.
International Review of Criminal Policy ..... Int'l Rev. Crim. Pol'y
International Review of Industrial
     Property and Copyright Law IIC
International Review of Law and Economics . . .Int'l Rev. L. & Econ.
International Tax and Business Lawyer . . . . Int' Tax & Bus. Lawyer
International Trade Law and Practice ....Int'l Trade L. & Pract.
Journal du droit international ........................J.D.I.
Journal of Comparative Business and
     Capital Market Law ....J. Comp. Bus. & Cap. Mkt. L.
Journal of International Arbitration .... J. Int'l Arb.
Journal of International Banking Law .... J. Int'l Bank. L.
Journal of Maritime Law and Commerce ....J. Marit. L. & Comm.
Journal of Space Law ....J. Space L.
Journal of World Trade ....J. World T.
Korean Journal of Comparative Law ....Korean J. Comp. L.
Law and Policy in International Business ... Law & Pol'y Int'l Bus.
Netherlands International Law Review ...... Netherl. Int'l L. Rev.
New York University Journal of International
     Law and Politics .... N.Y.U.J. Int'l L. & Pol.
Northwestern Journal of International Law
     and Business .... Nw. J. Int'l L. & Bus.
Nordic Journal of International Law ....Nordic J. Int'l L.
Notre Dame International Law Review ... Notre Dame Int'l L. Rev.
Ocean Development and International Law . . .Ocean Dev. & Int'l L.
Recueil des Cours ....Rec. des Cours
Revue africaine de droit international
     et comparé .... RADIC
Revue algérienne des sciences juridiques,
     économiques et politiques .... Rev. A.S.J.E.P.
Revue belge de droit international ....Rev. B.D.I.

Revue critique de droit international
    privé . . . . Rev. cri. dr. internat. privé
Revue de droit des affaires internationales . . . . RDAI
Revue de droit international et
    de droit comparé . . . . Rev. D.I. & D.C.
Revue de droit uniforme . . . . Rev. D.U.
Revue de l'arbitrage . . . . Rev. arb.
Revue du droit public et de la science
    politique en France et à l'étranger . . . . .Rev. D.P. & S.P.
Revue égyptienne de droit international . . . . .Rev. E.D.I.
Revue générale de droit international public . . . . .Rev. D.I.P.
Revue hellénique de droit international . . . . Rev. H.D.I.
Revue internationale de droit comparé . . . . .R.I.D.C.
Revue internationale de droit pénal . . . . .Rev. I.D.P.
Revue internationale de politique criminelle . . . . .Rev. I.P.C.
Revue trimestrielle de droit commercial
    et de droit économique . . . . Rev. trim. Droit com.
Revue trimestrielle de droit européen . . . . .Rev. trim. dr. europ.
Stanford Journal of International Law . . . . Stanf. J. Int'l L.
Texas International Law Journal . . . . Texas Int'l L.J.
Uniform Law Review . . . . Unif. L. Rev.
University of Miami Inter-American
    Law Review . . . . U. Miami Inter-Am. L. Rev.
University of Pennsylvania Journal of
    International Business Law . . . . .U. Pa. J. Int'l Bus. L.
Vanderbilt Journal of Transnational Law . . . . Vand. J. Transnat'l L.
Virginia Journal of International Law . . . . Va. J. Int'l L.
World Trade Materials . . . . .W.T.M.
Yale Journal of International Law . . . . Yale J. Int'l L.

APPENDICE 8

RECUEILS DE TRAITÉS

Air and Aviation Treaties of the World . . . . .A.A.T.W.
British and Foreign State Papers .U.K.F.S.
Canada Treaty Series . . . . .Can. T.S.
Consolidated Treaty Series . . . . Cons. T.S.
European Treaty Series . . . . Eur. T.S.
Journal Officiel . . . . .J.O.
League of Nations Treaty Series .L.N.T.S.
Recueil général des traités de la France . . . . Rec. G.T.F.
Recueil des traités d'alliance, de paix, de
      trêve, de neutralité, de commerce,
      de limites, d'échange, et plusieurs
      autres actes à la connaissance des
      relations étrangères des puissances
      et États de l'Europe . . . . .Rec. T.A.
Recueil des traités de la Société des Nations . . . . R.T.S.N.
Recueil des traités des Nations Unies . . . . R.T.N.U.
Recueil des traités du Canada . . . . .R.T. Can.
Série des traités et conventions européennes . . . . S.T.E.
Treaty Series (United Kingdom) . . . . U.K.T.S.
Treaties and other International Agreements
      of the United States of America 1776-1949 . . . . .U.S.B.S.
United States Statutes at Large . . . . .U.S. Stat.
United States Treaties and Other International
      Acts Series . . . . T.I.A.S.
United Nations Treaty Series . . . . U.N.T.S.

APPENDICE 9

RECUEILS DE JURISPRUDENCE EN DROIT INTERNATIONAL

Annuaire de la Convention européenne
     des Droits de l'Homme . . . . .Ann. Conv. Eur. D.H.
Basic Instruments and Selected Documents (GATT) . . . . . . B.I.S.D.
Canadian Trade and Commodity Tax Cases . . . . .T.C.T.
Collection of Decisions of the European
     Commission of Human Rights . . . . .Eur. Comm. H.R.C.D.
Common Market Law Reports . . . . C.M.L.R.
Common Market Reporter . . . . C.M.R.
Decisions and Reports (Eur. Comm. H.R.) . . . .Eur. Comm. H.R.D.R.
Décisions et rapports (Comm. Eur. D.H.) . . . .Comm. Eur. D.H.D.R.
European Human Rights Reports . . . . E.H.R.R.
Free Trade Law Reports . . . . .F.T.L.R.
Free Trade Update . . . . F.T.U.
Instruments de base et documents divers (GATT) . . . . . . .I.B.D.D.
Mémoires, plaidoiries et documents (C.I.J.) . . . . C.I.J. Mémoires
Pleadings, Oral Arguments, Documents (I.C.J.) . . . . .I.C.J. Pleadings
Recueil de décisions de la Commission européenne
     des Droits de l'Homme . . . . Comm. Eur. D.H. Rec.
Recueil de la Jurisprudence de la Cour (C.J.C.E.) . . . . . C.J.C.E. Rec.
Recueil des arrêts, avis consultatifs
     et ordonnances (C.I.J.) . . . . C.I.J. Rec.
Reports of Cases before the Court (C.J.E.C.) . . . . C.J.E.C. Rep.
Reports of Judgments, Advisory Opinions
     and Orders (I.C.J.) . . . . I.C.J. Rep.

Série A : Arrêts et décisions
(Cour Eur. D.H.) .... Cour Eur. D.H. Sér. A
Série A : Recueil des arrêts (C.P.J.I.) .............C.P.J.I. Sér. A
Série A/B : Arrêts, ordonnances et
avis consultatifs (C.P.J.I.) .... C.P.J.I. Sér. A/B
Série B : Recueil des avis consultatifs
(C.P.J.I.) .... C.P.J.I. Sér. B
Série B : Mémoires, plaidoiries et
documents (Cour Eur. D.H.) ....Cour Eur. D.H. Sér. B
Série C : Plaidoiries, exposés oraux
et documents (C.P.J.I.) .... C.P.J.I. Sér. C
Series A, Collection of Judgments
(P.C.I.J.) ...........................P.C.I.J. Ser. A
Series A : Judgments and Decisions
(Eur. Ct. H.R.) .... Eur. Ct. H.R. Ser. A
Series A : Judgments and Opinions
(Inter-Am. Ct. H.R.) ....Inter-Am. Ct. H.R. Ser. A
Series A/B, Judgments, Orders and
Advisory Opinions (P.C.I.J.) ..............P.C.I.J. Ser. A/B
Series B : Collection of Advisory Opinions
(P.C.I.J.) .... P.C.I.J. Ser. B
Series B : Pleadings, Oral Arguments and
Documents (Eur. Ct. H.R.) .... Eur. Ct. H.R. Ser. B
Series B : Pleadings, Oral Arguments and
Documents (Inter-Am. Ct. H.R.) .... Inter-Am. Ct. H.R. Ser. B
Series C : Decisions and Judgments
(Inter-Am. Ct. H.R.) ....Inter-Am. Ct. H.R. Ser. C
Series C : Pleadings, Oral Statements and
Documents (P.C.I.J.) .....................P.C.I.J. Ser. C
Trade and Tarrif Reports .... T.T.R.
Yearbook of the European Convention on
Human Rights .... Y.B. Eur. Conv. H.R.

APPENDICE 10

ANNUAIRES DE DROIT INTERNATIONAL

Canadian Yearbook of International Law . . . . Can. Y.B. Int'l L.
Chinese Yearbook of International
  Law and Affairs . . . . .Chinese Y.B. Int'l L. & Aff.
Current Law Yearbook . . . . Curr. L.Y.B.
European Environment Yearbook . . . . Eur. Env. Y.B.
Hague Yearbook of International Law . . . . Hague Y.B. Int'l L.
Harvard Human Rights Yearbook . . . . .Harv. H.R.Y.B.
Scottish Current Law Yearbook . . . . .Scot. Curr. L.Y.B.
Yearbook : Commercial Arbitration . . . . Y.B. Comm. Arb.
Yearbook of Air and Space Law . . . . Y.B. Air & Sp. L.
Yearbook of European Law . . . . Y.B. Eur. L.
Yearbook of Human Rights Committee . . . . Y.B.H.R. Ctee.
Yearbook of International Court of Justice . . . . Y.B.I.C.J.
Yearbook of International Environmental Law . . . . Y.B. Int'l Env. L.
Yearbook of Maritime Law . . . . .Y.B. Marit. L.
Yearbook of the Institute of International Law . . . Y.B. Inst. Int'l L.
Yearbook of the United Nations . . . . Y.B.U.N.
Yearbook on Human Rights . . . . Y.B.H.R.

INDEX